# Coming to Jesus for Life

## A Scientist Ponders the Divine-Human Mystery, From the Inside

Everett Myer

Published at Lulu.com

Published at Lulu.com

ISBN  978-0-615-26443-1 (paperback)

To Leona, my Sweets

# Preface

People who write theology books usually seem quite sure they have God figured out. Me? I have no idea. But I do know what works for me – and what doesn't. I hope that my musings on the divine-human mystery will, at least, do no harm. On the off-chance that some readers may be encouraged to persevere in their own quest to know and love God, I offer these humble thoughts. I pray that the Holy Spirit will cancel any error and magnify any truth found in these pages.

This book is unusual. For one thing, I have included dialogue from my personal prayer life. Some may think that these conversations reveal more about me than they do about Jesus. I can only say that I have done my best to record excerpts of what I sensed as I practiced listening prayer.

Secondly, at times I may seem to be making light of serious topics. Although I did not set out to write a humorous book, sometimes my playful side shows. There is a fine line between having fun and making fun. I would never make fun of Jesus. I rely completely on his life, death, resurrection and current indwelling. But the *way* he has rescued me from unbelief and despair has sometimes involved humor.

Lastly, I have addressed questions that most authors have the good sense to avoid. Sometimes, when I am struggling to make sense of difficult theological issues, Jesus seems to grant permission to take a Home Depot approach – "You can do it, I can help." Is do-it-yourself theology always a good idea? No, but the Holy Spirit sometimes gives insight if we sincerely ask.

I wrote this book for three reasons: to obey the call to "just write," to inspire hope in tired Christians, and to address some tough questions. I rely heavily on the Bible and personal experience. But, most of all, I have done my best to *listen* to the Holy Spirit, in both senses – hearing and obedience.

In addition to his direct teachings during times of private prayer, the Spirit has often taught me through others. I have read and am deeply indebted to C. S. Lewis, John Eldredge, Dallas Willard, and Edward M. Smith. Grant and Rosa Lee Smith are dear friends who have graciously helped me at crucial times in my faith journey. And, of course, I have no idea where I'd be without the steadfast love of the woman I call "Sweets," my wife Leona.

Jesus once chided the credentialed theologians of his day for diligently studying the Bible, yet failing to come to him for life.[1] But what does this mean today? How can we come to Jesus, now that he no longer physically walks among us? Trained as a scientist to carefully observe and document experience, I have recorded the account of my struggle to come to Jesus. I share my story in the hope that others may be encouraged to seek their own pathway to loving intimacy with the One who is Life itself.

# CONTENTS

# 1

# Chatting With an Invisible Friend

## A Voice from Beyond

I have never seen Jesus. He has never spoken audibly in my presence. At times I have wondered, how can I learn to love him if all I have as evidence are often hard-to-understand accounts, written by mostly uneducated followers, millennia ago? Were we meant to stumble through life, defending doctrine, fighting temptation, and singing songs about heaven to bolster our spirits? Is life on this earth a lost cause? Are we called to constant hard work serving the poor, always wondering if we are doing enough? Does this sound like the joyful life Jesus promised?[1]

After years of struggle, I am finally learning that God is always paying attention. He is fascinated with the details of our lives and wants to live them with us. Life is meant to be a guided adventure, not a lonely trek. Once I got serious about seeking intimacy with God, he began to teach me how to recognize his inner voice. When I learned to sit still and listen, he and I started having prayer conversations like this:

"You know what, Ev?"

"No, what, Lord?"

"Whenever I think about you, I can't help but grin."

"Why is that, Lord?"

"You are just delightful!"

"Wow, Lord, I wish more people could hear that from you. Why not interrupt a Super Bowl half-time show or a State of the Union address and say it clearly for all to hear?

"I *could* do that but I prefer to communicate using gentle whispers[2] and even more often, just thoughts."[3]

"Yeah, I noticed, Lord. Why?"

"I want to encourage a voluntary, loving response rather than the frightened or openly rebellious reactions that I often get when I show my power."[4]

"I can see that, Lord. I've noticed the same phenomenon in human relationships."

"Which ones in particular, Ev?"

"Well, you know, those with family, co-workers and *other drivers!*"

"Exactly, relationships thrive on mutual respect."

# Ancient Teaching

Many years ago Jesus said, "I am the Good Shepherd"[5] and the Shepherd's sheep "follow him because they know his voice."[6] He went on, "I have other sheep that are not of this sheep pen...they too will listen to my voice."[7] And again, "My sheep listen to my voice; I know them, and they follow me."[8]

On another occasion, Jesus said, "I have much more to say to you, more than you can now bear. But when he, the Spirit of truth comes, he will guide you into all truth...he will tell you what is yet to come."[9]

# Hearing my Shepherd's Voice

One day, after meditating on these Scriptures, I prayed a short prayer of gratitude:

"Thank you Daddy God, thank you King Jesus, thank you Holy Spirit of God, for honoring my questions with such reasonable and reassuring thoughts."

"You're certainly welcome, there, Kiddo. We[10] are delighted that you are waking up spiritually and opening yourself to the possibility of receiving truth as you are ready to understand it."

"Thanks, Lord. Can you please say a bit more about what it means for the Holy Spirit to guide me into truth?"

"Yes, Ev. The Holy Spirit will give you guidance that is based on and totally consistent with Scripture[11] yet is personal, specific, and practically applied to your situation each day."

"OK, Lord, I wonder why I've found it so difficult to sense such guidance."

Jesus seemed to reply, "When you first started your walk with me at age ten, you were a little young for that. But I must admit that you could have grown in your ability to detect my leading much faster than you did. Why do you think it took so long?"

"Well, Lord, several possible reasons come to mind:

1. I didn't know *how* to listen for your inner voice.
2. I was afraid of what you might ask of me.
3. I feared being misled by sinful desires[12] or Satan's temptations."[13]

"Sounds right, my son. How does it feel now?"

"I still struggle sometimes to sense the difference between your leading and my own wishful thinking. But I can usually distinguish your voice from Satan's, or from the general background noise of my own thinking. Of course, I still check what I believe I have received from you to make sure it is biblical.[14] Conversations with trusted Christian brothers and sisters are also helpful. Finally, I compare what I believe was your inner message, with observable facts."

"So, Ev, can you now trust my intentions toward you?"

I answered, "Much better than before, my King, but please help me grow."

"Of course, Kiddo," he replied. "Now just rest and let me 'love on you' a little while, OK?"[15]

"Yes, I'd really like that, Lord"

Fifteen minutes went by in the darkened study. Then I wrote, "You're the Man, Lord! You're the Man! You're the Man!"

And it seemed like he said, "Right you are there, Kiddo. And you're my Evy! I love you more than you can imagine!"[16]

And I answered, "WOW, Lord, What a gift!"

# A Personal Relationship

Imagine that! Is it possible that God, who is so far beyond my comprehension, actually knows and cares enough to call *me* Kiddo? What kind of imagination can make such a relationship possible? It must be one that only God can give. Is it like a child's – the kind we adults often label "overactive" or "misguided"? Wouldn't it be great if we could rediscover this childlike ability to sense realities beyond the merely physical? Cherished and encouraged, a child's imagination can grow into something much greater. Perhaps faith itself is mature, sanctified imagination.

Some children have an imaginary friend. Usually only the child can "see" and communicate with such a friend. As the child matures she comes to realize, perhaps with some sense of grief, that her friend is *only* a product of her imagination. Is God like such an imaginary, *unreal* friend? Some people would say so. For years I could point to very little personal experience to the contrary. Yet Christian preachers repeatedly insisted that nothing is more important than a personal relationship with Jesus Christ. I puzzled over that. To me, a personal relationship meant that there should be two-way communication. And yet, prayer, as modeled by my teachers, always seemed to be a one-way proposition.

In my evangelical church experience the services included no time to sit quietly and listen for any sort of reply from God. Bible reading and listening to sermons were the primary ways we were expected to "hear" from God. So I read, studied and memorized the Bible and listened to thousands of sermons. These were great ways to learn practical theology. However, it would be tragic never to grow beyond a basic understanding of propositional truth *about* God. A personal relationship *with* God is not only possible, but absolutely essential to living a life characterized by love, joy and peace. In fact, an intimate, joyful, interactive closeness with Jesus Christ must be sought above all else.[17] Seeking such intimacy with God trumps serving on church committees, giving a tithe or even helping out in the nursery. If you are tired of a life of trying hard to serve God while missing out on the power and joy that can come only from Jesus, read on. There is hope.

# How Does God "Speak"?

In the Bible there are numerous accounts where God spoke. In some cases God clearly used one or more of the five physical senses to communicate with humans. An angel would appear or a donkey would talk.[18] Even today some have had similar experiences. My wife Leona physically felt Jesus' hand on her shoulder while she was wide awake working in her kitchen. A close friend once heard Jesus speak audibly from the back seat of his car. But most Christians experience such moments only rarely, if at all. Precious as they are, such experiences are seldom regular and frequent enough to nourish a moment-by-moment, intimate relationship with God. Does God still communicate with human beings? Most Christians would say that he does, through Scripture, nature, other Christians, circumstances and observable answers to prayer. But no, I mean, *does he give specific thoughts and mental images to individual human beings on a regular basis?* Can a 21st century Christian have a personal, interactive, real-time relationship with God?

God is mysterious and infinitely creative. He feels free to use many different ways to communicate with us. Others have written at length on this topic. Dallas Willard's *Hearing God* is a thorough and thoughtful analysis of the overall topic.[19] However, my purpose is more limited. I hope to encourage Christians to recognize their Shepherd's voice as it comes to them inwardly in the form of thoughts, mental images and even feelings. Some Christians who have surrendered to Jesus' lordship and have a thorough understanding of biblical truth may still be missing out on spiritual blessings because they have not yet learned to hear from Jesus in personal, everyday, practical ways.

God has created us with marvelous powers of abstract thought, imagination and emotional sensitivity. He can use these to love, lead, convict, and comfort us. How does this work for me? After meditation on a brief passage of Scripture, or even while writing a few thoughts about my day, a question may come to mind. I address it to Jesus in my journal and then sit quietly and wait. Sometimes I get no thoughts, just a sense of peace. At other times he seems to say, "I can't answer that, at least not now." This reply is common when I ask "why" questions. But often, he gives me thoughts, sometimes just a word or phrase, maybe a brief conversation, a poem or even a mental image. In this way I am beginning to sense that Jesus knows who I am and is always paying attention. He really is *my* Shepherd, Friend and Brother.

## Is This for Real?

It is a common joke in our culture that anyone who claims to hear directly from God is insane. Insane people have committed horrible atrocities believing that God told them to do so. But, entirely sane folks *have* accomplished great acts of self-sacrificial love in obedience to direct Holy Spirit guidance. The Bible is full of accounts of God communicating directly to specific human beings. Even after the close of the biblical Canon, respected Christians have believed that they have conversed with God. In the 15th century Thomas à Kempis wrote *The Imitation of Christ*, over half of which consists of a conversation between "The Voice of Christ" and "The Disciple."[20] Much more recently, in 2005, Baker Books published *Questioning God* by Robert Don Hughes in which he recorded numerous prayer conversations. I agree with Professor Hughes who wrote "We need to have a close, continuing conversation going on at all times with the Holy Spirit."[21]

Jesus meant it when he said, "My sheep know my voice." As Jesus' followers, we should earnestly seek to grow spiritually until his voice becomes very familiar. Hard experience shows that *not* being attentive to his voice invites spiritual malnutrition and worse. And that is no way to live.

# 2

# Awesome Mystery

## Is God the Answer Man?

Once I realized that God responds personally to prayer questions, I began asking him about faith issues that had always puzzled me.

But I found that God does not always satisfy my curiosity. On the one hand Jesus promises to reward our asking.[1] However, God's ways are often far beyond our understanding.[2] As we humbly bring our questions to God, he decides how to answer.

Given our limitations, we should not be surprised when God does not explain everything. Even God's physical creation is incomprehensible. The sun is one of 100 billion stars in our galaxy, the Milky Way. But wait, there are 100 billion galaxies! Distances in space are mind-boggling. An object traveling at the speed of light would orbit the earth seven times in one second! Light travels from earth to the moon in less than two seconds. Yet at this speed, it takes light 200,000 years to reach the nearest galaxy outside our own.

Is you're head spinning yet? Actually it is. As you read, thinking you are sitting still, your head, as well as the rest of you, is speeding toward the east at about 1000 miles per hour, *spinning* around the earth's axis. In addition, you are wobbling with the earth as its axis tilts, revolving around the sun, revolving with our solar system around the center of our galaxy, and moving from the center of the universe along with our whole galaxy. You science enthusiasts may now go and look up the speeds of all these movements if you wish.

For *more* mental challenge, imagine how the universe can be infinitely large. If it is not, then it must have an edge. What, pray tell, is one foot beyond that edge? Did someone say incomprehensible?

Not only did God make it all. He also keeps it from crashing. The Bible says that Jesus holds all things together.[3] What a relief! In all my study of physical science, I never found a good explanation for gravity. We can describe *how* it works. We can calculate its effects well enough to travel to the moon and back. But exactly *why* is it that two objects are attracted to one another through space? Similar questions can be asked about subatomic particles. Why is it that protons and electrons attract one another? Scientists discover new insights regularly but so far no scientific theory explains why it all holds together. God simply states that he is doing it.

## God's Other Attributes

God has other mind-boggling characteristics and abilities. He had no beginning. If he *did* have a beginning, how can we explain what existed one minute *before* he came into being? And what do you call whatever or whoever created him?

Did you ever wonder how he can be present and communicate intimately with billions of people all at the same time? The Jim Carrey movie *Bruce Almighty* amusingly illustrates how difficult it would be to answer innumerable conflicting prayer requests. When Bruce questions why a loving God would not more readily give each person what they have requested, he is temporarily given God-like powers and responsibilities. Immediately, he is swamped with requests from people who want to win the lottery. Bruce decides to answer yes to all these requests and nearly creates a riot when everyone wins an insignificant amount of money.

But, beyond the answering of prayers, think about a God who promises to be present with each one of us all the time and who is able to *pay attention* to all the details of our lives. He has our hairs numbered.[4] That number is constantly changing, just like all the details of our lives. Think about the power it must take to keep such a database current.

Oh, yes, and God is not bound by time. Try to wrap your mind around that idea by this time last year. Does he predict the ancient past millions of years from now? I guess, from God's perspective, memory and foreknowledge were the same thing next Christmas. It makes you dizzy, doesn't it? I know my Microsoft Word grammar checker is starting to protest. You can see how it might be difficult for God to explain to us how his foreknowledge and our free will can co-exist. Obviously, even our language makes no sense if we disregard past, present and future. We are stuck in time; God is not.

# God's in Charge

As I came to know this mysterious and powerful God, I was amazed that anyone dares to play God. After Jesus had miraculously brought Lazarus to life, the chief priests and Pharisees called a meeting of the Sanhedrin. To do what? Discuss whether Jesus was *allowed* to raise Lazarus? Jesus had just brought a four-day-old corpse back to life and they still thought *they* were in charge? They said, "If we let him go on like this, everyone will believe in him."[5] Stop and think about this for a few seconds. Have you ever heard of anything so absurd? If he *wanted* to "go on like this" how were *they* going to stop him? They were unwilling to give up the illusion that they were in charge. They could not admit that they were a small part of something really big, much bigger than their own puny spheres of influence.

Of course, this was not the first (or last) time that creatures with free will were faced with the question, "Who is really in charge?" As I pondered the story of Adam and Eve's fall, I was initially at a loss to understand how it could have been a good thing to be unable to distinguish good from evil. But after praying about this question the following lines came to mind:

# Original Innocence

Pure adventure, no drudgery

No moral dilemmas, no trade-offs

No paradoxes

Pure intimacy, no loneliness

Pure love, given and received

Pure wonder, no disappointment

Pure glory, no gloom

Pure desire, no apathy

No temptation, other than to doubt his love

Come to think of it, that *does* sound like paradise.

But then mankind fell. How could it be fair that the disobedience of two people could ruin the human race and nature itself?[6] They had a choice but we are *born* sinful. They lived in Eden; our environment is subject to the curse. While I was praying about this, the thought came: once Adam and Eve fell, the only reasonable response was to shut down Eden and take a different approach. Only chaos would have ensued if each individual had been born innocent, some to parents still in Eden, some to those already banished. I also saw that, like Adam and Eve, we must all repeatedly make the same fundamental choice – whether to accept God's love and leading or to go it alone.

# What is Our Role?

Like Job, we seem to be part of a much larger drama. But why doesn't God give us a chance to study the script – at least the parts that pertain to us? One reason is that sometimes God's plan requires that we *not* know the outcome ahead of time. For example, when Jesus heard that Lazarus was sick he stayed where he was for two more days.[7] By the time Jesus arrived Lazarus had been buried for four days.[8] For Mary and Martha, the waiting must have been the worst part. While Jesus stayed put, Lazarus was dying. As they watched him worsen, grow weaker, slip in and out of consciousness, gasp for breath, and maybe deal with pain, they must have wondered, "What can possibly be keeping Jesus?"

Then Lazarus was gone. Still no Jesus. Jesus was not there to help them deal with their grief. He didn't show up in time to pay his last respects before the burial. Had Jesus forgotten them? They had seen and heard about Jesus' many healings. They knew he could have saved Lazarus, but he chose not to.

Four days after the burial, perhaps a week after they had first started to hope, Jesus finally arrived. Jesus himself was moved to tears. The waiting was hard for him as well. But, the Father's will came first. There was a divine purpose, an overarching need. The power of Jesus' invasion into human reality had to be demonstrated. What better family could there have been in which to show such power? Their faith, in spite of the pain and the questions, was like Job's. It was an unmistakable witness to the voluntary love of human beings for God. But just like a good fire drill, the test could not be pre-announced to the participants. The faith of the lovers of Jesus had to be entirely authentic. Had the end of the story been made known ahead of time to the "actors," they would have simply been playing a role. But it was *real* and the glory of God's power and love for his creatures and theirs for him stood as a shining object lesson.

## So What?

We are participants in something really big and we are not in charge. It's good we aren't since there is so much we don't know. Sometimes insights *do* come when we take time to ask and wait for the Spirit's teaching. But we need to understand that God may have a greater purpose in mind. As in the story of Lazarus, it may not be possible for God to answer our questions. But in my experience, fresh insights come just often enough to keep me asking.

Our understanding of reality is partial at best.[9] Yet, we can count on God to show us what we really *need* to know. Then we must respond appropriately. In John 12:1-10, there is an account of a dinner in Jesus' honor at the home of Mary, Martha and Lazarus, after Lazarus' raising. Martha served. Lazarus enjoyed life. Mary adored while she poured perfume. Judas objected. The chief priests plotted and a curious crowd watched. What a story! The hero is honored. The villains couldn't be more treacherous. The friends celebrate. The dead man breathes! And, the curious check it all out. A thumbnail of the *big* story – the love story that is God's grand creation![10]

# 3

# Who Are You, Lord?

## A Big Question

Some questions are crucial. Lying on the Damascus road, blind and bewildered, Saul asked such a question. "Who are you, Lord?"[1] Like Saul, we need the answer. Yes, we need to know God's name, but even more, we must know his character. If we wonder deep inside whether God is cruel and unfair, we will find it nearly impossible to trust him. Jesus said that the most important commandment is to love God passionately with all that is in us.[2] But, if we think of God as predominately angry and judgmental, we will likely keep our distance. Such intellectual and emotional roadblocks to intimacy can exist in the minds of the most sincere seekers – those just beginning to seek as well as mature Christians longing for a deeper sense of closeness with God. One such roadblock for me has been the idea of a wrathful God.

# Is God Cruel?

The Bible says that God is both holy and loving.[3] He is capable of wrathful judgment as well as abundant mercy.[4] But is God ever cruel? Some traditional Christian interpretations of the Bible make God appear to be absolutely sadistic! What kind of being would set up a system in which a majority of human beings take the wrong road in this life[5] and consequently suffer in hell eternally?[6] The epitome of such a view of God and the human predicament is Jonathan Edwards' fearful vision of God's wrath portrayed in the sermon "Sinners in the Hands of an Angry God." Addressing the unsaved in his congregation Edwards said, "The God that holds you over the pit of hell, much as one holds a spider, or some loathsome insect over the fire, *abhors you*, and is dreadfully provoked: his wrath towards you burns like fire; he looks upon you as worthy of nothing else, but to be cast into the fire; ...you are ten thousand times more *abominable* in his eyes than the most hateful venomous serpent is in ours."[7] (emphasis mine) He went on to emphasize that hell's torments are eternal and that heaven's inhabitants will adore God's great power and majesty whenever they look into hell and see the damned in agony.

If this is the truth about God and the afterlife, how could Jesus possibly have delayed his public ministry for more than a decade while people all around him were dying and going to such a hell? If Edwards' vision is real, why did no sermons in the book of Acts warn of such a terrible fate?[8] If very few find salvation and the rest suffer forever, why would Christians ever have children? Can we be *that* certain that growing up in a Christian home will assure that our children will decide for Christ? What would we think of a human being who would torture even the worst criminal for twenty-four hours – let alone for eternity? If eternal agony is truly God's plan for most of the human family, why would he have given us a conscience that is so totally repulsed by the very thought? Are we to imagine that a God who welcomes the prodigal son back, looks for the one lost sheep out of one hundred,[9] and tells Peter to forgive 490 times[10] would suddenly become eternally *unmerciful* the moment we drop dead?

# God is Merciful

I cannot accept that God is, or ever will be, cruel and unmerciful. The life, death and resurrection of Jesus Christ will not allow such a conclusion. Likewise my own experience with Jesus shows that he is anything but cruel. He does at times get angry at stubborn sinners.[11] But numerous Bible passages show that God's love lasts longer than his wrath. Exodus 34:6-7 portrays him as compassionate, gracious, slow to anger and forgiving. In Exodus 20:5-6 we see that God's love lasts for a thousand generations and his punishment for only a few. Isaiah 54:8 speaks of God's anger as momentary compared to his everlasting kindness and compassion. In Psalm 30:5 we read "For his anger lasts only a moment, but his favor lasts a lifetime." Psalm 103:9 says "He will not always accuse, nor will he harbor his anger forever."

# What about Hell?

So what are we to do with the traditional doctrine of hell as a place of eternal conscious torment with no possibility of mercy – not even a merciful death? If you are like me, you usually try not to think about such questions. For most of my life I had succeeded in convincing myself that because a loving God is also just and righteous, and because he has chosen to give us a free will, there must be real consequences for bad choices. The nature of those consequences seemed to be unavoidably described in passages such as the story of the wicked rich man and Lazarus[12] and in Revelation 20:10 which speaks of the lake of burning sulfur into which the "beast," the "false prophet" and the "devil" will be cast and where "They will be tormented day and night for ever and ever." True, at that point the population of the lake was exactly three, but in verse fifteen we read "If anyone's name was not found written in the book of life, he was thrown into the lake of fire." Is it the same lake? Will wicked humans also be tormented day and night for ever and ever? This passage does not say for sure but innumerable Christian preachers have insisted that all who die unrepentant will suffer eternally and have used such passages to urge sinners to accept Jesus Christ as their personal Savior. At age ten I was one of the many thus "scared into the kingdom." Since then, on the few occasions when I would allow myself to ponder it at all, I am ashamed to admit, I would tell myself, "Well, at least my family and I won't have to suffer such a fate."

However, as God's compassion for others floods my heart, I am compelled to rethink such a narrowly smug position. Can I love God passionately with my whole being, including my mind, if I continue to believe he would countenance the eternal torture of most of his human children? For me, the answer is simply no. So I have a dilemma. Either

God is not love or the traditional view of the *nature* of hell is wrong. Is there a third possibility? Is this question one of those "unsearchable judgments" of God[13] that we should not even try to understand? For me it cannot be. Why? I cannot love God wholeheartedly while holding to the traditional view of hell. As I have previously stated, I know God is not cruel. I am therefore forced to conclude that hell is not a place of eternal conscious torment.

I know I am not the first to have reached this point. C. S. Lewis dealt with the issue in *The Great Divorce*.[14] In it he describes hell as a dreary town in a perpetual drizzle. Its inhabitants are periodically given the opportunity to board a bus bound for heaven. Most don't even make it onto the bus because they are bickering and fighting while waiting in line. Some do go, are met by one of the saved, and a few are able to trust God and submit to his love and lordship. But most get right back on the bus and return to the dreary town to await ultimate darkness. He does not mention fire or any sort of pain. Of course, C. S. Lewis' writings are not Holy Scripture and he freely admits in the preface that this work is "…solely an imaginative supposal…."[15] However, he must have known that to publish such a book would provide a window into his thinking. Apparently, he did not believe in eternal torture or in no second chances after death.

# Alternative Interpretations

What *does* the Bible say about the ultimate fate of those who have lived a wicked life here on earth? There are several alternatives to the traditional doctrine of eternal conscious torment. One, sometimes called annihilationism or conditional immortality, teaches that unrepentant sinners will be judged, punished for a period of time and then destroyed.[16] This view is supported by familiar scriptures such as John 3:16 that speak of those who would *perish* if it were not for God's love. Another is Romans 6:23, "For the wages of sin is *death*, but the gift of God is *eternal life* in Christ Jesus our Lord." (emphasis mine) In fact, if immortality were automatically bestowed on all at birth, what would be the sense of the Genesis passage in which God said, "The man has now become like one of us, knowing good and evil. He must *not* be allowed to reach out his hand and take also from the tree of life and eat and *live forever*."[17] (emphasis mine) Let's look at just one Psalm, the 37th. Here the wicked are said to "wither…and die away," "be cut off," "be no more," "not be found," "perish," and "vanish like smoke." The psalmist writes "he soon passed away and was no more; though I looked for him, he could not be found," and "all sinners will be destroyed, the future of the wicked will be cut off." Those who believe the Bible teaches conditional immortality say Scriptures that speak of eternal punishment[18] mean that the *result* of the punishment is eternal, irrevocable oblivion not that the *process* of punishing lasts forever. John Stott, a well-respected evangelical Christian leader, holds this view.[19] For a thorough treatment of this interpretation of biblical teachings on the afterlife, please read *The Fire That Consumes* by E. W. Fudge.[20]

Another alternative view, for which there is also considerable biblical evidence, is Christian universalism. In this view, God will ultimately "…bring all things in heaven and on earth together under one head, even Christ." This is to take place "… when the times will have reached their fulfillment."[21] Christ himself said, "But I, when I am lifted up from the earth, will draw all men to myself."[22] Then there is the soaring passage in Philippians that reads in part "…that at the name of Jesus every knee should bow, in heaven and on earth and under the earth, and every tongue confess that Jesus Christ is Lord…."[23] Some argue that this passage means that the damned will confess Jesus' lordship out of fear or by coercion just as the demons believe and shudder.[24] But in 1 Corinthians 12:3 Paul wrote that "…no one can say, 'Jesus is Lord' except by the Holy Spirit." Would such unwilling worshipers be temporarily given the Holy Spirit to enable them to say "Jesus is Lord" only to have him taken away again so they can be tortured for eternity? Perhaps, but it would seem less than loving.

The possibility of the eventual salvation of all allows us to raise a fascinating question. Is God great enough, in some way incomprehensible to us now, to take into account his love, his holiness, his election and our free will so that there is a happy ending for all? Is it conceivable that he could find a way to deal with even the stubborn, knowing rebellion of the wicked and bring about their salvation without violating their freedom? It certainly seems impossible, but as Jesus himself reminded us "… all things are possible with God."[25] In *What Does the Bible Really Say About Hell?* Randolph J. Klassen further develops the case for biblical universalism.[26]

Although the scriptural evidence seems to lean toward conditional immortality, my heart keeps rooting for the eventual salvation of all. For those who protest that either view removes the incentive to repent, I merely point to the Hebrews passage where the writer concludes "It is a dreadful thing to fall into the hands of the living

God."[16] I certainly do not want to risk even ten minutes of divine punishment, let alone a year or two, especially if it is followed by missing out on eternal joy!

Others may ask, "Isn't even conditional immortality inconsistent with a belief in a loving God?" For me, it depends on how one answers another burning question. That is, how can it be fair that people who have never heard of Jesus will be held accountable and punished?

# Is God Unfair?

Does God allow billions of humans to be born, knowing that many will never have a chance to consciously decide whether or not to accept Jesus as their personal Savior? Many of us in the evangelical and fundamental Christian traditions have grown up hearing very strong teaching on the necessity of belief in Jesus for our salvation. Scriptures often used include John 14:6 where Jesus himself said "I am the way and the truth and the life. No one comes to the Father except through me." Likewise Acts 4:12 where the apostle Peter says "Salvation is found in no one else, for there is no other name under heaven given to men by which we must be saved." But what about those who, for whatever reason, have never heard the name of Jesus, let alone the full story of his atoning work on their behalf?

Before we go further, let me be clear; I am a born-again evangelical Christian. In fact, on the very morning of this writing I attended an evangelical service at my home church. The pastor gave an invitation during which he led seekers in a simple but profound "Jesus prayer." More than thirty people responded by looking up and "agreeing with the pastor" that they had taken this important step. I love when that happens. I was one of the loudest clappers when the congregation was invited to rejoice together with the brand new believers. It is a great blessing in this life and the next to have heard and received the gospel of Jesus Christ. What I am about to propose is by no means an attempt to undermine evangelistic efforts in today's world.

# What about Nurk?

However, I have often wondered about the fate of the North American plains native who lived 800 years before Christ. Let's call him Nurk. Nurk could not read or write. In fact no one in his tribe could.

Nurk had no idea there was a nation of Israel. The Old Testament stories of God's interaction with his chosen people were totally unknown to him. He certainly had never heard of Jesus or been given a chance to respond to an "altar call." But Nurk was the kind of man who would rise early and welcome the new day with a sense of awe. The beauty of the sunrise, the sleepy songs of waking birds and the scents of wild flowers would stir in him the strong conviction that someone great must have created all of this. As he prepared for the day's hunt he would look skyward with an open, thankful heart and ask whoever was there for safety and a blessing as he went out seeking the necessities of life. When successful, he would share generously with others who had been less fortunate. In these ways Nurk was very much like Cornelius the Caesarean centurion who, even before he knew about Jesus, was described as "devout and God-fearing; he gave generously to those in need and prayed to God regularly."[27] Through the experience of being sent to this man by God, the apostle Peter learned that "God does not show favoritism but accepts men from every nation who fear him and who do what is right."[28] But Cornelius was especially blessed to have lived at a time and place to be able to hear the story of Jesus. While he was still listening "the Holy Spirit came on all who heard."[29]

But back to Nurk. Like millions of others around this planet and throughout history he was, through no fault of his own, prevented by historic and geographic circumstance from hearing the gospel of Jesus. The apostle Peter was not sent to Nurk. Although I cannot be absolutely sure that he was not visited by an angel, scripture does not suggest that such visitations would have been common. Yet, I firmly believe that Jesus loved Nurk every bit as much as he loved the apostle Paul, Mother Teresa, or Billy Graham.[30]

So what about Nurk? A few scriptures address this question. In Romans 1:20 the apostle Paul wrote "For since the creation of the world God's invisible qualities – his eternal power and divine nature – have been clearly seen, being understood from what has been made, so that men are without excuse." Psalm 19:1-4 also speaks to this question: "The heavens declare the glory of God; the skies proclaim the work of his hands…There is no speech or language where their voice is not heard. Their voice goes out into all the earth, their words to the ends of the world." Apparently, these inspired writers believed that nature itself was sufficient evidence of God's existence and love so that people who had only these are still accountable. But how does this fit with the clear statements that we can be saved only by Jesus' name or only through Jesus who is the Way?

# Prayer Thoughts

As I was studying the gospel of John recently I came to Jesus' teaching in 5:19-30. After reading the passage I was baffled. In fact, I told Jesus that I felt a complete inability to comprehend what I had been reading. First of all, in verse 19, Jesus says he "can do nothing by himself" and in verse 30 he says, "I judge only as I hear." But in verse 22, he says "…the Father judges no one, but has entrusted all judgment to the Son." Well, which is it, I wondered. At this point I admitted my consternation to Jesus, sat in my prayer chair, turned out the lights and waited. After a little while, Jesus seemed to say:

"I am the Son of God. I am the Judge. All human beings will face me for judgment. Those whom *I* judge to be good will be given eternal life. Some will have had an opportunity to hear of my life, teachings, substitutionary death and resurrection and will have made a well-informed decision to accept or reject my offer of salvation. Of this group, I will judge to be good those who have accepted me and my atoning work on their behalf. Those who willfully rejected me will be in trouble. Their punishment will be just and fair.[31]

Now, with respect to all the others who, like Nurk, did not have such a clear-cut opportunity to decide, I (Jesus), in my divine omniscience, will judge which ones responded *appropriately* to my less detailed, yet unmistakable, revelation available to all by way of observation of my creation and by listening to the internal witness of their own conscience.[32] These I will judge to be good and will welcome into my kingdom. Those who, on the other hand, rejected the evidence and lived wicked lives will be punished appropriately."[31]

Now, Ev, can you see why it is true that no one can come to the Father except by me? I AM THE JUDGE! Since I have experienced what it is like to be human, and since I endured the torture and death necessary to save you and others, *I get to decide* which ones will live eternally with me.[33] And yet, because of the mystery of the Trinity, my judgment will be fully initiated, approved, sanctioned and ratified by God the Father as well."[34]

At that point I thanked Jesus for his help in understanding a little better that difficult passage.

# Fair, Yes, But No Fool Either!

How will a loving Jesus judge those who had no opportunity to hear about his love for them? In short, *mercifully* and with full knowledge of what each person *would have* decided if they had heard the gospel story.

Some may fear that this position will undermine the sense of urgency evangelicals have for mission work. I would counter that a theology that damns huge numbers of our fellow humans simply because of the place and timing of their births is even *more* detrimental to outreach. If we teach such a theology we risk driving away anyone who thinks deeply about Christ's claims. Additionally, once they are converted, they could find it very difficult to love such a God wholeheartedly.

How does all of this apply to modern-day seekers who *do* hear the gospel of Jesus but who can't bring themselves to accept it because, for example, they were trained in childhood to be strict Muslims, or because they were sexually abused by a priest or pastor, or because they can't stand the thought that their already dead non-Christian family members may have to face a time of punishment or even be eternally lost? I do not know. I can only beg Jesus, who will be the judge, to look on *all* of us needy folks with mercy. But I do know this. The people that upset Jesus the most while he walked this earth were *not* the ones that were confused, grief-stricken, emotionally scarred or struggling to find their way. Instead, they were the ones who knew better and who still stubbornly and knowingly opposed him.[35] Let us fear above all else being found among that group.

# 4

# The Divine-Human Dance

## Is That the Doorbell?

Imagine a suburban home. It's late afternoon on an October Tuesday. The children play happily. Their laughter mingles with the noise of a TV commercial. A doorbell sounds. Mom is not sure if it's their doorbell or the one on TV. She says to her oldest, "Hey! Jessica, listen! Is there someone at the door? Would you please go see who it is?"

Jessica peeks out the sidelight and runs back to the kitchen. "It looks like Jesus," she whispers.

With some fear, Mom opens the door. Sure enough, there is a bearded man in robe and sandals. His eyes dance and his grin is enormous. "Hi, I'm Jesus. I was just in the neighborhood and thought I'd stop by for a chat. May I come in?"

"Jesus, I can't believe it! You should have called. This place is a mess. But, now that you're here, by all means, please come in. In fact, we were just about ready to sit down to dinner. Would you care to join us?"

"Why, I'd love to. I thought you'd never ask!"

# The Ultimate Dinner Guest

Many people wonder if God is approachable. Does the almighty Creator of this stupendous universe ever even notice us – such tiny specks, such seemingly insignificant bit players in this unimaginably huge drama? The answer, incredibly, is yes. Not only does he notice us, he wants to come to dinner! He says, "Here I am! I stand at the door and knock. If anyone hears my voice and opens the door, I will come in and eat with him, and he with me."[1]

What happens at dinner? Friends visit – that's what. Neither host nor guest does all the talking. There is give-and-take, two-way conversation, sharing of ideas and mutual enrichment and encouragement. There may even be some debating. Jesus said, "I will…eat with him, *and he with me.*" It doesn't sound like a lecture, a sermon or even a committee meeting. Instead, it's an invitation to chat, over some good food – nourishing, refreshing, and fun. Yes, there may also be some gentle challenge involved, but the picture is predominately one of mutual respect, hearing one another out, being relaxed, "chewing the fat" or in today's lingo, "hangin." Can you imagine having this type of relationship with God? Please do. You just need to open the door and give your consent. He will gladly start to make it happen.

Some may be thinking, "Oh, but you have no idea what a mess it is inside. I must clean house first before I would dare invite Jesus to dinner." But he is already at the door! He *did* call first, many times, through the prophets and his own life, teachings, death and resurrection and now by the nudges of the Holy Spirit. Now he's *at the door!* If you open it and give your consent, *he* will do the housecleaning![2] Believe me, he already knows about the mess. He wants to visit anyway! The mess may be a direct *result* of keeping him waiting outside. Oh, yes, *you* may not be able to enjoy the visit as much *while* he is cleaning up the mess, but *he* will be absolutely delighted. He knows just what needs to be done to make your heart a fit place for a friendly dinner conversation. Once you consent, he will begin, gently but firmly. You may not always be sure exactly what all he is doing but *he* already can envision the sparkling, hospitable, and peaceful heart he plans to give you as a result of this marvelous remodeling project.

## Where Does He Knock?

Jesus' knocking on our heart's door refers to more than our initial conversion. In fact, the context of this verse[1] is a message to the *church* at Laodicea and includes the statement, "Those whom I love I rebuke and discipline."[3] He knocks at any door that we have never opened at all or that we chose to close in his face. Even those who have held him at a distance for years are urged to open to him. His grace is glorious. Peter's sermon to the Jews in the third chapter of Acts illustrates Jesus' long-suffering love. In verses 12 to 20 he tells them in effect, "Face it guys, you messed up big-time and you deserved to be incinerated on the spot, but instead, what God *really* wants is for you to turn *toward* him with love and gratitude. You need to acknowledge your part in the biggest screw-up of all time, killing the *source* of all life, for pity sakes! You need to let Jesus in and let him draw you close." He called them "brothers" and said he knew they "acted in ignorance."[4] He even gave their *leaders* the benefit of the doubt. These were some of the same people whom John the Baptist called a "brood of vipers"[5] and whom Jesus referred to as rotten hypocrites.[6] Talk about a mess! Even the Laodicean Christians whom Jesus considered so distastefully lukewarm that he wanted to "spit them out"[7] were the very folks that he offered to eat dinner with.

## Family!

Not only are we encouraged to invite Jesus to dinner, we are also urged to extend long-term hospitality. Jesus himself said, "If anyone loves me, he will obey my teaching. My Father will love him, and we will come to him and *make our home with him*."[8] (emphasis mine). Here, we are encouraged not to think of this relationship as just an occasional dinner conversation, or even a one-night or weekend sleepover, but a permanent family arrangement! Jesus and his Father will move in and become family. Family members are committed to one-another. Family members encourage, make allowances for, and even argue with one-another. Family members care enough to tell each other when a shirt label is sticking up or a breath mint is needed. In God's family, unlike some of our earthly ones, he is always "there for us," but we must open the door.

# Check This Out!

Right after Jesus invited himself to dinner, he said, "To him who overcomes, I will give the right to sit with me on my throne, just as I overcame and sat down with my Father on his throne."[9] Wow, those must be truly king-sized thrones! What does one do while seated on a throne? Check out the view like a little boy invited up to the cockpit of an airliner by a kindly captain? I don't think so. Jesus said we will sit on his throne just as he sits on the Father's. Jesus was certainly no small boy checking out the view. What then does this promise mean? Think about it. What does one normally do on a throne? Could he possibly mean that we will help to govern, make decisions, take responsibility, even rule? Is it possible that one reason to sit down over dinner with Jesus is to learn to "overcome" so that we will be ready to govern with him in some heavenly realm? Maybe we can begin to learn, even now, to offer leadership in our own current spheres of influence. There is biblical support for both. In Genesis 1:28 we read that God made us to "rule over…all the earth." Likewise, Revelation 20:6 says "Blessed and holy are those who have part in the first resurrection. The second death has no power over them, but they will be priests of God and of Christ and will reign with him for a thousand years."

# What Kind of Relationship Is This?

Is it possible – dare we even suggest – that God might actually listen to human beings and change *his* mind about something? Do dinner-guest friends do this? Yes! Do family members do this? Yes! Do fellow heads-of-state sometimes learn from one-another? Yes! Is there any biblical evidence that God ever listened to a human being's prayer and then changed his mind about an action he had been considering? Well, there *is* this incredible story from Exodus 32:7-14:

> Then the Lord said to Moses, "Go down, because *your* people, whom *you* brought up out of Egypt, have become corrupt. They have been quick to turn away from what I commanded them and have made themselves an idol cast in the shape of a calf. They have bowed down to it and sacrificed to it and have said, 'These are your gods, O Israel, who brought you up out of Egypt.'" "I have seen these people," the Lord said to Moses, "and they are a stiff-necked people. *Now leave me alone*, so that my anger may burn

against them and that I may destroy them. Then I will make you into a great nation." But Moses sought the favor of the Lord his God. "O Lord," he said, "why should your anger burn against *your* people, whom *you* brought out of Egypt with great power and a mighty hand? Why should the Egyptians say, 'It was with evil intent that he brought them out, to kill them in the mountains and to wipe them off the face of the earth'? *Turn* from your fierce anger; *relent* and do not bring disaster on *your* people. Remember your servants Abraham, Isaac and Israel, to whom you swore by your own self: 'I will make your descendants as numerous as the stars in the sky and I will give your descendants all their land I promised them, and it will be their inheritance forever.'" *Then the Lord relented*, and did not bring on his people the disaster he had threatened. (emphasis mine)

How shall we view this passage? We could say:

1. "God is not really like that. The Old Testament writer was merely reflecting an outmoded, even pagan, view of an angry, anthropomorphic (human-like) god that had to be appeased and cajoled by the more sensible priest – in this case Moses." Or
2. "The Old Testament never really made sense to me anyway. That was the old dispensation which cannot be directly applied today." Or
3. "Moses was a special case; it wouldn't really work that way for the ordinary Christian." Or
4. "God was just pretending to be angry to test Moses." Or
5. "Maybe we should accept the account at face value and seriously try to discern what it teaches about the divine-human relationship."

To me, the last option seems most worthy. Perhaps you would prefer one of the others or still another one I've missed altogether. But for now, please hear me out.

It seems to me that this story suggests an amazing truth about God. He *does* listen to his creatures; he does actually respect the thinking of his faithful saints. Like Moses, they are the ones who "overcome." Moses overcame his own selfishness and loved God and others first.[10] Is it possible that God can have a reciprocal relationship with his spiritually mature, fully-surrendered children? The Bible says God made mankind in his image.[11] Does this mean we can think independently? Dare we even entertain such a thought? Could God actually make a creature with an independent, creative mind – one that can actually suggest something new to his creator? Could God be enriched and influenced by the thinking and prayer of a person whom he created?

How God's sovereignty and our freedom co-exist is a great mystery. The Bible says, "Every good and perfect gift is from above, coming down from the Father of the heavenly lights, who *does not change* like shifting shadows."[12] (emphasis mine). Does this mean God is impassive, aloof and unresponsive? No, he is not immutable in that sense. There is plenty of biblical evidence, such as in this Exodus 32 story as well as in the gospels, that God *responds* lovingly, creatively, even angrily sometimes, to what his creatures do and say. I suspect, rather, that the clear meaning of the passage above is that God is not flaky, capricious, or unreliable. It's a good thing too, since he wields such great power.

But let us return to the question, can a human being ever have an idea that God would consider a serious intellectual contribution? Would he ever have occasion to think, concerning something you or I said to him, "Oh, I had never thought of it that way before, perhaps I *should* reconsider!"? The Exodus 32 story seems to suggest, incredibly enough, that it could happen! Admittedly, however, the story of Moses convincing God to change his mind stands pretty much alone in Scripture. Jesus did not put up with much "back-talk" while here on this planet. His numerous differences of opinion with Peter are illustrative. Jesus even called Peter "Satan" at one point![13] Jesus himself, in Gethsemane, was unable to convince the Father that there had to be a better way.[14] So what should we actually expect to happen if we open the door to Jesus' knock? In other words, what is the *nature* of this personal relationship we are promised? Let's start with prayer.

## Does Prayer Make Any Sense?

As a young Christian, I found it easiest to pray prayers of gratitude. There are many Scriptures that urge us to be thankful. Psalm 136 is just one example. I could always understand thanksgiving prayers. All good gifts *do* come from above.[12] Even blessings that come seemingly as a result of our hard work are made possible only by God. He has given us the unearned gifts of health, intelligence, physical stamina, and support of family, friends and others that make sustained effort possible.

Prayers of petition, on the other hand, have been more puzzling. Although, as the Lord's Prayer shows, it is quite appropriate to ask that God's will be done on earth and that he lead us not into temptation, it seems almost presumptuous to ask God for anything more specific. How can any human expect to know God's will well enough to ask him for rent money or for healing from a particular incurable disease, for example? His ways and thoughts are far above ours.[15] Since, according to the classical view, God knows everything, past, present, and future, how can our prayers possibly make any difference – except perhaps in our own attitude? Prayers of intercession present similar issues. How can we possibly know God's specific will for *someone else?* For that matter, if the person for whom I am praying is unaware of my intercession, how can there be even an attitudinal benefit?

Through the study of the above Scriptures, we can perhaps grasp one way in which prayer *might* work. If God in Christ wants to come to dinner, wants to move in and live with us, is willing to share his throne with us, and would listen to Moses and change his mind about an action he had planned to take, on an issue about which he was very passionate, maybe – just maybe, it *does* make sense to ask him for something we need or even to beg his mercy for someone else! Is it possible that our prayers may actually change the course of history by influencing the mind of God? James asserts in 5:16 that "the prayer of a righteous man is powerful and effective." The story in Exodus 32 seems to suggest that one possible reason for the effectiveness of prayer is that God may actually do something different as a result of our prayers!

## Was Moses a Special Case?

I am struck with Moses' character. What a man! He was filled with such selfless love for God's people that he was willing to give up his own salvation if necessary to save them.[10] Filled with compassion for those great sinners, he begged God repeatedly to spare them. I want to meet such a man! He took responsibility. He *ruled* the way Christ rules, with sacrificial love and a servant's heart. He was brave beyond words. Imagine putting it all on the line, standing up in the face of God's mighty wrath and daring to take an opposing position! Who of us would have such courage? Would any be willing to give up his very own place in God's Book of Life? What an inspiring example of an "overcomer"

Moses was. And think about this story for a moment – what an example of God and man acting as "co-rulers!" Could this possibly be a true picture of how God viewed this event?

# A Deep, Sweet Mystery

It is clearly a great mystery. It seems way too much to hope for, or better, far too scary a responsibility! How could God, the mighty Creator and Ruler of the universe, possibly invite us needy, sinful creatures to be his friends, family members and co-rulers? It may be that the key is his foreknowledge. He knows that once he is given the OK to come in and clean house for a long while, once we have shared many dinner conversations and enjoyed countless sleepovers, he will be able to renovate our hearts[16] to the extent that we actually will become overcomers like Moses. By that time Christ-like compassion will be our very nature. To get to that point, however, will probably take a lot of listening prayer, most likely quite a bit of silence, on both our part and God's,[17] and, finally, a deep, wordless communion during which it may be difficult to know who is influencing whom.

Prayer is indeed sweetly mysterious. Adele Gonzalez describes it like this.

> "The English word *prayer* comes from the Latin verb *precari*, which means to 'entreat or beg.' This definition indicates that we always stand in need before God, even when petition is not our intent. In prayer we do not speak *about* God; we speak *with* God. We choose to become present to God who is always present to us and to respond to the One who continually seeks to communicate with us. Prayer is offering God hospitality and opening ourselves to a deepening, personal relationship. In prayer we communicate with God verbally or silently, and we allow time and space for God to communicate with us. To pray is to surrender ourselves to God and to open our hearts, understanding and wills to God."[18]

Centuries ago Thomas à Kempis wrote, "It is a great art to know how to converse with Jesus, and a great wisdom to know how to keep Him. Be humble and peaceful, and Jesus will be with you. Be devout and calm, and He will remain with you."[19]

Thomas Keating describes times of spiritual dryness as an "emptying" and a "purification of the unconscious." The result of this process, he writes, is humility and "As humility grows, so do compassion for others, submission to God, and the kind of confidence in God that leads to self-surrender."[17]

All these saints stress humility, receptivity and surrender. It is just such an attitude that permits us to get up, open the door and invite Jesus in, no matter how messy our hearts are at the moment. There are probably dusty, cob-webby rooms in our hearts of which we are not even aware.[20] As Jesus shows them to us and knocks on each door in turn, may we keep saying, "Come in, Lord Jesus, you are invited, by all means, please come in!" And may our mealtime and late night chats, and times of silent communion, be sweet and deep and life-giving.

# 5

# No Longer Willing to Miss Out

## Death and New Birth

Comatose, Dad lay dying. For several days Leona and I kept watch. At one point she whispered, "Just think, you'll soon have two heavenly fathers!" Then she hugged me as I laughed and cried. During his last night I slept in the empty patient bed next to his. A Scopolamine patch on his chest helped him breath freely. Oral Morphine, given mercifully by his nurse every two hours, stilled his restlessness. When he died the family was there. My sister exclaimed, "Ohhh! I could sense his spirit going up!" I felt nothing of the sort. As usual, I seemed to have the spiritual sensitivity of a block of wood. All I felt was sad relief that the month-long process, after the final big stroke, was finally over. "Oh well," I thought, "that's just me, the 'concrete thinker,' I suppose some of us are just practical, left-brained and unemotional." But somehow I felt cheated and secretly wished for a greater sense of the supernatural. Was real intimacy with my Creator out of the question for me? My dad had died, but a deep heart longing was born that night.

# Seeking Closeness

Almost two years later, I sat for hours at my first weekend contemplative retreat and complained earnestly to God. "Lord, if you really want to have a relationship with me, why are you so coy? You know where I am. If you wanted my companionship like I've always been told, why, pray tell, did you give me *five* senses for interacting with the physical world, and precious little with which to discern spiritual reality? How can I be friends with a person I cannot see, hear or hug? How can I possibly obey the first and greatest commandment to love you with all my heart, soul, mind and strength, if you and I can't even have a five-minute chat?" I had read of others with similar questions,[1] but now I was begging God for *my* answer.

If God answered me at that time, I didn't hear him. But in a very practical way he *did* answer. During that weekend Leona and I learned to know a wonderful couple, the retreat center hosts and leaders. Let's call them Jim and Mary Ann Miller. We liked them so much that when they asked us to help them teach a 28-week spiritual formation course called *Companions in Christ* (CIC),[2] we agreed. Well, actually, Mary Ann and Leona had discussed it initially. Leona told Mary Ann that she was sure I would not be interested. I wanted to help teach a Christian Thought course. But shortly thereafter, as we shared lunch in a small, delightful Pennsylvania Dutch restaurant along the Lincoln Highway, just east of Lancaster, Pennsylvania, Mary Ann and Jim brought up the topic. After we had chatted a bit, Mary Ann asked, "Ev, would you be interested in helping to teach?"

Almost against my will, I heard myself say, "Yes, I would." As it turned out, it was one of the three or four best decisions I have ever made. I believe that I had help, now that I think about it. Right there in that little restaurant, God was starting to answer my question about how to grow into intimacy with him.

# Halting First Steps

For the first time in many years, I had made a decision to spend time each day alone with the Lord, completing the exercises for the course. At the beginning I would hurry through them, doing two or three at a time, then skipping several days. In fact, some weeks I did all five on Saturday morning! I had made a commitment, so, in my usual plodding way, I dutifully followed through. I did not really expect much to happen but to my surprise and delight, what gripped me first was the *sheer joy* I would often feel at the end of the group sessions each Sunday afternoon. For two hours we had shared openly and the Lord Jesus had paid us all a visit. I remember thinking, *It feels like I've just had a soul bath.*

Since we had started the course in January and planned a summer break, it had not taken me long to realize that I would have to miss a significant number of Pittsburgh Steeler football games. At that time it seemed to me that Jim and Mary Ann did not care too much about football since they had set the meeting time for 1:00 to 3:00 Sunday afternoon! When I agreed to this schedule I viewed it as a real sacrifice. I was surprised to find that I felt much better after a CIC session than after a Steeler game, even when the Steelers won! Of course, these were pre-Ben Rothlisberger games! Still, the sense of joy and intimacy I felt during and after those meetings whetted my appetite for more of the same.

About half way through that first CIC year, I prayed, "Lord, I want some sense of your presence. This life-long silence, or at best, on very rare occasions, a very brief thought or vague mental image, is wearing pretty thin. Could your voice perhaps be not quite so still and small for a change?" I sensed no answer at all.

On another occasion, about that same time, after I had meditated in total silence for fifteen minutes, I wrote, "Nothing. No thoughts – other than rehashing the happenings of the day. No feelings – except slight annoyance at the neighbor lady across the street hollering at a screaming child. No more rest or peace than I had felt initially. Perhaps even a little rise in stress level because of a feeling of resentment at being ignored." The following Sunday, however, as I was sharing my account of what I had thought was a wasted fifteen minutes, the thought came very clearly, "Yes, Ev, I heard that woman and child too." Thus he reminded me that all the while I had thought he was ignoring me, he was, in fact, right there, quietly sharing my experience.

Just a few days later, again after fifteen minutes of silence, I wrote, "Tonight I seem to be able to sense only the external: the aching beauty of the evening sunlight shining on the mountain maple florets swaying in the breeze outside our living room windows, the soft strains of hymns playing on the Bose CD player, the manly rumble of the neighbor's Harley as he takes it for a gentle spin around the block, the sheer joy of being alive to enjoy all you have made, directly and through your creatures. Thank you, Lord." The beauty of those external creations spoke to me wordlessly, deep inside, and I wept. My wooden heart was starting to soften!

# Can You Relate?

Perhaps some of you would say that your spirituality quotient is also very low. Are you tired of feeling left out when others' faces beam with the joy of God's touch? Do you wonder whether the spiritual numbness you feel most of the time is a congenital, irreversible condition? Perhaps you were wired concrete and practical on purpose? Maybe God needs some down-to-earth folks to help keep the intuitive ones in touch with reality. Maybe these will be the ones able to take quick, decisive action in some future emergency. There may be some truth here. People with this type of temperament are needed as fire fighters and airline pilots, for example. But does this mean that such decisive, practical people can never experience the joy of intimacy with God? Absolutely not! God gave all of us *both* sides of our brains. We can be sure he will use whatever abilities he gave us during those pre-natal knitting sessions in our mothers' wombs.[3] We need only give our consent so that he can start his marvelous inner renovation.[4]

# Desire Is Key

Whether we are "head people" or "heart people," most of us are at times convinced that there must be more to life than we have yet experienced. In a sense, this will always be true. We were created for another world. John Eldredge wrote at length about this in *The Journey of Desire*.[5] However, in addition to this general longing that will be fulfilled only when "Death is swallowed up in victory,"[6] some may also be sensing the special hunger that comes from the lack of a life-giving closeness with Jesus. For those who feel a soul-stirring and are thinking, "Could this be me?" take heart. There is hope. Please do not settle for less than Jesus wants to give you. Please ask for faith to believe that Jeremiah 29:11 might actually apply to *your* life. God said, "For I know the plans I have for you," declares the Lord, "plans to prosper you and not to harm you, plans to give you hope and a future."

God not only has plans for us, he will also act. In Ezekiel 11:19 God said, "I will remove from them their heart of stone and give them a heart of flesh." Can we believe that he will do this for each of us personally and specifically? What inward and outward evidence will there be that God is acting in your life? How long will it take? These details vary. He uses a wondrous diversity of methods, especially suited to each of us individually. Balaam heard from his donkey![7] Saul was blinded and knocked to the ground by a heavenly flash of light.[8] Jonah was swallowed (and vomited) by a great fish![9] Elijah heard a "gentle whisper."[10] But many of us will probably have an experience more like that of the Ethiopian eunuch.[11] For him it took Scripture study, a pilgrimage, an angel, the Spirit, a faithful Christian and still more Bible-based teaching. He needed a *lot* of help hearing from the Lord. His heart was open. He had gone to Jerusalem from Egypt, a really long journey by chariot, and was already heading home, *still* not getting it! God saw that this sincere seeker had not yet received what he needed to be able to draw close. So God acted. He provided a way for this hungry soul to be fed.

In my case the desire was ignited and stoked by a series of midlife events. Ten years ago I was sure I had lost Leona. Her persistent abdominal pain forced a late-night trip to the emergency room. They admitted her. Various imaging procedures showed a confusing array of abnormalities including fluid in the abdominal cavity. Nurse Leona knew this was one of the signs of ovarian cancer. Once ovarian cancer has progressed to this point, survival is unlikely. During the weeks of diagnostic procedures leading up to surgery we prayed, asked many others to pray, memorized scripture and hugged each other a lot. I remember one evening alone in the bathroom thinking, "I believe I am going to lose her!" I wept with disappointment. It seemed cruel that just at a time when we finally were learning to really *enjoy* our marriage, she was going to be taken away. As it turned out, the surgeon found three different kinds of *benign* tumors and Leona is still healthy. But my world had been rocked. About six months later Dad died. God used these two painful events, some tough personnel issues at work and some personal battles I'll discuss later to motivate me to begin taking seriously my need for a close, personal relationship with him.

## An All-night Wrestling Match

Jacob's story may also help some of us. For years he had lived by his wits. Yes, God had blessed and led him in marvelous ways. But much of his life he took the helm himself. Then there came a night, right before he was to meet Esau, when Jacob wrestled with God. Jacob would not let go – even after he had been injured. Jacob said, "I will not let you go unless you bless me."[12] The Bible says "Then he blessed him there."[13] As with many biblical stories, details are missing. Exactly who was the "man" with whom Jacob wrestled? If he was God or even an angel, what possible sense does it make to say that he "could not overpower" Jacob?[14] Why should we not consider it a spiteful act that Jacob was permanently injured? What does it mean that even after the hip injury the "man" still had to *ask* Jacob to let him go? What was the nature of the blessing? Was it more than just the name-change? I can't answer these questions. But one thing seems clear. God blesses those who persist – who simply *refuse to settle* for anything short of his best for their lives.

# God the Trickster?

It reminds me of an occasion when I had read in Acts 13 the account of Paul and Barnabas being thrown out of Pisidian Antioch by "God-fearing women of high standing." God-fearing? High standing? They booted Christ's apostle out of town! After this ignominious finish to the revival meetings, the evangelists shook the dust off their feet and "were filled with joy and with the Holy Spirit."[15]

After trying unsuccessfully for some time to make sense of this somewhat bizarre series of events, I admitted, "Lord, you are truly in charge. Your ways are far above mine and your thoughts are way beyond my poor attempts at comprehension. But I *do* want to be filled with joy and with the Holy Spirit. So, would you please do *that* for me, Lord, in spite of my inability to understand this passage?"

At this point I sat still and waited for *thirty minutes*. Nothing. No joy. No thoughts. No mental images. *Just plain, blind silence.* I finally wrote, "Well, I guess not this time. OK then, Lord, *be that way!* I am not going anywhere. I am just going to trust you, even in the silent darkness. If you're tired of me hanging around you'll just have to kick me out yourself because I am *not* leaving on my own."

Immediately the thought came, "Good, that's my man. I'd hate to see you go anywhere – just when we were starting to get along so well."

Startled, I wrote, "Why you trickster, you! Hide and seek is it?"

"Nah, just kidding a bit. Where's that sense of humor I gave you?"

"That's not fair!" I replied. "Having you pretend to hide from me is *not* funny. In fact, it's terrifying!"

He seemed to answer, "Exactly. But you know I *do* like it when you are willing to *insist* on staying near, even when I temporarily withhold obvious rewards."

## Why Does God Often Seem Coy?

John Eldredge believes that God has a feminine side. God wants to be pursued. He wants to know we are willing to fight to be close to him.[16] God wants us to earnestly seek intimacy with him. Is it too much of a stretch to say he wants to be courted? This may be one reason why God sometimes acts coy. Others also come to mind. He may want us to be really *sure* that we want his love and leadership. Otherwise, the nature of the relationship can so easily become coercive, given the vast power difference. Alternatively, he may simply be respecting our personhood, teaching us humility, or testing our co-ruler potential. Sometimes I suspect God wants to step back a bit so that we will learn to lean on each other. In this way he can draw us toward the unity that is basic in his Trinitarian universe. (Chapter 21) It may even be that what seems like divine reticence is, at times, merely an inescapable by-product of our limited grasp of mind-boggling reality.

There is probably some truth in all of the above. However, at the root, I believe the process is about the need to regain some measure of original innocence – at least in the sense that we once again can walk with God in the cool of the day without feeling a need to hide.[17] We need to be honest. No spiritual fig leaves are allowed or needed on this journey back to our Daddy God. But he is sensitive to our spiritual shyness and gives us time and space in which to grow. We must trust his judgment as to the details of method and timing. Our part is to *continue to invite* his closeness, to *consent over and over* to his mysterious inner workings. If we do that, God will work wonders.

## What Will it Look Like?

Simeon and Anna give us a glimpse of what a lifetime of walking with God can become.[18] Imagine with me what it may have been like to have been in the temple that day.

I see people, clothed in robes of rough cloth, sandaled feet dusty, even grimy, and smelling like people do who bathe once every week or two. The odor of burning feathers, cooking meat. The smoke from the wood fire on the altar stings my eyes a little. A couple brings a tiny baby boy for his eighth-day consecration. Simeon is there – well known as a man close to the Lord. He seems to have a direct line to the Father. His prayers are often answered. He is a gifted listener to the Spirit. After long practice his spiritual sensitivity comes naturally. When he sees the baby his face immediately lights up! He just *knows* this is the one, reaches for the child, prophesies and gives thanks aloud. I and others are drawn into the spirit of the occasion. We smile and feel warm and comforted. Simeon tells the mother about a sword that would pierce her heart. I'm not sure if even *he* knows what that means. I surely don't. As I am pondering that, a second confirmation comes. Anna, the temple bag lady/full-time saint, who just loves spending time as close to God as possible, also sees the baby. Her husband died many years ago. She lives on meager gifts of food that people give her. The Lord is her caretaker. She trusts God fully and wants only to spend her remaining days in his presence. She also gives thanks and explains who this child is – the redeemer we have all been hoping for. He is the freer of captives – Jews subject to Rome and maybe much more? I will definitely have to keep my eye on this child.

Could we ever become as spiritually sensitive as Simeon and Anna? Why set out on such a daunting quest? We could all come up with good reasons, I'm sure. Here is my list for starters:

1. His Spirit draws us.
2. Living without God gets too painful after while.
3. We learn, finally, that counterfeits cannot deliver on their promise of lasting meaning and joy.
4. We realize that others have something really cool that we know we want to get in on! We are tired of pretending. We are tired of missing out.

Once we get to this point, we need to tell God. When we finally do, I imagine he dances a little jig, claps his hands and says, "Ohhh, goody! *Now* look what we'll be able to do for her! Just you watch! It'll be a HOOT!" And the adventure begins.

# 6

# Imagination and Faith

## Trapped?

My career was going nowhere. Well above my pay grade, upper managers were making big decisions about the company's future. Job security was a distant memory. Retirement was not yet thinkable. Huge deadlines loomed. There I sat in my basement office, staring out at a barren, earthen bank, with two soccer-ball-sized rocks. Looking almost straight up, I could see the bottom two feet of several small trees, and a few swatches of blue sky. On this gorgeous day, I felt boxed in by concrete, trapped in time, stranded in space – a captive of unimaginable distance. But truth slowly settled in. Although physically stuck in that office, at that time, I was still able to move imaginatively to a host of varied and beautiful destinations – even to God's kingdom, right next to his heart! God gave me a precious glimpse of new spiritual possibilities, right there in my basement office.

## What is Christianity?

All my life I have heard that Christianity, rightly understood, is not a religion but a personal relationship with Jesus Christ. No matter how much I agreed cognitively, living this truth had been a struggle. I would read or hear sermons on biblical accounts of human beings who conversed with God, saw and were spoken to by angels, dreamed prophetic dreams, saw visions and even heard God speak aloud from the sky. But whenever I tried to recall any direct, personal communication from Jesus Christ, I could think of only one experience from my teen years. I had been praying to God despairingly after one more failure, "Lord, what is ever going to become of me?" After agonizing for fifteen minutes I had a mental image of Jesus walking over to my bed, sitting down on its edge, and saying simply, "It'll be OK." Although I cherished the memory of this encounter, I eventually came to realize how profoundly sad it was that this experience stood alone as the only direct evidence of Jesus' personal love and attention.

It was not that I had been openly rebellious. I was in church every Sunday, had listened to thousands of sermons, preached about two dozen myself, served as a missionary teacher for three years, led numerous small group Bible studies, taught a high school course on the life of Christ and read the Bible and prayed more or less regularly. Nevertheless, the personal relationship was mostly absent. I was basically failing at what I have now come to see was a performance-based, sin-management type of Christian religion.

Perhaps it wasn't quite that dismal. There were times when a particular Scripture, song, or instance of natural beauty would move me deeply and I would sense God's presence and love. But these were rare punctuations in the long, run-on sentence that was my life.

During this time in my personal desert outback,[1] almost the only way I could sense Jesus' leading was by what I had come to think of as "the call." That is, at four or five crucial points in my life such as my conversion, career changes, and church moves, I had heard God's "voice" as a gentle but persistent idea or mental urging that kept coming to mind, often for days, weeks or even months until I finally acted. If I was not completely sure that it was the Lord, I would put off responding until I was so convinced by the sheer persistence of the idea that I finally took action. One such call was the one that led me to overcome my natural shyness and phone Jim Miller to inquire about my first contemplative Christian retreat.

# Honest Wrestling

At the retreat, the Millers led Leona and me in a study of Psalm 27. Written guidance that they provided for a three-hour period of silence and prayer included this question: "Is there something you are waiting on the Lord for in your life?" They encouraged us to "Write a prayer to God expressing your feelings and hope for your life." I wrote this:

> Lord, I am tired. Life seems harder than necessary. Why this struggle to learn to live by faith, only to then go to heaven where such skills will apparently no longer be needed? What's the point? Why the tendency to get the blues? Why the craving for fatty, sugary and salty foods? Why the need to relate to difficult people? Why must I worry about the economy, retirement finances, homeland security, higher taxes and cancer? I hope you know what you're doing, because I often can't figure things out. I hope I can learn to trust you more and sense your presence better. You seem awfully hard to contact most of the time. I have never seen, touched, smelled or heard you. True, I have had rare occasions when I believed I sensed you through a "touching" of my emotions. There have also been times when I believed that you influenced my thoughts. But then again, at other times, when I thought you were giving me mental guidance, it turned out that it had been just my imagination playing tricks. How do you expect me to know the difference? I am getting tired of playing mental games. Sometimes I can convince myself that I have Holy Spirit guidance only to find that once again it was just me. If you wanted me to be spiritual and to live by faith, why did you give me such an aptitude to observe and understand the tangible world and such a weak sense of immaterial reality?

# Breakthrough

Jesus took this anguished heart-cry seriously. I believe he was actually delighted that I was willing to be this honest. Since that time, Leona and I have been learning to co-operate with the Holy Spirit as he communicates with us using our ordinary human abilities to think abstractly, to imagine and to be emotionally sensitive. Through instruction in and practice of an array of tried-and-true spiritual disciplines (as well as some unusual ones he seems to have designed just for us – see Chapter 14), we have been learning to invite the Holy Spirit to address very specific concerns in our daily lives. What a blessing! After a lifetime of struggle and several years of intense searching, I am finally getting over my spiritual shyness[2] and beginning to experience an interactive, real-time, personal relationship with Jesus Christ.

However, let me be clear. I have still never knowingly seen or heard an angel, heard any audible divine words (from the sky or otherwise) or had a supernatural vision visible to my physical eyes. I have had one prophetic dream and one occasion when I seemed to feel Jesus' hand in mine, physically. Routinely, however, my relationship with Jesus consists of various forms of prayer and his communication to me through the Bible, oral and written messages from other Christians, open and closed "doors" and mental images and thoughts. It is this last part, the mental images and thoughts, often in the form of conversations, which I then write down, that he has been using for some time now to deepen our relationship.

Even after considerable practice though, my spiritual "hearing" and "sight" are imperfect. Recently, after I discovered that I had misread God's leading while buying a Christmas gift for my wife (she did not like the earrings and I took them back later), I wrote the following:

## Mystery

My Master, the mystery man

Figure him out? See if *you* can!

"You flummox me, Lord

Perhaps that's your plan?"


"I didn't say," he seems to reply.

"I know you didn't, that's why I asked why!"

"Some day I'll say when we meet in the sky!

You'll be able to bear more truth bye and bye.

Meanwhile, what is it that you *really do* need?"

"Why don't *you* tell me?" I plaintively plead.

"What do I promise, how do *you* read?"

"Your peace, joy and love," I finally concede.

"Astonish me, Lord, I'm open to you."

He seems now to say, *"Now watch what I'll do!"*

# Why So Difficult?

For many years I had felt trapped – stymied in my attempts to know and love God. I wondered why God so rarely communicated in obvious, physical ways. Some insights came recently as I studied John 20:10-18. This is the account of the empty tomb when Mary Magdalene stayed behind – lingering at the tomb after the disciples had gone home. Jesus, in his new, glorified body appeared to her and she thought he was the gardener. Why was it consistently difficult for people who had known Jesus well to recognize him, now that he had risen? It's unlikely that there was any other-worldly radiance since Mary mistook him for an ordinary laborer. There was a difference that threw them off initially. We are not told what it was. But what caused them to *recognize* him? In Mary's case it was something about the way he said her name. In the case of the men who met Jesus on the road to Emmaus it was the way he broke the bread.[3] It seems clear that the recognition was more at an emotional level than merely visual or auditory. If so, maybe it's not so strange that today we often sense Jesus at an abstract, intuitive level, rather than physically. Perhaps there is something about our created nature that requires us to come to him with our *whole being* in order to consistently interact. It seems that we are designed so that if we want to connect with Jesus, we must learn to use more than just our physical senses.

Why might God operate this way? Perhaps our Creator, who knows intimately how he made us, longs for each of us to let him draw out our full potential. Does he sometimes intentionally withdraw conscious feedback in one area in order to give incentive to develop another? For example, in my case, does he at times stop answering intellectual questions in order to encourage me to develop my creative, intuitive abilities? If so, is it also true that he may cause spiritual dryness for "heart people" in order to urge them to become more intellectually muscular? Could this whole enterprise be God's gracious way of leading us to develop the ability to actually love him with all our heart, soul, mind, and strength?

At times God meets us right where we are, in our most familiar mode of operation. Or, he may completely surprise us. Saul of Tarsus was a scholar, but Jesus did not send him a learned professor. He got Saul's attention with a blinding flash of light and then sent a simple believer to heal and baptize him.[4] Naaman was a distinguished military officer yet God spoke to him through a foreign servant girl and a prophet who did not even bother to come out of the house to meet him![5] God can also see potential we never dreamed we had. Moses, a fugitive shepherd with a speech impediment, was amazed that God called him to a role requiring him to speak publicly.[6]

Gideon, the fearful farmer, was threshing wheat in a winepress, hiding from the Midianites, when an angel appeared to him and said, "The Lord is with you, mighty warrior."[7] Gideon was so unsure of himself and his call that he asked for repeated signs. Even after the angel made fire spring from a rock, Gideon still asked for the famous fleece sign, twice![8] God was incredibly patient with Gideon. He met him right at his point of need, over and over again, steadily building up his confidence, drawing him out of his fear. I can almost hear God saying, gently but firmly, "Gideon, come up a little higher. Go ahead, it'll be OK. I've got you covered. There you go, just take the next step. Now see, that wasn't so bad after all, was it? If you slip and start to fall, I've got a firm grip on the safety rope, you can just start again. That's it, see, isn't this fun?"

Does the God portrayed in these and other biblical accounts still work with his people, leading them, step-by-step in the personal life pathway he chooses for each? Many experienced Christians affirm that he does. But if we ask how this relationship with God works, we are often simply told that we must live by faith.

# Faith

Biblically, faith has several meanings. The writer of Hebrews, in 11:1, defines faith as "being sure of what we hope for and certain of what we do not see."[9] Paul writes that while we are still in this body "We live by faith, not by sight."[10] Sometimes faith means our confidence that God can heal and save us.[11] At times it even refers to Christianity itself.[12] Here I'd like to explore the Hebrews 11:1 concept of faith as a spiritual sense that goes beyond natural sight – a mysterious ability to know with a deep assurance that God is present, and always has our best interests at heart.

Not only can we know this in general, but it is possible, frequently, to experience specific, personal examples of his presence and love, individually and in community. We shouldn't be surprised, however if it often seems like we are squinting – straining to make out an image in a dull, primitive mirror.[13] Consequently, we must usually really *want* to connect; we must be *very sure* that we *crave* his involvement with us. He can then choose to "speak" in that personal way, or accomplish that personal healing, or show us that personal thought picture, or give us that deep sense of peace, any or all of which may lead to the joyful moment of recognition, "He's *here!* It *is* him! Hallelujah!" Although it may often seem like we are using a smudged mirror, at least it is not a piece of black construction paper.

# The Holy Spirit's Role

There are many ways God reveals himself to the honest seeker. Today the work of the Holy Spirit is paramount. In Ephesians 1:17 the apostle Paul wrote that he keeps "asking that the God of our Lord Jesus Christ, the glorious Father, may give you the Spirit of wisdom and revelation, so that you may know him better." Even though the biblical Canon is closed, there is a sense in which God still reveals truth to the ordinary Christian believer. There is no evidence that Paul was praying this prayer for the Ephesians because he expected each of them to write more New Testament books. In fact, he plainly states the reason for his prayer, so that they could know the Father better. The focus is on the divine granting of whatever insights may be needed to deepen their (and our) relationship with God the Father. It is just such a deep knowledge of God that can begin to make it possible for us to love him whole-heartedly.[14]

Such knowledge is not always verbal or even cognitive. But even when I can't find words to describe it, I can often sense that God is at work, marvelously, deep inside, renovating the foundations of my life.[15] Real life evidence regularly confirms this mystical sense. Just ask my wife.

# 7

# The Two Most Important Things

## Sensing His Love

In August of 1999 I had back surgery. Lying in my hospital bed that night, feeling alone and vulnerable, I prayed, "Lord, I need some sense of your love. Since I am a visual person, can you please give me a mental picture of your love for me?" And then I waited. Almost immediately, a cherished childhood memory came to mind. I was three years old. It was a sun-drenched Saturday afternoon. Daddy was home and had time to hold me. I was sitting on his lap, facing him. As he hugged me, gently rocking the old chair, I snuggled in against his strong, warm chest and felt completely secure in his love. Now, years later, there in my hospital bed, I knew Jesus was showing me that he also has time to comfort me.

Five months later, during a church training session on the baptism of the Holy Spirit, its scriptural background and various manifestations, Jim Miller, whom I did not yet know personally, spoke a few words of wisdom.

"We must be careful as we discuss this topic. We should not think that what we are looking for is an 'it,' that is, a certain type of experience. But rather, we are on a life-long journey with a person."

And I thought, *Yes, and right now I am looking for ways to connect with that person.*

Two years later, after my first contemplative retreat and during a course on listening prayer, I was given another mental image. It was April. Good Friday was coming soon and I was dreading it. I hate anything gory. I am repulsed by even the *thought* of pain. But as I contemplated Jesus' ghastly death on my behalf, suddenly, in my mind's eye, I saw myself on my knees with my arms stretched wide, looking up at Jesus on the cross. This in itself was surprising to me. I rarely raise my hands at church, even though I attend a church where it is encouraged. But in this mental gesture I seemed to be opening myself to whatever he had for me. As I knelt there, Jesus seemed to stretch forward and look down at me. His love, interest and concern, for me were so plain on his face that all I could do was respond with a prayer of gratitude. "Thank you, Lord, for this powerful mental image, given to me, the 'concrete,' imagination-challenged scientist. I *do* sense your love for me like never before!"

About ten months later, during the third week of the *Companions in Christ* course that Leona and I were helping Jim and Mary Ann Miller lead, we were directed to read Ephesians 3:14-19. Paul wrote to the believers at Ephesus:

> "I kneel before the Father, from whom his whole family in heaven and on earth derives its name. I pray that out of his glorious riches he may strengthen you with power through his Spirit in your inner being, so that Christ may dwell in your hearts through faith. And I pray that you, being rooted and established in love, *may have power*, together with all the saints, *to grasp* how wide and long and high and deep is *the love of Christ*, and to know this love that surpasses knowledge – that you may be filled to the measure of all the fullness of God." (emphasis mine)

## Recognizing God's Love

It struck me then how essential it is to have God empower us as we seek to sense his love. How can we tell if thoughts we have are growing from his love? Jesus' love is active, personal, bottomless, constant, hilarious, creative, freeing, cuddly, all-inclusive and cool. His love creates, pursues, rescues, teaches, comforts, provides, protects, leads, plays, laughs, reconciles, sustains, endures, confronts, convicts, encourages, forgives, calms, strengthens, carries, inspires, sets free, gives hope, enlightens, and accompanies. He does not accuse, condemn, confuse, belittle, show contempt, imprison, bully, grandstand, nag, depress, scare, make nervous, mislead, mock, shut down, dismiss, abandon, relegate, ignore, or reject. Hallelujah!

## Accusation or Conviction?

Once we are paying attention, it is usually easy to distinguish between loving thoughts from God's Spirit and non-loving ones from our Enemy. But the difference between conviction and accusation can sometimes be difficult to spot. When I am feeling guilty and want to discern whether it is legitimate Holy Spirit conviction, I ask myself, "Am I feeling belittled or hopeless? Do I feel confused and trapped?" If so, it is accusation, from Satan, not conviction from the Holy Spirit. Conviction will bring honest sorrow but with it often comes a gracious offer of a way out. Perhaps a specific act of restitution will come to mind or a practical idea of how to do better the next time. Accusation is usually more general like "Wow, Ev, are you ever a hopeless case, it seems you'll never be able to get it together. I surely wouldn't want to be in your shoes. Jesus is coming back and, boy, is he mad!" On the other hand, conviction may well bring a godly fear but tends to be more specific, "Ev, that was pretty dumb, wasn't it? Do you really need to keep taking that risk? Think how much better it would be if you were to simply come to me for some loving when you start to feel that way. How about it, Kiddo? I'm always here and I have much more for you if you'll only give me a chance. OK?"

## What Is Most Important?

Once we are able by God's power to sense his love for us, to what response does he call us? In the gospel of Luke the story is told of a lawyer who stood up to test Jesus.[1] "Teacher," he asked, "what must I do to inherit eternal life?"

"What is written in the Law?" Jesus replied. "How do you read it?"

The lawyer answered: "Love the Lord your God with all your heart and with all your soul and with all your strength and with all your mind, and love your neighbor as yourself."

"You have answered correctly," Jesus replied. "Do this and you will live."

Matthew records a similar event.[2] Here the lawyer is identified as a Pharisee and his question is slightly different. He asks, "Teacher, which is the greatest commandment in the Law?"

Jesus replied: "'Love the Lord your God with all your heart and with all your soul and with all your mind.' This is the first and greatest commandment. And the second is like it: 'Love your neighbor as yourself.' All the Law and the Prophets hang on these two commandments."

## But How Can We Do This?

These admonitions to love God and others are well-known to students of both the Old and New Testaments.[3] But how many of us feel we know how to obey them? How can we love a God who usually remains invisible, silent and out of reach physically? And how do we love people who are often weird, stubborn, and sometimes even cruel?

In my case, God was merciful and long-suffering. He continued to work with me until I was ready to admit that *I really did not have a clue how to obey either one of these commandments.* He patiently waited until I was ready to give up my own failing self-effort attempts to "live the victorious Christian life." Yes, I had often prayed for God's *help.* I would ask him to "Help me, Lord, to live for you today, to love the unlovable" and so forth. But it was still *me* trying to do the loving, setting the agenda and asking him to empower *my* efforts, not asking him to *lead* me in the specifics of whom and how I was to love. Furthermore, I usually put the *second commandment first!* He was waiting for me to do what I finally did in that hospital bed after my back operation. I had to simply come to him, in the midst of heart-bankruptcy, and beg for a vision of *his love for me!* As the Bible says plainly, "We love because he first loved us."[4] It was only when I finally gave up trying to obey these two great commandments and admitted my total inability to do so, even with his "help," that I could begin to *see his love for me,* and really start living the God-life.

After several more years of searching, the Holy Spirit teaching I received went something like this:

My son, once you are radically honest with me, once you put in the time and learn how to *listen* to me, once you overcome spiritual shyness, once you wrestle with me until you are blessed, once you renounce substitutes, once you have opened yourself to inner healing, once you persevere through times of spiritual dryness, you will get to the place where you *cannot help but love me!* For, to know me *is* to love me.

## Radical Honesty, Scary But Essential

But it was not easy. The times of brutal honesty and wrestling were especially scary. For example, at one point I was reading Luke Chapter 14 where Jesus said, "If anyone comes to me and does not hate his father and mother, his wife and children, his brothers and sisters – yes, even his own life – he cannot be my disciple." He goes on, "In the same way, any of you who does not give up everything he has cannot be my disciple."[5]

I prayed, "Well then, Lord, I suppose I cannot be your disciple. I absolutely refuse to hate my wife and children. In fact, you yourself taught that to be angry with someone is as bad as murder.[6] I refuse to murder my wife and children!" I noticed that even the commentators who normally write copious notes at the page bottoms in my *Life Application Bible* did not have a word to say about Jesus requiring people to hate their families.

Since God did not answer immediately, I went on, "Obviously, Lord, you did not mean this teaching to be taken literally. I get the impression that you felt that many in the crowds thronging around you at the time were there only for the 'goodies' you were doling out – healings, food, calming of storms and so forth and that this teaching was your way of getting their attention. You seemed to deliberately use hyperbole to shock them into taking a serious look at what true discipleship required."

In Luke 14:31-32 Jesus spoke of a king who despaired of fighting a war against another much stronger army and sent a delegation to surrender. In response to these verses I prayed, "Lord, many times in my life I have felt just like that king who could not possibly win the next battle, let alone the war. So what are you suggesting? That I should give up and go away? Well, I'm *not* going to do that either! I guess you're just stuck with this particular hanger-on. And as far as giving up everything I have is concerned, that is not fair either. As you know, since you made me, I cannot live without food, water, clothing and shelter. Even intimacy with you would be very difficult for me without a Bible, a notebook and a pen."

At this point Jesus seemed to chuckle and step forward a bit as if to signal it was time for him to get a word in edgewise. "OK, Ev, I hear you. As you have clearly pointed out, my words here were chosen to jar the shallow, not to chastise the committed. I was talking about *priorities*. I want you to love me above all else. I want you to value our closeness, you and me, as if it were a priceless, irreplaceable pearl.[7] I want you to be willing to *give up big chunks of your time* to work at our friendship. Your time is your life, after all. And I see you doing just that. I am *thrilled* because I remember when you would not give me much time or thought at all. I know how unhappy you were then. It really hurt my heart to see you in such pain. Let's stay close. I have even more joy to give you as we walk together."

# Priorities

Often sincere Christians try to obey the second most important commandment first. That is, we try to love our neighbors as we do ourselves without first loving God. It is understandable that we might be confused on this point. Jesus himself taught the 'Golden Rule': "So in everything, do to others what you would have them do to you, for this sums up the Law and the Prophets."[8] He was right in the sense that if we *could* do this without first loving God, we'd have it made. But of course we can't. Many people who think they can are confused about the biblical message. They may be getting their Bible knowledge from sources such as the TV sitcom, Dharma and Greg. Recently, Greg admitted that he had not yet read the Bible. Dharma said, "Well, then, let me save you some time. The first part says 'Don't mess with God' and the second part says 'Be nice to people'" Funny, but wrong, wrong, wrong! Both parts of the Bible clearly teach "Above all else, love God!" In Luke 14 Jesus emphasizes that *he* must come first. We must love him with such a passion that our love for others, even those closest to us, will seem like "hate" in comparison! The backwards approach, trying to love others first does not work. For a while we can convince ourselves that we are "socially aware." We may even go for long stretches of time serving the disadvantaged while paying very little attention to the relationship implied in the first and greatest commandment. But, inevitably, if we work at it long and hard enough, this approach leads to burn-out or at least to a dutiful, joyless life that falls far short of God's best for us.[9] If, however, we come daily to Jesus for life[10] and make his "touch" our first priority, we will begin to experience his love for us and he will give us the power we need to love him. Then, we may begin to notice, probably to our surprise and delight, that we are starting to have authentic compassion for other people, even the ones we may have avoided before!

# Jesus, Our Example

Jesus practiced what he preached. Think about his earthly life. He was thirty before he even started his public ministry.[11] We know that he had started to prepare when he was twelve by spending time in his Father's house, the temple.[12] Although we are not told exactly how he spent the eighteen intervening years, there is evidence from the record of his public ministry the he must have spent considerable time in Scripture study and prayer. During his forty days of temptation alone in the wilderness his ready knowledge of the Old Testament made it possible for him to parry each satanic suggestion with one of his famous "It is written…" responses.[13] If Jesus had been like many of us, don't you think he would have been tempted to get out there and start teaching, healing and casting out demons long before age thirty? Imagine seeing blind men, lepers, lame beggars and people hungry physically and spiritually for what only he could provide – year after year for nearly two decades. Why wait so long to get started with the "real work" of his life? We cannot say for sure, but I suspect the answer is pretty simple. He had an ongoing, intimate prayer relationship with the Father, and Jesus was not about to go public until God the Father said so! During those decades of preparation he most likely developed a pattern of periodically finding solitude, sometimes all night, to pray and seek the Father's will.[14] Over and over he would later tell his disciples that he did nothing except the Father's will.[15]

A careful reading of the gospels does not allow the notion that Jesus knew the Father's will effortlessly because he (Jesus) was divine. If this had been the case, why did he need extended periods of prayerful solitude? Why would he have prayed so excruciatingly in Gethsemane? At times Jesus invited his disciples to come "to a quiet place and get some rest."[16] At others times he went away alone.[17] Obviously he was not a hermit. His public ministry was so people-oriented that sometimes he allowed himself to be drawn to helping needy folks, even when he had planned to take a break. It was almost as though he couldn't help himself because of his deep compassion for the leaderless throng.[18] But even Jesus could not go on indefinitely, serving the needy, without times of closeness alone with the Father.

Similarly, David spent years watching sheep, hiding from King Saul and writing psalms before he assumed his throne. Saul of Tarsus, even after Jesus spoke directly to him on the Damascus road and Ananias had healed and baptized him,[19] spent three years in Arabian solitude receiving revelation from Jesus before he began his active ministry.[20]

In contrast, today it seems that the first and greatest commandment is to serve on committees. Sadly, Christian leaders often follow a business model, deciding first what new, worthy program is needed and then rallying people (and even God?) to support it. Is it any wonder that many well-meaning Christians appear to be overworked and joyless? The Protestant Work Ethic, however good it may be for progress in a human sense, often militates against the humble, surrendered love relationship that Jesus said must be our first priority.

# Driven or Led?

Loving Jesus first is not easy. In fact, our human nature *fights* walking closely with Jesus. *We* want to set the agenda and manage the programs. We feel we can best justify our existence by showing that we can "plan the work and work the plan." If we are honest we must admit that often it is nearly impossible to trust Jesus to lead us one-step-at-a-time. We are often so afraid of the *uncertainty* inherent in the love-God-first life that we are willing to be *driven* rather than led. But we are not nails, golf balls or cars. Down deep we really don't *want* to be driven – even by very worthy goals or purposes. Jesus never said, "I am the sheep driver. I gather the sheep into the fold, tell them what purposes should drive their lives and then drive them out into the world to do their best to live up to these ideas." Now, I admit that ideas are powerful and once we are sure Jesus has given us a specific *next-step*, we absolutely do need to take prompt and effective action. But, cut off from a deep intimacy with Jesus, propositional truth and programmatic objectives take us only so far, and sometimes even in the wrong direction.

# What Then Shall We Do?

At this point some are protesting, "Yes, but isn't it true that Jesus said we must carry our crosses daily[21] and that the way we *show* our love for Jesus is to obey his commandments[22] and feed his sheep?[23] Are we not to go into the world and make disciples?[24] Yes, to all of the above. But the *first* and *greatest* commandment is still to love God passionately with all that is in us. If we will *first* do that, he will then give us the specific, personal *next-step* commands that we must obey to both show our love for him and to accomplish his will on earth. He will show us, each one, to what *part* of the world we should go and *when, which* of his sheep we should feed and *how.* And he will give us *his* compassion, deep down inside, for our neighbors. Only then can we really begin to obey the second most important commandment.

Putting love for God first is effective because *he* is then the one at work in us "to will and to act according to his good purpose."[25] He does not drive us; he leads us. If we follow him we cannot go wrong. He will have plenty for us to do, but our primary reason for being is to spend time loving him. If we think the main reason he made us is to run errands for him according to biblical principles, we will trip over our own feet. The dance works only if we let him lead.

# 8

# Can We Talk?

## Twentieth Century Pharisee?

In one sense I was extremely fortunate. My parents did their best to "bring [me] up in the training and instruction of the Lord."[1] They took me and my brother and sister to church and Sunday school every week. Serious illness or impassable roads were the only exceptions. But, as Mennonites, we were also taught that regular church attendance was not enough. Living out one's faith during the week was also necessary.[2] The commands of the Bible were taken very seriously and often quite literally. For example, women took the apostle Paul's admonitions to allow their hair to grow uncut and to cover their heads during prayer as normative.[3] They wore a special head-covering at all times, except while sleeping, since the Bible also instructed that Christians should "pray continually."[4] It never seemed to occur to anyone that by the same logic, since men were to have their heads *uncovered* during prayer,[5] a man should never wear a hat except in bed! Men were urged to wear a straight-cut (Nehru-style) suit coat and no necktie since Christians were not supposed to outwardly adorn themselves.[6] I wore such a "plain suit" as a young man until I realized that this drew *more* attention to my external appearance than wearing a conventional suit and a tastefully selected necktie.

The strictest moral code was emphasized. Fighting pride was valued so highly that praising someone in public was very rare because it might lead to "destruction."[7] Even telling someone good news from one's own life was often met with stern silence as this seemed too much like bragging. Telling the truth at all times was so important a virtue that we learned to be extremely careful to qualify our statements for fear we might, even inadvertently, utter an untruth and find ourselves excluded on the judgment day.[8]

Human sexuality, although affirmed for married couples, was considered a strong temptation to sin and embarrassing to mention in public. My parents cancelled the local daily newspaper subscription on several occasions partly because department store ads used pictures of partially unclothed models. Dressing modestly was a high value. Skirt and sleeve lengths were often prescribed in churches and schools. Going to the movies, smoking, dancing and drinking alcoholic beverages were all strictly prohibited.

Another strong emphasis was to keep ourselves from becoming "polluted by the world."[9] We believed that we had to control as much as possible our exposure to the evil external influences of a corrupt culture. This led to a subculture that emphasized "separation from the world." It played out in many ways – not owning a television, turning the volume down on the radio during cigarette and alcohol commercials, urging children not to go to college, and placing such an emphasis on guarding doctrinal purity that the body of Christ was forever being splintered over the most ridiculous minutia. Some groups split over whether or not members were allowed to own a radio!

However, I almost feel ashamed of myself for being critical of my upbringing. I realize that being conscientious and taking one's faith seriously have their good points. I enjoy many benefits because of my morally upright heritage. And, to be fair, I must mention that in addition to all the emphasis on good works, I was taught the importance of having a personal relationship with Jesus Christ. We often heard that "God has no grandchildren." The importance of having an individual conversion experience, being "born again," was stressed.[10] The basic tenets of traditional Christian doctrine were preached regularly and at annually scheduled revival meetings. Such meetings were held each evening for one or two weeks and usually included at least one night when the topic was "hell." I and many other youngsters were thus "scared into the kingdom." Once converted, we were taught that to maintain a close walk with our Lord we should read the Bible and pray daily. Sunday school and Christian elementary school teachers set up contests and games that required us to learn the books of the Bible and to memorize numerous Scripture passages. As a result I am still reaping the benefits of having God's word hidden in my heart.[11]

Yet, what stuck with me as I grew up was that the *most important* things about the Christian life were to live it out daily in practical ways, to be victorious over temptation, to defend doctrinal purity, and to *work hard* serving the Lord and those less fortunate. Others may have *called* themselves Christian, but we believed *we* were one of the few groups that really lived it! Other Christians may have had a blind spot about loving their enemies,[12] but *we* were willing to suffer defenselessly for our faith. Biblical and *Martyr's Mirror* stories about Christians, especially Anabaptist ancestors, being horribly tortured and killed while refusing to recant were told and retold and we were expected to be willing to live up to their example, should it ever come to that.

Did someone mention pride? Wow, what a blind spot! I marvel at the ease with which admirable intentions can co-exist with such a self-righteous attitude.

# Brokenness

Well, I think this has gone on long enough. Suffice it to say, I grew up a "Mennonite of the Mennonites." Paul knew all about this self-righteous condition.[13] I thought I had the "all things"[14] *and* a personal relationship with Christ. Therefore, it was my job to "get my act together" and to help others. Imagine my chagrin when, after decades of trying to live a good Christian life, I finally came face-to-face with the undeniable fact of my brokenness. The insight came as I read John Eldredge's *Waking the Dead*. In his chapter "Deep Restoration" he describes those of us who are "broken-hearted" as having "habits we cannot quit or patterns we cannot stop, anger that flies out of nowhere, fears we cannot overcome or weaknesses we hate to admit."[15] He goes on, "Yet another indication of a house divided is the 'on again, off again' personality. One day you are kind; the next day you are sullen and angry." Such a person is "hard to read, you never know what you're going to get." He further describes a broken-hearted person as "completely different depending on what part of his heart he's living out of. He is not whole-hearted."[16] I recognized myself in this description. Suddenly I knew that, despite all that was good about my life up to that point, my heart was not whole. Did I inevitably and repeatedly find myself doing things I knew were wrong and didn't want to keep doing? Yes. Did those closest to me have to wonder each day "which Everett" they would see? Yes. Were my fear, anger and sense of abandonment always there, just under the surface, ready, at the slightest provocation, to express themselves in a sour mood, old-fashioned irritability, or even an angry verbal outburst? Yes. Was I alternatively withdrawn or angry rather than at peace, "at home in my skin"? Yes. I had to admit it; by these criteria my heart *was* broken. But how did it get that way, and what could be done about it? As I prayerfully considered these questions I recorded tentative answers in my journal. Upcoming chapters contain some of what I learned. But, first, let's think a bit about victorious Christian living.

# Trapped in Romans 7

For years, my life had been like the one Paul described in Chapter 7 of his letter to the Romans:

> "I am unspiritual, sold as a slave to sin. I do not understand what I do. For what I want to do I do not do, but what I hate I do…For I have the desire to do what is good, but I cannot carry it out. For what I do is not the good I want to do; no, the evil I do not want to do—this I keep doing."[17]

Theologians have debated whether Paul was writing about his life before his conversion or afterwards. Those who argue that this passage must refer to his plight prior to conversion point out that he also wrote that others should "Follow my example as I follow the example of Christ"[18] and that he had "fought the good fight…finished the race" and "kept the faith."[19] How could someone who continues to be a helpless slave to sin say either one? Others have held that Paul was simply admitting that even as a Christian there are times of temptation and moral failure.

Although it is difficult to know to what life phase Paul may have been referring, many Christians would agree that we have at times, even years after our conversion, struggled mightily, and sometimes unsuccessfully, to live victoriously. I have heard sermons about living as a "carnal" Christian. That is, one who has accepted Jesus as Savior but not Lord. Was that me? In a sense, at least at a deep heart level, it may have been. That is, although I would have *said* Christ was my Lord, I did not know his voice well enough, or obey him consistently enough, to live a life of true discipleship. For example, I struggled, mostly unsuccessfully, with compulsive overeating.

# Christian Victory

Edward M. Smith describes the difference between "moment-by-moment victory" and "maintenance-free victory."[20] Moment-by-moment victory is abstinence from sinful behavior in spite of emotional pain and with considerable effort and struggle. In my case, over the years I had individual moments of victory but the overall tone of my life was joyless struggle. Much of my life could have been characterized by what Smith calls the "cycle of defeat."[21] He describes this as "a deceptive cycle that is common in Christian circles. It teaches that when I am *defeated* by some sin I need to *confess* it, *repent* and turn from it, *adjust* my attitude, strategy and approach to dealing with it, and then *perform* or try harder."[22] Such an approach is a manifestation of a *performance-based* view of how to live as a Christian.[23] As such, the power of the Holy Spirit is missing and the cycle repeats itself *ad nauseum.*

In contrast, Smith and others teach that there really is the possibility, in specific areas of temptation, to be *totally freed from the struggle* and to be able to rest in Christ's provision of "maintenance-free victory."[20] For example, as in the case with my own bondage to compulsive overeating, we can find healing or deliverance from whatever is the root cause of the compulsion. The root cause may be a vow that we have made in childhood or a deep-seated lie suggested by Satan at a vulnerable moment years ago. Once these vows or lies are identified and dealt with by coming to Jesus for deliverance and truth, we can experience an amazing degree of freedom from that particular compulsion (bondage to sin) without simply becoming re-enslaved by another compulsion. When this happens, I believe that Jesus has moved us forward to a Romans 8 life condition in which we are "more than conquerors."[24]

What does this feel like? In my case, the difference is that when the temptation presents itself, it comes as a thought but not an overwhelming compulsion. The decision still has to be made. The will still must be exercised. But it no longer seems *necessary* to give in. My emotional *survival* no longer depends on receiving the temporary high of indulgence in that particular counterfeit. In some cases, we may be totally freed from the temptation to the point that it no longer even crosses our mind. Does this mean that we will never again struggle with sin in a

Romans 7 sense? Not necessarily. The Holy Spirit progressively reveals areas of sin and unbelief in which we need to once again come to Jesus for truth and healing. However, my experience has been that turning over control of my life to Christ in one area, while regularly consenting to his lordship and inviting his presence, has made it easier for me to experience the Romans 7 to Romans 8 transformation in all areas of struggle with sin. How can we co-operate as Jesus moves us from Romans 7 to Romans 8? Let's start with an overview.

## Who Will Rescue Me?

Sanctification, living as a disciple of Christ, is a life-long experience. The first pitfall to avoid is our tendency to view it as *our* project and to ask Jesus to *help us*. If we fall into this trap, we run the risk of having recurring Romans 7 experiences that involve *the same* hang-ups, hurts and habits. If instead we constantly face up to our total inability to help ourselves and insist on coming to Jesus for love, leadership, provision, power and joy, that is, *life itself*, we will be amazed at how he will transform our hearts. Does life then become dull and boring? Not if we continually keep abiding in him. He will see to it that we will always have a growing edge. He will progressively show us more ways in which we need to be surrendered to his leading. He will keep giving us challenges that will ensure that life in him will continue to be an adventure.

My wife and I purchased a cute motto some time ago with the saying:

What we are is God's gift to us

What we become is our gift to God.

It seemed true when we bought it and actually sums up pretty well the emphases of our teachers as we grew up. But the theology is just wrong. In fact, what we become is *also* God's gift to us! I suspect that as long as we live as though we can make ourselves into some sort of gift for God, he graciously works to show us the error of our ways. He doesn't want us to try to redo ourselves. He wants us to be his friend and to consent to *his* makeover project designed especially for us.[25] As long as we are *trying our best* to live the victorious Christian life, we are placing ourselves under the law anew, right back in Romans 7.[26] Not that we are no longer saved, but, for that time, on that particular issue, we have stopped being the clay and usurped the role of the potter. As long as we are thus occupied we are limiting our freedom and growth to what we can accomplish in our own puny strength. What a tragedy that so many well-meaning Christians settle for such self-imposed limitations.

To the extent that a respectable, even godly, upbringing encourages us to rely on our own strength, it is a trap. We must sooner or later come to the place where we, like Isaiah, realize that "all our righteous acts are like filthy rags."[27] Only then can we open ourselves to Jesus and let *him* make us a new creation.[28]

# Our Part

What is our part? It has to do with choice, but not in the way we often think. It is a current cultural fad to teach ethics generically. Children are taught the importance of having "values" and "making good choices." It seems to me that this is merely a new way to talk about living under the law – right back in Romans 7. Rather, the choice we need to make, moment-by-moment, is "Will I try to go it alone or will I abide in Jesus?" If we choose rightly here, the power will flow. The Holy Spirit will show us, moment-by-moment, what we should do next and will give us the motivation, power and love we need to do it. Sometimes he chooses to remain uncommunicative. This may mean that he is working non-verbally, perhaps at a subconscious level. If so, we may not see the evidence until some time later when we face a stressful situation with surprising resilience and love. At other times, his silence means that he is simply waiting for us to take action on a *next-step* he had previously given. In any case, we must allow the difficult circumstances of life to drive us to Jesus. If instead we merely take them as a reason to exercise our wills more resolutely, to practice self-control with more determination, or to resolve to more consistently make better choices, we are, I am sorry to say, doomed to a joyless life of struggle and hardship. We are then trying to serve God without tapping into the power of Jesus' resurrection and are in Paul's famous words, "to be pitied more than all men."[29] The relationship with Jesus really is at the heart of living a joyous Christian life. If you *must* work hard at something, please work at that.

I lived that joyless, struggling life way too long. My hurting heart needed to be healed. I desperately needed to get out of Romans 7! Once I admitted it to Jesus, he started to work.

# 9

# Heart Healing

## Worry about Scarcity

I am an adult child of normal parents. Even so, childhood wounding was at the root of my inability to trust God's provision. Psalm 23 was one of the Bible passages I had memorized as a child. Although I knew all my life that the Lord was my shepherd, I discovered several years ago that I did not really believe it, not deep inside, at the operational level of my psyche. This was related to my father wound.[1]

I have often heard folks complain that their fathers were good providers but that they were "never there for them." Well, my father was there for me, big time. Not only was he warm, creative and humorous, he was *literally there*. For most of my childhood he worked in his own cabinet shop just behind our house. Unfortunately though, our family was always poor. I realize now that compared to many of the world's poor, we were pretty well off. We never went hungry or slept in a cardboard box, but money was always scarce. I can still remember the month my parents had to borrow money because they could not scrape together seventy dollars to pay the rent. I saved *all* my allowance for *five years* to buy a baseball glove.

My parents wanted me to learn "the value of a dollar." I did. The problem was, I also concluded that I could not rely on my earthly father to be a good provider, at least not compared to many of my friends whose fathers were more financially secure. My parents openly discussed our family's money worries during my most impressionable years. Finally, when I was thirteen, Dad abandoned his dream of running a successful family business and went to work as a truck driver. From then on, even though the family income was still low, at least there was a steady paycheck. But the damage had already been done. I had come to view Dad, and by extension my heavenly Father as well, as an unreliable provider for my physical needs. In fact, as soon as I was able to start earning money, I was expected to "pay money home" in partial repayment of my support up to that time. This setup seemed to fit with what I had been taught about God. I had come to mistakenly believe that he primarily required my faithful *service*.[2] It only made sense, I reasoned, that since I must serve God and others, I needed to first support myself. In order to be in a position to make a contribution, I had to first avoid being a burden. In addition, whenever I would read verses like Psalm 23:1, I would immediately go into a "yes but" mode of thinking. My mind would go to the Hebrews 11 passage where at least some of the faithful are described as wandering about "destitute," and worse.[3] Though some do miraculously receive financial blessings in this life,[4] our family was not among them. I would simply have to get a decent education and a steady job. In other words, *I would have to be my own shepherd.*

# Hard Teachings

I struggled with passages like Luke 12:22-34 in which Jesus taught against worry over material necessities. Jesus said, "Consider the ravens: They do not sow or reap, they have no storeroom or barn; yet God feeds them."[5] Yes but, I reasoned, even a raven goes out and finds food. He may not be engaged in agriculture, but he is certainly a hunter/gatherer. He does not simply sit and wait for God to place food into his beak. After Jesus talked a bit about how God provides for lilies and grass he said "Sell your possessions and give to the poor."[6] Taken literally and to its logical conclusion, this command is problematic. If I sell all my possessions and give all the proceeds to World Vision and then go and sit naked in the local park, I may freeze to death. If, instead, I delay my radical obedience until summer, chances are I might survive and have my needs provided for in the nearest mental institution. Or, if a shocked but compassionate passerby were to give me clothing and food, or even if God were to drop provisions from the sky, I would once again be obliged to sell even these gifts and give the proceeds to the poor. Naked in the park all over again! And what about the poor people who receive my handouts? Should they also resell what I had given *them* and redonate the proceeds so that *they* are again naked and starving? Clearly, such an interpretation is ridiculous. In fact, an earlier verse says that our heavenly Father knows that we do need the necessities of life.[7] So what does Jesus mean? His point must have been that inordinate *concern* about one's physical needs is a bad idea. It certainly was for me.

## A Stubborn Vow

Some may be thinking, doesn't the apostle Paul write in his second letter to the Thessalonians that "If a man will not work, he shall not eat"?[8] I am not advocating irresponsible laziness. Dependence on Jesus as my Shepherd and being willing to work for a living are not mutually exclusive. But to somewhat angrily make up my mind that *I will see to it that I will never be poor again* went way beyond normal acceptance of the responsibility to earn a living. It took a while for the Lord to show me how damaging such a vow could be.

I *did* worry about money most of my life. I hated having my options in life limited by constant cash flow problems. Some years Dad's cabinet business cleared only $3,500. My first job paid forty cents an hour even when the minimum wage was $1.25. For years I found it impossible *not* to worry about finances. In fact, I found that once I had landed a good professional job, *I worried much less* than I had while destitute. Thus, the thought of selling most of my possessions and giving away the proceeds sounded to me like a *prescription* for worry rather than a solution to it. My experience was that using public transportation and sharing garden tools with neighbors made life more complicated and stressful, not simpler, as some suggested.

Nevertheless, as long as I believed at a gut level that I was on my own, I was in bondage. For me, this was idolatry. One exercise suggested by the authors of the *Companions in Christ* spiritual formation course was to compose a "reverse paraphrase" of Psalm 23.[9] Imagine if this familiar Psalm went like this:

The Devil is my harsh taskmaster

I will always be hungry, yea, starving and parched

He maketh me to jump up and down on sharp gravel – barefooted

He pusheth me over a 600 foot cliff

He sendest me out to wander about in pitch darkness for no apparent reason

Even when life seems perfect, I will always feel a deep sense of impending doom

His night stick beateth me silly

He feedeth my enemies a scrumptious feast while I am sick as a dog and can't stand the thought of food

He poureth used motor oil on my head and it drippeth from my chin

Surely, all kinds of bad stuff will keep happening to me for the rest of my born days

For life is indeed a bummer and then we die.


How many of us live as though this were the real Psalm 23? Have we learned not to expect much, so as not to be disappointed? Do we belittle our desires for happiness and significance, repeatedly reminding ourselves that we are only pilgrims in this life? Is worry our constant companion while gratitude seldom visits? If so, these may be hints that we really believe the reverse version of Psalm 23. God can heal this spiritual brokenness. Here's how I know.


# Compulsion

I was a chubby child, enough so that I earned the nickname "wobbles" because of the way I looked running the bases of the softball diamond. Most of my life I battled a compulsion to overeat. For years I would diet, lose thirty pounds, and then put them back on, over and over, all the while enduring the sad looks and disapproving comments from family and friends whenever they would notice the regaining part of the cycle once again kicking in.

I realize that some chronically overweight folks have a medical problem. Others are "normal" people who do not have a true compulsion to overeat, but are simply opportunistic overeaters and under-exercisers. But for people like I was, who eat to feel better, who eat when they're sad and eat when they're excited, who find themselves snacking when not hungry – just because they feel tense, who may be using the treadmill an hour every day so they can continue to overeat, who hate to start a new round of dieting because feeling even a little physical hunger triggers almost unbearable emotional stress; people like us need to just give it up! Let's face it, *there is something very broken inside.* But there is hope. Jesus longs to rescue even the most desperate.

# The Road Back

Near the beginning of my first time through the 28-week *Companions in Christ* (CIC) experience[10], I read Psalm 81. In verses 8-16 the Lord says, "Hear, O my people, and I will warn you – if you would but listen to me, O Israel! You shall have no foreign god among you; you shall not bow down to an alien god. I am the Lord your God...Open wide your mouth and I will fill it. ...If [you] would but listen to me [you] would be fed with the finest of wheat; with honey from the rock I would satisfy you." The thought question was, "What is the character of your heart when it is listening [to God]?[11] Prayerfully, I wrote, "When I am listening, I am humble; I am at peace, not in a hurry. I am *expecting a surprising blessing*...I am accepting my place as creature, not creator." God wants us to be still and listen. If we will do that, he will provide for our needs. No foreign, counterfeit god such as more food, more sex or more shopping can satisfy. Only God can.

Six months later, the CIC authors directed our attention to Romans 7 in which Paul described his struggle to live out what he knew to be right.[12] The suggestion was to "Find places in your life where you identify with Paul's struggle and describe them in your own words."[13] My response was honest. "I find it very difficult to rely on the Lord instead of food when I feel low or lonely. Food is so tangible, immediate and sensual. The Lord [seems] so intangible, silent and abstract." In the next exercise, we were directed to read 2 Corinthians 12:1-10 in which Paul spoke of his "thorn in the flesh." One of the questions was "What weakness embarrasses you?" I wrote, "My weakness is food and my tendency to gain weight. This is obvious to all. I cannot overeat in secret without the evidence showing up for all to see." (Fortunately, I had never considered bulimia as a solution to this dilemma.)

Six more months went by. As I was starting through the CIC experience with a second group, we were reading Ephesians 6:10-17 where Paul urges us to "take up the whole armor of God." The CIC authors asked "What inner and outer forces routinely uproot your faith, sap your inner strength, or undermine your courage to "stand firm" in Christ's love?[14] I responded that the force (Devil's scheme)[15] most at work was my fear of poverty. Then, for the first time, this question came to mind, "Is this why I tend to overeat?" Oddly enough, when in the same exercise the question "What armor do you need to take up?" was asked, I replied, "I need to take up the *belt* of truth.' Without it I could be caught with my pants down – embarrassed and vulnerable." It strikes me now that the Holy Spirit was getting me ready for the time when my physical belt became a reminder of a precious truth.

About a month later God touched me deeply while I was reading Psalm 139. In verses 15 and 16 the psalmist says "My frame was not hidden from you, when I was made in the secret place. When I was woven together...your eyes saw my unformed body." I sobbed uncontrollably. I thought of all the self-loathing I had suffered for so long about "my frame." Suddenly I realized the precious truth that he knew all about "my frame." Yes, he knew long ago, *during the design phase*, what my physical and emotional tendencies would be. He also knew the potential that he would build in for my body to be vital and strong.

The next month we studied the account of the woman whose body was bent double for eighteen years.[16] She was "crippled by a spirit." Unlike times when an evil spirit possessed the person and Jesus rebuked the demon directly,[17] this time he spoke to the woman. It seems that even though Satan caused the illness, he had not possessed her will. Jesus simply said, "Woman, you are set free from your infirmity." And she was! After meditating on this story, I prayed, "Lord, show me how I can be free from my *compulsion* to overeat. If this is caused by an evil spirit or Satan, would you please rebuke it or him. If not, would you please work to heal the broken places in my heart that motivate this *self-destructive behavior*. Lord, if I am to be 'set free from this infirmity,' *you* must do it. I cannot do it by trying harder!"

This was the first time that I had recognized my overeating as a compulsion with a possible spiritual and/or emotional cause. The fact that this insight came as a result of prayer makes me think it was from the Holy Spirit. Although I was not aware of it at the time, it could be that Jesus' healing had already begun.

Another month passed. Looking at a photograph of myself, I was disgusted with how fat I looked. I prayed, "Lord, if you knew me so well and actually formed (knitted together) my physique as Psalm 139 says, why do I have such a struggle with overeating?" Immediately he seemed to reply, "Ev, you need to get that book by Ed Smith called *Healing Life's Deepest Hurts*."[18]

Four days later, as Leona and I were bringing a CIC session to a close in our two-story living room, we suggested that the group spend a few minutes in silent prayer. After a bit, while my eyes were closed, I received a mental image of Jesus standing above and in front of me. He was either very tall or standing on a platform. He was holding a large Horn of Plenty full of all kinds of candy bars and other small, wrapped food items. As I "watched" he lifted it and poured them down onto me so that they piled up waist-high all around me. He said nothing, but the meaning was clear. I no longer needed to worry about scarcity. I could rest assured that whenever I needed good food, there would be enough. There would no longer be a need to store up calories in my body as a hedge against possible future shortages.

After four more days, I was meditating on the story of Jesus' healing of blind Bartimaeus.[19] The blind man shouted, "Son of David, have mercy on me!" Jesus called him over and asked, "What do you want me to do for you?" What did he *think* the man wanted, better hearing? Of course, Jesus knew, he just wanted Bartimaeus to say it. Then Jesus healed him.

As I thought about this story, I realized that my problem wasn't excess adipose tissue. It was not bad eating habits. It was not lack of self-control. It was not lack of knowledge about how to eat healthily. In my case, it was not a medical problem. My body responded nicely when I ate properly and exercised. My problem was clearly a spiritual and emotional one. At the root of my eating compulsion lay fear of scarcity. I prayed, "Lord, I want a deep, unshakable trust in your love and your promises to care for me. Lord, help me to trust in your bounty." At this point he reminded me that I still needed to read *Healing Life's Deepest Hurts*. So I did.

In this book Ed Smith explains that sometimes emotional pain and compulsions stem from traumatic childhood experiences. If the emotion aroused is stronger than the present circumstance warrants, it is a hint that there is buried pain left over from events earlier in life. We need to follow the negative emotion back to its origin in our memory. Often the pain is caused, not by the memory itself, but by false beliefs embedded in the memory.[20] I began to write down all the specifics of my poverty-stricken childhood. One that I did not detail above seems now to be trivial compared to the very real poverty many suffer daily. But I include it here to illustrate that even what seems trivial from an adult viewpoint, can be the basis for gut-level emotional compulsions.

# Chevy "Heaven"

As a teenager I loved to drive. For two or three years before I turned sixteen and could get a driver's license, Dad allowed me to drive the family vehicles in our driveway. As I backed the car out of the detached garage, turned it around and drove it the eighty feet to the house, I longingly pictured the day I could drive out onto the street and go somewhere on my own. The young men that were my neighbors were a few years older. The father to the west bought his son a brand new '57 Chevy. Five years later my neighbor to the east received a new '62 Chevy. A few years later a close school buddy announced that his father had just given him a new '64 Chevy. All of these were stylish two-doors with lots of V-8 power. When I first got my license, I had the choice of two family vehicles. One was a hand-painted (with a brush!), fire-engine red '53 GMC pickup truck and the other a black, six-cylinder '46 Chevy. Within a year I bought my Grandfather's '55 Chevy. It was a battleship-grey, four-door sedan with a six-cylinder engine. It got me from point A to point B but with none of the style or power that I craved. I thought at the time that it did not really matter. Was I simply being envious? I honestly don't think so. At the time, given my family's financial difficulties, I was just glad to be able to afford independent transportation. But the stark reality of the unequal distribution of resources was not lost on my teenage mind. And, I did not believe that there was anything to be done about it other than to *stuff my feelings* and determine to do better for myself – *by my own efforts.*

# Insight

The next morning, during our prayer time, I mentioned to Leona that I was in the midst of a process of following the emotional "smoke trail" back to my childhood hurt over being poor.[21] She asked for an example. I told her about the cars. It made her cry. Then she shared an amazing insight. She said, "Perhaps you felt especially vulnerable as a child because of your father's asthma." Dad's poor health constantly lurked as a threat to even what little financial security we did have. I realized the truth she had spoken, and began to weep. I felt very much like the scared little boy again. As I wept I asked Jesus to heal me in that place of deep heart brokenness, that soul-scarred spot. I thanked him and then came the question, "Will I actually feel noticeably more freedom from this fear in the near future?"

He seemed to reply. "Ev, I'm so glad that you have received this insight by my Spirit's leading through Leona. Stay close to me. I *do* have a very real Horn of Plenty, both physical and spiritual, that I long to make available to you. I will heal you in this area of hurt."

I replied, "Thanks, Lord, I'm here and I invite you at all times to be with me and to work on my unbelief and to give me confidence in your bountiful provision.

Love,

Ev

P.S. Lord, is my compulsive overeating a symptom of this deep-seated insecurity about the necessities of life? Is this similar to Andrew's story in *Healing Life's Deepest Hurts*?[22] Andrew's childhood wounding resulted in compulsive homosexual urges that plagued him every day even though he had abstained from acting on them for eight years! According to author Ed Smith, 'Andrew held the mistaken belief that abstinence means victory. This is not victory. Victory occurs only when the battle and struggle are over – for good. ...Months later [Andrew] wrote, "I have not had one homosexual urge in over three months, and I have not had to work at it! Before this freedom, I could not go an hour!"

These thoughts occurred to me, I think they were from Jesus: "Andrew's thinking changed. His freedom was real. Now he could rest. He had experienced true emotional, spiritual and physical release. *Ev, you can too.*"

"Oh, Lord," I answered, "how I wish this could be true for me in my overeating compulsion. *Dare I even hope* for such a miraculous healing?"

Marvelously, his reply was "Yes, a thousand times yes, my dear son! And you do not have to fix it. Just *let me* do it. I will take as much time and care as needed so that you will not be traumatized. Just stay close, I have wonderful plans for your future!"[23]

# Christian Fatalism

My parents did their best. Dad's parents had taken him out of school at the end of eighth grade. Basically, he was an indentured servant for his father between ages thirteen and twenty-one. He received his room and board but no pay. Mother's parents also removed her from school after the tenth grade and took her to a different city where she worked as a cook and maid for a wealthy family so that she could pay money home. Just sixteen at the time, she had really liked school and wished to continue. My grandparents were not ogres, just dirt poor and struggling to survive the Great Depression. These experiences, combined with various health issues and financial pressures led to my parents holding a world view which, for lack of a better term, I will call Christian Fatalism. I would summarize it this way:

> Life is uncertain and sometimes even cruel. We can consider ourselves blessed, as Christians, if we make it through life without being tortured or martyred like many Christians were before us. In short, this life is a lost cause. As Christians though, we can look forward to having it better in heaven.

# Healing!

For years I subscribed to a similar life philosophy. But now Jesus seemed to be stepping in with renewed hope. Based on Jesus' personal and specific promise of healing for me, I prayed, "Lord, is there already a degree of healing? How will I know?"

He began to ask me the following series of questions:

1. "Well, Ev, start paying attention to your *attitude toward food*. For instance, is it as important as it used to be that you eat just because it is *mealtime*? Do you sometimes just skip or delay a meal because you are engaged in an interesting activity?"

I replied, "As a matter of fact, Lord, that changed almost as soon as I began taking the anti-depressant six months ago! What a difference!"

He came back with, "See, Ev, I've already been working on that woundedness, partly through the medication, which, by the way was also my idea, and partly by way of the healing I have been doing in your heart even before you understood the nature of your brokenness. You had asked me to start working as soon as you became aware that your heart was broken, and I started right away. But I can do even more now that you are ready and actively pursuing healing."

2.  Next Jesus asked, "Do you sometimes make decisions involving food differently than you would have in the past?"

I answered, "Yes, Lord, just this morning I was sitting in a meeting at work. At 10:50 am it became obvious that, for me, this particular all-day training session was a complete waste of time. My thinking at first was 'Well, if I stay until lunch, I will get a good lunch free and then I can decide whether to go back for the afternoon session.' But almost immediately I thought, 'No, I should not waste an hour and a half just to get a free lunch.' So I excused myself and left. For me, that was evidence of a new-found freedom."

3.  Jesus then asked, "Do you find your urges to snack between meals less frequent, and, when you do snack, is the urge to binge less compelling?"

"Yes Lord, yes, yes yes! Already true! Amazing! At the weekend conference a few days ago I ate one helping at mealtime although seconds were offered. One time I even totally forgot to eat dessert! Also, I felt very little desire to snack between meals even though the snacks looked yummy and were always available. And this morning I had absolutely no urge to go to the vending machine for a snack even though I had eaten a small breakfast."

4.  Several hours later Jesus said, "Another question, Ev, do you totally rule out the possibility of fasting as a means of grace (spiritual discipline) for yourself?"

"As a matter of fact, Lord, I used to, but no longer."

"See, Kiddo," he responded, "isn't that in itself a miracle?"

"Amazing, Lord! Thanks for calling all this to my attention. These are evidences of healing that you have already been doing!"

5. But there was still more. At home later he asked, "Ev, are you gaining weight?" "No, Lord, I have actually lost 5 or 6 pounds over the last six months."

6. "Is your belt getting tighter?", he asked next. "Actually no, it is getting a little looser lately."

"See what I'm saying?" he inquired.

"Yes, Lord," I answered. "This evening for dinner I had a salad and one pork chop and I didn't even feel hungry for dessert."

The next morning I actually weighed myself. I had lost *eight pounds!*. My belt was in the next tighter hole comfortably for the first time in years. I had *not been trying* to lose weight. I had been working at my relationship with Jesus! Never before in my life had I ever lost weight or waistline girth except when I had been totally focused on doing so and even then with great difficulty.

I know, some may be skeptical at this point. They're just dying to ask, "Was it just a temporary, small, medication-induced weight loss?" The simple answer is no. First of all, as Jesus' questions showed, the most profound change was in my *attitude* toward food. That renewal has lasted. In addition, I went on to lose a total of twenty-six pounds and four inches from my waist without dieting at all. I have maintained these losses for four and a half years. Furthermore, when I stopped taking the low dose of anti-depressant[24] for six months, the eating compulsion did not return nor did I gain weight. Now, every morning when I put on my pants I can see the external, scientific evidence of the miraculous inner healing Jesus worked in me. For me, "belt of truth" now has a precious new meaning!

# Compulsion vs. Sinning

Do I ever overeat? Occasionally, yes. But the *compulsion* to do so never came back. Let me explain. In John 5 Jesus healed a man who had been crippled for thirty-eight years. Jesus asked, "Do you want to get well?" Even though the man's answer was whiny and expressed very little faith or hope, Jesus said, "Get up! Pick up your mat and walk."[25] And he did. The man had lain there almost four decades! Imagine how atrophied his leg muscles must have been. But Jesus didn't say, "Call for your friends and have them take you to the physical therapist and in six months you will have enough strength to get up and walk." No, Jesus restored his full muscular strength and his sense of balance right then and there. The man did not hobble, shuffle, stumble or totter. He stood up on his fully restored legs, stooped down and used his restored core and upper body strength to pick up his mat and walk off. And at that point he didn't even know who Jesus was![26] But later, Jesus found him at the temple and warned him to stop sinning.[27]

I feel like that man. For about the same amount of time, I was crippled emotionally. Jesus' healing of my overeating compulsion has been pure and complete gift. But like the former cripple in John 5, I must stop sinning. Just because I am now free from the *compulsion* to overeat does not mean that I cannot still commit the sin of gluttony. I can still be tempted to overeat opportunistically. But, since I am no longer oppressed by the compulsion, it is *much easier* not to sin. In Jesus' strength, I can now successfully resist the temptation to overeat without feeling the emotional pain that used to accompany abstinence from gluttony.

## An Ongoing Journey

Let me summarize. Although, at the moment of break-through, I sensed a miraculous and surprising release from life-long bondage, the process leading up to that point was not so mysterious. Jesus used a series of experiences to prepare me to receive his gift. Some of these were joyful like the point early in that first *Companions in Christ* course when I realized that sharing deeply with God's children brought me more joy than watching a Pittsburgh Steelers football game. But I would have missed even that had I not obeyed when asked to help teach *Companions in Christ* in the fall, on Sunday afternoons, from 1-3 pm.

Other experiences were painful: watching my parents die, living through the scary time when I thought I was going to lose my wife to cancer, being disgusted by pictures of my fat self, and getting so depressed that I could just barely drag myself out of bed and to work. Even after I had started to recognize my Shepherd's voice, there were *large blocks of time* during which I was "on the road" with Jesus.

Several years later Jesus was still working with me on the issue of fear of scarcity. Although it no longer was expressed as a compulsion to overeat, I had begun to suspect that it was not completely gone. Our church small group leader asked what we would like the group to pray for us about. Suddenly I knew what it was. I said, "Ask that God would give me a more generous heart." One week later I participated in a one day personality-type workshop.[28] I scored abysmally on the questions relating to being a generous person. According to that survey I was not. Exactly one week later, at a one-day retreat, my co-leader, Jim Miller led us in a meditation on Matthew 6:19-34. Here Jesus urges us not to be slaves to our worry about money. One of the thought questions was "What do I sense Jesus is calling me to do through this passage?"

I answered, "To let go of my fear of scarcity and to be willing to take *small steps in a generous direction*, as he points them out to me."

Since the breakthrough on the overeating compulsion issue I have retired from my corporate, middle-management position. My income is now only twenty-five percent of what it was while I was working. So, of course, Jesus would pick *this* time in my life to teach me about generosity! Once again, did I dare hope that Jesus could work *this* miracle? Could he lead me to even this new level of freedom from concern about material things? I am happy to report that he has begun to do just that.

# 10

# Lies That Bind

## What Do We *Really* Believe?

Jesus said, "If you hold to my teaching, you are really my disciple. Then you will know the truth, and the truth will set you free."[1] If truth sets us free, what is it that ties us up in knots? Lies, of course! Lies we learn subtly, in our innocence, usually very early on. Things we believe deep down, at the "gut level." Lessons we have learned about how life *really* works, we think, as opposed to the way preachers and Sunday school teachers have told us it should. These lies were often suggested by Satan at times of emotional wounding caused by the inevitable hard knocks of life. These untruths seemed right to us at the time, so we agreed with the Deceiver and have lived accordingly ever since, often without conscious awareness of the deception. As a result, experiences we face in everyday life repeatedly trigger emotions and urges that are stronger than the current situation warrants. Until we become aware of these hot button issues and invite Jesus to replace them with healing truth, we may find that it is very difficult to live a consistently Christ-like life. We may struggle with compulsions or addictions or a tendency to over-react in stressful situations.[2] Each person's wounding, consequent erroneous beliefs, and paths to freedom are different but there are common themes and practical ways to come to Jesus for truth and healing. One example from my life was the belief that I was ultimately responsible to provide for my own physical needs (Chapter 9). Here I detail a second personal example.

## I'm Just Not Good Enough

I used to enjoy Al Franken's skits on Saturday Night Live in which he played a needy soul with a mock self-help show called "Daily Affirmations with Stuart Smalley." Just before he went on stage Stuart would try to bolster his nearly non-existent self-confidence by telling himself, "I'm good enough, I'm smart enough, and doggone it, people like me!" The mere fact that he had to keep telling himself this was evidence that he didn't really believe it. At the time, I couldn't see how much I resembled that fictional character. But I now know that a thematic lie plagued me most of my life. Thematic lies are created when similar experiences recur over extended periods of a person's childhood.[5] This one probably resulted from the fact that my naturally boisterous, passionate and even somewhat irreverent nature was in conflict with a strict, moralistic upbringing that valued quiet, unemotional niceness and viewed creative, male energy with suspicion. Sometimes my natural absent-mindedness also caused trouble. As a result, I was often convinced that I was *unacceptable*. This had been going on for so long and so frequently that there was an accompanying sense of hopelessness. Here is how it showed up most recently.

About a month ago, while I was cleaning up the kitchen after lunch, Leona asked a question and made a statement. "Everett, why do you put the dirty dishes on the counter above the dishwasher rather than directly into it. I often find myself having to put them into the dishwasher after you have left the area. I'm tired of having to do that." Immediately I was flooded with emotion – a mixture of anger and fear – and lashed out verbally. No sooner had the hateful words passed my lips than I recoiled in shock at their vehemence and malice. Within seconds I recognized them for the sin that they were, and apologized profusely. But I also recognized this over-reaction as a classic example of being "triggered" – having lie-based emotional pain exposed. As soon as possible I went to Jesus seeking insight and emotional healing.

"Why does this stir me up so much, Lord?" I asked. "I thought you and I had already dealt with this whole super-neatness issue before. You know, that, as a boy, I had only the top of one chest of drawers as my own personal space in a small apartment. Every Saturday I had to arrange my things neatly enough to please my super-neat mother. I hated that job. There seemed to be no good place to put things. About a year ago I brought this memory to you, Lord. You showed me a mental image in which you swept all the stuff off the chest of drawers onto the floor, sat down on the floor across from me and said, 'This is why I made you, to spend time with me, not to constantly chase the perfectionist ideal of a super-neat living space!' So, Lord, why does this type of mild criticism still pain me so much?"

He didn't seem to answer so I began to describe my feelings. "I feel penned in, trapped, imprisoned by my mother's and my wife's expectations when all I really want is to be free to wander and explore." After about ten minutes of letting my mind drift back, searching for a memory that felt most like these current emotions, I arrived at another one Jesus and I had already visited. As it turned out, it had nothing to do with keeping a neat house. However, the emotional content, feeling unavoidably trapped by others' expectations, was very similar.

As a small boy (aged two to four), I was expected to sit still and quiet in church. On a regular basis I could not accomplish this unnatural act, no matter how hard I tried. Consequently, Dad often spanked me at home after church. Although the spankings never left marks and were not done in anger, they were hard enough that I always cried hard during and for a little while after. Now, the pain of being repeatedly criticized for not being neat enough around the house feels a lot like that earlier pain. As I prayerfully considered this memory, the lie seemed to be "If I do not perform perfectly, painful consequences are inevitable." The truth the Spirit of Jesus gave was "Failing to always meet Leona's expectations for neatness will not cause her to divorce you and, furthermore, *I* do not expect legalistic perfection."[6]

I then watched for a similar event to find out if there had been real healing. Two days later, Leona questioned me about something I had misplaced in the bathroom. I did not get triggered! In perfect peace and good humor I explained my action logically and in a way that made her grin with amusement. Later I prayed, "That, dear Lord, was a miracle!"

"Neat, huh?" he said.

"Very neat, Lord," I replied.

# And Furthermore

But Jesus was not yet finished. He had dealt with my fear of immediate, dire consequences but there were other lies embedded in the same memory. A few days later, while Leona and I were praying at the end of the day, she told me that she wished I would pray more often for certain loved ones. Although she meant it as an expression of her desire for unity with me in prayer, I over-reacted. I perceived her comment as a stinging rebuke. This time I did not fight back but I felt chastised and very angry. "Why must she find fault, over and over?" I wondered.

Later in private I prayed, "Lord, for years Leona has wanted me to take spiritual leadership in our home. Now that I am moving in that direction she takes exception to *how* I pray, or *don't* pray. Maybe Ed Smith is right. Maybe you are using her suggestions to uncover my lie-based thinking.[7] But I thought I *had* dealt with this before. Right now I feel like just getting into the car and driving away, perhaps permanently!"

Jesus seemed to reply, "So Ev, don't hold back, just come right out and tell me how you *really* feel!"

So I did. I said, "I feel hopeless, invalidated and unfairly picked-upon. I feel angry, hen-pecked and alone. My best friend in the entire world thinks I'm unacceptable in many ways. What am *I* supposed to think?"

At this point I stopped and sat still and allowed my mind to drift back. Once again, the memory that felt most like my current emotions was the one where I was riding home in the back seat of Dad's '37 Chevy. It was dark outside – most likely after a Wednesday evening prayer meeting. I was about four years old. Once again I had failed to meet Dad's expectations to be quiet and still enough while kneeling on the hard wooden floor listening to adults mumble prayers into the backs of church pews for an hour or more. What I did, specifically, I can't remember. But I do know I had not *intentionally* misbehaved. Nevertheless, Dad, as was his way, had promised to give me a spanking when we got home. Other fathers took their "rutchy" (Pennsylvania Dutch lingo meaning antsy) boys to the church basement and "got it over with." But not my dad. His theory seemed to be, it'll make a more lasting impression if the boy has to worry about it all the way home. Well he was right. Decades later I was *still* dealing with the emotional consequences.

Anyway, back to the memory. I was in the car, during the thirty minute ride home, hoping against hope that Dad would forget about the spanking. I felt trapped, unacceptable and hopeless. Hopeless in two ways – I knew he'd remember, he always did, and I knew I'd misbehave again and the terrible cycle would go on forever. I was so unacceptable that my own dad spanked me repeatedly, trying to change my active little boy nature! Not only was my natural exuberance and physical energy not validated, it was judged to be evil and deserving of painful punishment.

Two things seemed very true:

1. I was unacceptable, and
2. My situation was hopeless, i.e., I would *always* be unacceptable

# Ah, Truth!

I asked Jesus to come and bring truth. After a minute or so I "saw" him, in my mind's eye, checking my account on a computer screen. He had reading glasses part way down his nose and a medium-length, salt-and-pepper beard on a kindly face, lit softly by the light from the lap-top screen. He typed a few strokes, checked the screen again and then said, "Humph, your account is paid in full. In fact, you have an infinite line of credit. Not $10,000, not $1,000,000, infinite, I say!"

"Really, Lord?" I asked, "I've never had a line of credit like that before."

"You know what this means, don't you, Ev?" he asked with a grin.

"Yes, Lord, it means that I *still* have credit, and to spare! Whoopee!"

And then came a realization of truth – *I no longer misbehave in church*. So it wasn't hopeless, after all. And, it's not hopeless now either, because just as I *grew out of* my tendency to misbehave in church, both Leona and I are continuing to grow spiritually. Then Jesus checked the computer again and said, "It wasn't your fault, even then. It went on your dad's account. You were actually a victim of a mild form of physical abuse. Although you did deserve some of your spankings later on when you were willfully naughty, *these* were not deserved. You were just an active little boy. You simply *could not* consistently behave like an adult in that type of church service. Your parents and the church should have made provision for age-appropriate activities. To force you to sit or kneel still and quiet for that long was *just plain wrong*. Your church does not expect it of today's children. You recently enjoyed watching your three-year-old grandson as he got soaked up to his waist running repeatedly through a big rain-water puddle. That's the kind of thing little boys are supposed to do! You were **not** unacceptable; it was your dad and the church that were missing the mark."

Then I asked the Lord how all this related to the current situation. He seemed to say, "You are acceptable when *I* say you are acceptable, regardless of what Leona or anyone else says or thinks.[8] As I said, your account is clear. You are already doing what I am asking of you. If at some future time I lay a burden on your heart to intercede for specific loved ones in prayer, you will of course do that as well, right?"

"Absolutely, Lord"

He went on, "And furthermore, it is not hopeless. You will not always be so sensitive to Leona's suggestions."

# Confirmation

Three days later a marvelous thing happened. Our bedroom and bathroom are separated by a pair of French doors. In the cold months we like to sleep in a cool bedroom while using a space-heater to warm the adjoining bath. To make this work, we must keep the doors closed as much as possible. Leona mentioned that she had noticed that these doors had been left open on several occasions. I knew by the way she said it that she was pretty sure that I was the culprit. *I did not get triggered!* Out of perfect peace I merely said, "I have no conscious memory of leaving them open, nor did I intentionally do so. But, it was probably me. I will try to remember to shut the doors. I probably got careless over the summer when it didn't matter, and now I need to retrain myself. *Would you please remind me as often as you notice them hanging open?* That will help me do better!"

The contrast from the dirty-dishes-on-top-of-the-kitchen-counter incident was dramatic. That time I had fought back viciously. Now I found myself *asking her to "nag" me* as often as necessary! I prayed a brief prayer of gratitude. "Thank you, Lord. You came through again. What a wonderful miracle, to have sweet peace in a place that had been so painful!" Then, as I often do, I asked for more insight. "So why was my response so different?"

The truth I realized in that moment was, "I now know that I am acceptable to God. Criticism of a certain behavior is not evidence that I am a bad, unacceptable person. It is merely a request for me to make a reasonable effort to improve that particular behavior. Both God and Leona love me completely and want nothing but the best for me. Especially God, but Leona too. A request from either for me to behave better in a particular way is merely that, not further evidence that I am fundamentally and hopelessly flawed.

## Thoughts on Mind Renewal

How do these experiences fit with biblical truth? What did Jesus mean by an "infinite line of credit"? I was brought up in the Arminian tradition, taught to be wary of anything that smacked of Calvinism or "eternal security." It is not my intention to try to resolve this doctrinal dilemma. I am not a theologian nor do I believe that the validity of Jesus' message to me, "you have an infinite line of credit," hinges on the outcome of this debate. For me, the "I'm not acceptable" lie was never about my ultimate salvation. Even though I knew I was saved, I *still felt unacceptable in practical ways in everyday life,* unable to achieve the level of performance *that some folks expected.*

But I still couldn't quite let the Arminian question alone. I prayed, "Lord, if my account is clear and I have an infinite line of credit,[9] why is repentance and forgiveness still necessary when I sin?"

He answered, "Even a person who has money in his account must go to the automatic teller machine (ATM) and withdraw cash as needed."

"Yes, Lord, I know. I must confess and repent and receive your grace by faith." Then I couldn't help myself; I had always wanted to ask him this question. "But, Lord, what if I die suddenly between the sin and the confession?" (This fear is a well-known drawback of interpreting Scripture from an Arminian perspective.)

Jesus seemed to reply, "Well, what if you die on the way to the ATM?"

"Then I wouldn't need the cash, would I, Lord?"

"Now you're getting it, Kiddo."

"But Lord, I protested, "it seems like you are mixing up past and future. In the natural example, I need cash for future expenditures. In the case of a sin I have committed, I need the grace for a past offence."

He said with a grin, "Hey, Kiddo, I AM!"

"Are you saying, Lord, that in your "beyond-time" economy my line of credit works both retrospectively and prospectively?"

"Something like that, Ev. I'll be better able to explain that once you have your new heavenly brain. But, also, I can see your heart. I know your intentions. You want to remain close to me. So your account is clear, with an infinite line of credit. Together we will use those times, when you sin, as training and growth opportunities. I am not looking to cut you off at the slightest provocation. You and I have a marvelous future together!"

"But Lord, that sounds an awful lot like eternal security."

"So what?" Jesus asked. He went on, "Just *try* to make me let you go now, my boy!" It was almost a playful dare!

"Oh no, Lord," I replied in horror, "don't even *think* that! What I have come to experience with you is way too precious."

## Acceptable or Not?

So, am I unacceptable? Only if I think I must be perfect to be loved. In this life there will always be room for growth and improvement. But I must never agree that my natural human limitations make me unacceptable. That lie sounds like one our Enemy told Eve in the Garden of Eden. He said she could be *like God* if she ate the forbidden fruit.[10] To think that I am unacceptable as long as I still need helpful suggestions from God, my wife, and others is just baloney. *I need to relax and get used to being human and needing a lot of help.* Some suggestions will have merit (of course, all of God's do), while others should simply be ignored. Jesus will show us the difference.[11]

## Is There Hope for Us All?

It is likely that we all have woundedness from childhood experiences and believe some lies that need to be dispelled by a personal encounter with Jesus. When a current event causes a flood of negative emotion that seems out of proportion to the immediate stimulus, truth-based healing may be needed. Ask Jesus to show you how he wants **you** to get free. Do *not* think that, if you struggle with some of the same lies I have described, that just reading, and cognitively agreeing with, the truth I was given will necessarily result in your own release. You need to "hear, see, sense or realize" the *particular truth* that Jesus has *especially for you.* Only he can give you truth at that deep-down, operational level that will free you to "grow up into him."[12] Some folks may need professional psychiatric care and/or medication. Some are helped by a spiritual director, pastoral counselor, or prayer minister. Some may benefit from Theophostic Prayer Ministry. Others may study and apply Christian spiritual practices such as Centering Prayer[13] or the Ignatian Exercises.[14] Whatever pathway Jesus chooses for you, please know that he wants you to be "transformed by the renewing of your mind."[4] Go for it!

# 11

# Enjoying Life in a Scary World

## Fear Itself

The Bible says, "perfect love drives out fear."[1] But what does this mean? If we are afraid, are we necessarily unloving? Of course not; some fear is good. Imagine standing on a huge boulder on the brink of a sheer, 3000 foot cliff. There are no nearby trees or shrubs. You are outside the safety railing. There are no friends within arm's reach. In this position, a good, stiff gust of wind might be just enough to start you falling over the edge. Healthy, realistic fear should kick in, causing you to step back to a safe distance.

Anyone who has ever cared for a young child will agree that, at first, he has a *fear deficiency*. As soon as he can, he will climb up onto anything available and step fearlessly off the edge. Before he can safely play unsupervised, he must *learn* fear. Obviously, this is not the kind of fear that love eliminates.

At the other extreme of the fear spectrum lie the phobias. These are pathological, even paralyzing, unrealistic fears. A person with claustrophobia may avoid elevators. Someone with an extreme fear of heights (acrophobia) may have suffered strong anxiety just reading the first paragraph of this chapter. (Sorry, I should have warned you.)

But this chapter is not about everyday, realistic fear or any of the extreme phobias. Nor am I dealing here with "The fear of the Lord"[2] – a "reverential awe of God."[3] No, I'm addressing the fear that gets in the way of trusting God. The New Testament Greek word most often translated "fear" is *phobos*.[4] A few times it is also translated "terror." This is the word used in 1 John 4:18, "There is no fear in love. But perfect love drives out fear, because fear has to do with punishment. The one who fears is not made perfect in love." Another Greek word used much less often is *deilia,* which means timidity or cowardice.[5] This is the word used in 2 Timothy 1:7, "For God did not give us a spirit of timidity, but a spirit of power." Thus, if we go through life timidly, always being afraid of criticism or punishment, we are missing the best that God has for us.

This kind of fear, while not paralyzing like an extreme phobia, limits our ability to trust God's goodness and protection. Often it is a gut-level, reflexive emotion and in many cases may be connected to lies we learned in early childhood's emotionally traumatic experiences. It can also be partially caused by how our parents viewed life and how teachers and preachers interpreted Scripture or even by the stories that were told and retold as we were growing up. If, for example, we were raised by timid parents who often reminded us that our ancestors suffered for their faith, we may be convinced that life is more dangerous than joyful.

As we know from experience, some of us are naturally more shy and fearful than others. A combination of genetic, environmental and biochemical factors can cause such differences. When fear is extreme, psychotherapy and medication may be needed. But even for normally functioning folks, common fear, timidity and an over-concern for personal safety and security can greatly limit our ability to live a joyful, creative and productive life.

## Is Life Sometimes Frightening?

Of course. God often allows sinful and stupid people to act as they choose. Even nature causes great human suffering. No matter how hard we try to be careful and follow all the safety rules, ultimately, we are not in control of outcomes. For his own reasons and according to a script to which we are not privy, God sometimes allows a breach in the protective perimeter his angelic SWAT team normally sets up around us.

In light of these inescapable facts, how is it that we can face each new day, go "outside" and enjoy life? Only God can give us a "spirit of power."[6] Here is how it happened for me.

## Dealing with Scary Memories

Some of my earliest memories are of my mother warning me to be on the lookout for the neighboring farmer's escaped bull or the rabid fox that had been seen nearby. Dangerous, out-of-control animals thus played a significant role in my childhood imagination. But this imagined danger became vivid reality on one occasion. While I was playing in the driveway not far from the road, I heard a tremendous racket. A two-mule team raced down the road toward me. To my horror, I saw that no driver was on the empty hay wagon they were pulling. Running at top speed behind the wagon were two Amish men. They were losing the race! The mules were paying no attention to their shouts. In my three-year-old mind I felt completely vulnerable. Dad explained later that the mules were simply heading home after a long day of work. "But," I thought, "How could he be sure? After all, the Amish men seemed quite concerned as they passed our house, still running and shouting, no closer to gaining control of the rampaging beasts. Could Dad *guarantee* that the next time the mules got loose they wouldn't make a little side-trip into our driveway and kick the life out of my tiny body?" I didn't even ask. I just knew he couldn't. Thus was born in me a strong fear of mules and horses. On numerous occasions after that, whenever I would hear the clip-clop sound of approaching horses or mules, I would run into the house and hide. I remember hiding behind the closed, windowless garage door. I did not even want the horses to *see* me! I had a pretty severe case of equinophobia – complete with nightmares!

It was while I suffered under this strong fear, that the most emotionally traumatic event of my early childhood took place. My younger brother and I had been playing behind our house and were running along its side toward the front, planning to go inside. He was two steps ahead of me. As we rounded the corner, my worst fears were suddenly realized. There was a huge horse directly in front of us. He was so startled by our sudden appearance that he *reared up on his hind legs!* While I was momentarily paralyzed by the sight of his flailing legs and sharp hooves directly above me, my brother rushed into the house and *locked me out!* I frantically pounded on the door, yelling for Mom to come downstairs and let me in. (We lived in a second floor apartment reached by an indoor staircase.) All my hollering and banging made the horse react all the more as the Amish buggy driver desperately yanked on the reins trying to get him to back away from me before his front hooves returned to earth. I was sure I was going to be crushed to death. I knew Mom could not get to me in time. In my panic, it never occurred to me to run back around the corner of the house. I felt helpless and hopeless. I was terrified and alone with no one to help (I thought). The lies that settled in at that time I can now recognize:

1. I am all alone in a terrifying world.
2. No one can save me in time.
3. I am doomed to a painful death.

As I "relived" this memory during a prayer ministry session several years ago, a picture came to mind. Jesus was standing with his arms outstretched like a huge school crossing guard. His back was to the rearing horse and he was looking down at me with love and concern. He was BIG, so big that I could hardly even see the horse behind him! He seemed to say, "I've got you covered. Don't worry about the horse. I made him too and he doesn't scare me. In fact, he's scared too. And, he should be ashamed of himself for being afraid of such a little guy like you."

In my mind's eye, Jesus seemed to get even bigger. At the same time the horse slowly lowered his flailing front hooves. Then I could just barely see the Amish man craning his neck to look around Jesus' waist at me with a sheepish grin as if to say, "Sorry about all that, little fellow!"

Jesus, once again normal human size, went over and sat down on the driveway with his back to the closed garage door, and crossed his legs. Since he was wearing a full-length robe, this posture made a nice lap. I couldn't help but run the three or four steps to him and sit down there. How cuddly and totally safe it felt. I sensed his whiskery cheek against the top of my head as he held me. The Amish man got out of his buggy and led the horse, *now totally calm*, over to where Jesus and I were sitting. The horse seemed curious. He leaned his big head down and pushed his wet nose forward until both Jesus and I could not help but pet him. It was as though Jesus was caring for the horse at the same time that he was reassuring me. The Amish man was standing there with a bemused grin on his face, taking it all in. I suddenly realized that *there was no longer any need to go inside!*

Life-giving truth began to flood my mind:

1. I need not continue my life-long pattern of running away whenever things get scary, because Jesus is big and strong and is with me all the time. I'm also pretty big now myself.
2. I am not trapped. *I'm already outside*, deeply immersed in the grand, wild "outdoor" adventure of life with Jesus, who makes it both fierce and safe at the same time.
3. I no longer need to escape "indoors" because Jesus can transform the more risky "outdoors" into a peaceful, even *comical* tableau.
4. I'm actually *glad* my brother locked me out so I could learn this lesson.
5. I don't have to keep eating compulsively to make myself bigger and stronger.
6. It's OK to be wise and make reasonable preparations for emergencies, but my survival does not depend only, or even primarily, on my own efforts.

A few days later this poem came to mind as I studied Psalm 46:

# I AM

(A meditation on Psalm 46)

Be still

Chill

Choose not to fear

For I AM here

I AM

I just AM

I AM always with you

I inhabit all life events

I do not cause evil

But when it happens
I AM here


I hate evil
*But it doesn't scare me*
The evil doer cannot escape me
The godly are never abandoned


I AM aware
Of the most insignificant hurt
As well as the most overwhelming tragedy


I AM
Your creator
Your sustainer
I AM the sustainer of ALL creation
I AM above all, yet in all


If you seek me, you *will* find me


I AM your peace
Your only hope for true peace
Choose to trust me
Choose not to fear


Give up striving
Give up self-effort
Give *me* your unsolvable life puzzles
And *watch me work!*

From beginning to end

For I AM

The beginning and the end.

## Yes, But

Wouldn't it be nice to end the chapter here? Ahh, but I suspect that some readers are asking, "Yeah, this is all very comforting if we are helpless little children. But, as grown-ups, are we never supposed to take *action* to defend ourselves and the weaker ones near us?" David, the psalmist, warrior and king, also pondered this question. In Psalm 27 he wrote that he longed for nothing more than to behold God's beauty in the safety of the temple.[7] On another occasion, however, he asked *God* to punch his enemies in the mouth! In Psalm 3:7 David wrote, "Strike all my enemies on the jaw; break the teeth of the wicked." God as Almighty Pugilist? One clearly wants to be on *his* side in any cosmic brawl! Yet we know David also did plenty of real, physical fighting and killing of his own.[8] The apostle Paul wrote in the New Testament that God establishes earthly governments to restrain and punish wrongdoers. Lethal force may be needed.[9]

One day several years ago I had a heart-to-heart "chat" with Jesus on the question of how active we should be when forced to deal with dangerous human beings.

"Lord," I prayed, "I'll be honest. At this point I seem to be unable to love my enemies. The best I can muster right now is to try to avoid them. Some evil people are determined to kill all human beings who do not convert to their religious sect. How should we respond? Should we simply try to talk them out of it and, failing that, renounce our faith – or let them kill us? Any of these options seem like letting the Devil have a field day. I don't get it. Why put us here on this planet in the first place if we are simply supposed to give in to evil? (My upbringing was strongly pacifist.) By experience, I have learned that when I stand my ground with reasonable firmness – not throwing a fit, but making it clear that I will not tolerate being treated with contempt – people respect me. Typically, they apologize and we are then able to work together."

"You're right, Ev. There is a difference between loving your enemies (or those who oppose you on some issue) and just letting them walk all over you. In a sense, when you play the doormat role, you invite those with evil intentions to further stray from my will in their lives.

Sometimes calm, reasonable confrontation is the *very best* response to the antagonistic behavior or contemptuous attitudes of others."

"But Lord," I pushed further, "what about a madman who enters a crowded restaurant and starts shooting randomly? Certainly a calm, reasonable confrontation in such a situation would probably not work. Wouldn't it be better to hit him with a chair while he is reloading? How else would one 'do good' [10] to such an enemy? Offering him a nice piece of lemon meringue pie would probably just make me the next victim."

I went on, now asking about the people on the hijacked Flight 93 on September 11, 2001. "They knew that, if they did nothing, they, and *many more* innocent victims on the ground, would be killed. If one has to choose between loving a few enemies and saving the lives of lots of decent folks, and there is at least a *chance* of changing the outcome for the better, how is a strict pacifist approach ethical? In this case, the perpetrators were going to die anyway. By taking action, the brave passengers of Flight 93 were able to save the lives of perhaps hundreds of unsaved people on the ground, thus giving them more opportunities to come to repentance. Even if it did mean sending a few hijackers to meet their Maker a few minutes earlier than they would have otherwise, was not this the ethically superior choice?"

In reply, Jesus seemed to say, "Trust me in this. If you ever find yourself in a similarly dangerous emergency and, if you take an action with which I disagree, I will either stop you or I will do as I did in Gethsemane – repair the damage. If, however, I do want you to stop the evil activity, that's how it will work out. How's that?"

"That sounds like a plan, Lord." I agreed.

Why, some may ask, do I even include this discussion on resisting evil humans in a chapter on fear? Originally, I thought that if I could prayerfully pre-think this issue it might help me know what to do if I ever found myself in a particularly scary situation. One principle of emergency response preparedness is that thorough pre-planning, as well as training in conditions that simulate an emergency, can reduce fear and confusion if the worst actually happens. I'm sure I would consider forcible resistance only as a last resort, if at all. I would do my best to avoid the confrontation if possible. I would certainly not go looking for opportunities to pick a fight or to take revenge after the fact. But, if it were possible to *prevent* torture or carnage, I trust that the Holy Spirit would lead me to do the right thing.

# Cosmic Fear

For me, there was at least one other major cause of fear. Growing up in a Christian Anabaptist tradition, I often wondered, would I recant under torture? This question was especially poignant since I was also strongly taught an Arminian view of salvation. Founded by the sixteenth century Dutch theologian, Jacobus Arminius, and later championed by John Wesley, this doctrinal school holds, among other things, that one's personal salvation can be lost, since continued salvation is conditioned upon continued faith.[11] Coupled with that was a strong teaching on hell as eternal, conscious torment. As a small child, I was emotionally traumatized by the horrific prospect of being forced to choose between unbearable present pain and eternal pain in hell.

As I was praying about this several years ago I wrote, "Lord, I am *not* suffering now. Your yoke *is* easy and light. This burden I am bearing right now, this *fear of possible future pain*, is not from you. You are the one who gave me the mental picture of the scary horse being transformed into a calm, curious friend. Therefore, Lord, this fear is not based on present truth about my life. But I can't seem to shake it lately. So I give up trying to figure it out. I am willing to be freed from it. Would you take it away, Lord Jesus, and just let me rest in your arms, please?"

At this point I prayed contemplatively for about twenty minutes. Then I wrote, "The nearest I can tell, this fear comes from the lie that *I am responsible to keep myself saved*. Therefore, if I am ever subjected to too much pain for too long, I will loose my faith and my salvation and end up in hell eternally damned."

Jesus asked, "My beloved child, Ev, do you think in a million years I would *ever* let that happen?"

"Doesn't make much sense, does it Lord?" I replied

Then Jesus asked three more questions:

1. "Could you save yourself in the first place?
2. Were you able to conquer your eating compulsion by yourself?
3. Could you be peaceful in your own strength?"

"No, no and no," I admitted.

"So why would you think it is your job to *keep* yourself saved if you were ever under duress? That's *my job*, Ev. And I am fully capable to complete the work I have begun in you and to 'present you faultless' when this life is done."[12]

"Yes, Lord Jesus, that's what I want, more than anything: to be completely faultless, blameless, pure and beautiful in your eyes!"

Jesus assured me, "Yes, my dear son, you *already are* and there's nothing anyone can do to you that will ever change that! Look back at Psalm 37:6, 'He will make your righteousness shine like the dawn.' In the unlikely event that you are ever forced to recant, *it will not count*. Under such coercive conditions, you would not be making a free-will choice and it would not be held against you."

# Relief

(Meditation on Psalm 37)

As pure as the driven snow
As peaceful and bright as the dawn
This, now, I most surely know
Is how my portrait is drawn.

Only you can keep saving me, Lord
And you surely are up to the task
By you I am loved – yes, adored
I now can discard every mask.

I thought that *I* had to stay saved
I feared I'd renounce you when stressed
But my road to Glory is paved
With *your* saving power, I'm blessed!

Nothing I do while in pain
Will be counted against me, I know
For you know that I *want* to remain

As pure as the driven snow.

No matter what evil men do
They never can *force* me to fall
They'll vanish like morning dew
And I will inherit it all!

# Real Life Test

As usual, after a prayerful encounter during which I am pretty sure mind renewal has taken place, I looked for evidence in a subsequent life experience. Would I remain calm in a situation that would have normally caused fear and anxiety? Fortunately, I have not been threatened with any situations involving severe pain but I will share one that was rather scary.

In March of 2005 I traveled to New Haven, Conn. on a business trip. During my morning presentation it started to snow – hard. At 11:30 am, rather than going to the planned client lunch, I decided it would be best to get to the airport as soon as possible. I was booked on a 6:00 pm flight out of Hartford. Perhaps I could get an earlier flight. The forty-five mile drive would have normally taken about an hour. But not this time! After waiting over an hour for a limo, we started out. It was snowing horizontally in a 50 mph gale. The limo driver had to stop three times to clear ice and snow from the windshield wiper blades. Traffic barely moved. Numerous drivers had pulled off the road. It took more than three hours to drive to the airport. Normally I get quite irritable and anxious in such situations. This time I sat *completely relaxed the whole time!*

I arrived at the gate with only fifteen minutes to spare. It was still snowing hard and now it was dark. I expected the flight to be cancelled any minute, but they loaded the plane on time. The U. S. Airways Express Embrair taxied out onto the apron. A deicing truck drove up next to the plane, on my side just in front of the wing. The boom began to move up and then stopped. Several minutes later it slowly lowered to the ground and the worker climbed out of the spray cab and walked over to the truck and got in. Nothing happened for about ten minutes. Nothing but more blowing snow. Then the captain informed us that the *deicing truck had broken down* (was it frozen?) and would have to be *towed* away from the plane!

Just then I had the strong sense that Jesus was nudging me with his elbow and, with a mischievous grin, asking, "Isn't this fun? Just look what a show I am putting on for you!"

"You are just *nuts*, Lord", I exclaimed. "You are a wild man! I want to *party* with you! And what a *drama freak* you are! A three hour trip! Getting me here just in time! You just *had* to make it exciting, didn't you? You *had* to test my new-found peace and ability to surrender control to you. As my brother Bob said at church on Sunday, you *are* my *personal trainer.*"

All he said was, "Wasn't that a hoot, my man?"

"As I said, Lord, you are crazy. You're just nuts. *And I love it!*"

About an hour later, the first truck had been removed. The second one had deiced the plane (we hoped!); we were sitting at the end of the runway. Snow was still going straight across, blowing from left to right, as we sat looking down the runway. The plane was shaking in the crosswind. Just before we started the takeoff roll, a man halfway up the thirty-passenger cabin shouted, "I'll give him a 50-50 chance of taking off safely!" Not only was I *not scared*; I was actually *enjoying the wildness!* Only Jesus could have made that possible. From that point on, the flight was uneventful. I did learn later, however, that ours was the last flight out before they closed the airport.

# 12

# The Red Root of Bitterness

## Big Weeds

A preacher once told this story. A man was toiling in the hot August sun, pulling weeds in his vegetable garden. His pastor paid him a surprise visit and remarked, "That's a fine garden you and the Lord have there!"

The gardener straightened up, wiped sweat and joked, "Yeah, and you should have seen it when the Lord had it all to himself!" Of course, we know that weeds resulted from the fall[1] and some of the most beautiful places on earth are ones God *does* have all to himself! But if you've ever tried to keep a vegetable garden neat and weed-free, you know how the sweaty man felt.

As a boy I hated weeds; some were worse than others. In eastern Pennsylvania one of the worst was the red root pigweed, *Amaranthus retroflexus*, or just "red root," for short. These were the giant sequoias of garden weeds. They grew four to five feet tall and measured over one half inch in diameter at the base. The tap root, yes, it was definitely red, could reach six to twelve inches into the ground. No friendly little chickweed, this fellow! Don't even think of pulling it out of a mature potato patch unless you are ready to harvest at least two stalks of potatoes.

Anger can be like such a weed – especially anger that has grown into resentment and bitterness over an extended period of time.[2] As a high school biology student I did a research project that involved growing weeds from seeds. I remember how easy it was to uproot very young red root plants. But, once they had grown all summer, they became formidable. Anger is like that.

## Discovering Heart Weeds

In May of 2004 I attended a *Wild at Heart* weekend in eastern Pennsylvania. One of the reasons I chose to attend was that we were invited to come prepared to shoot clays on Saturday afternoon. That sounded like my kind of men's retreat. But once I was there, I felt compelled instead to spend that afternoon working my way through Chapter 4 of the *Wild at Heart Field Manual*.[3] This chapter was entitled "The Wound." As I answered Mr. Eldredge's excellent series of questions, one theme emerged persistently. As a child, I was repeatedly told that my natural fierceness was evil. My parents were convinced that my strong will and my passionate emotional make-up were sinful. My "will had to be broken" and my emotions controlled. I'm starting to get angry now just thinking about it! ............ (There, now that I've prayed and read my daily *Get Fuzzy* desk calendar cartoon, we can go on.)

When small, my younger brother often provoked me to anger. He was fifteen months younger than me and we had many fun times together. But, periodically he would spice things up by "pushing my buttons." I cannot remember what he would do or say but I became so angry that I would chase him and pound on him until he would stop his impish laughter and yell for Mom. Invariably, this would end in Mom's intervention on *his* behalf. Apparently I never hurt him seriously because he kept coming back for more. This scenario must have happened at least twenty times a year for five or six years.

I remember wondering why Mom never reprimanded *him* for intentionally provoking *me*. She would just say, "No hit for talk." I was left with bottled up anger, not so much at his teasing, as at what I saw as her unjust reaction. After years of this, some "truths" about life began to settle in:

1. It is better not to allow myself to feel anger – it only motivates behavior that gets me into trouble.
2. Life is intrinsically unjust and there is nothing I can do about it.
3. It is always my fault.

I know now that these were lies, but I lived for decades as though they were true.

Fearing my own passion, I began to build a false self. I learned to instantly suppress my anger. I could feel myself shut down emotionally. I was actually pleased at this ability to "numb out." I avoided infuriating situations and people as much as possible. Failing that, I would stuff my feelings, remain outwardly calm and play the "nice guy" role. My life philosophy became one of swallowing my pride, fitting in, and being *way too cautious*. In John Eldredge's words, I became the "passive man."[4] Some nasty side-effects of this strategy showed up over time. I noticed that whenever I had to confront anyone, I would tense up to the point that I would hardly be able to find the right words. Even when I did speak, I would do so with a nervous, quavery voice. Whenever I allowed someone to disrespect me, I would suffer through 2-3 days of self-recrimination. I would sometimes take out my anger on the wrong people later. At other times I resorted to sarcastic humor or other passive-aggressive stratagems. In order to cope, I would often tell myself, "It doesn't matter. It really doesn't matter."

I finally realized that I had never really killed any of that suppressed anger. It was still there, just below the surface, making my life an emotional hell. No wonder; I was living a lie. God had not designed me to be an emotional zombie. He had "wired" me to feel injustice strongly and to do something constructive about it. Not to be an out-of-control violent man, but certainly not the super-cautious person I had become.

I prayed, "Lord Jesus, I need healing concerning the lie that I am somehow *flawed* because I react passionately when I experience or see injustice. *Your* Word says 'In your anger do not sin.'[2] *You* made a whip and drove out the temple-desecrating cheats.[5] *You* verbally blasted the scribes and Pharisees, angrily denouncing them in public![6] Dare I realistically hope for healing in this area?"

"Yes, Ev, a thousand times YES!" he replied with delight, as though he had been waiting for 50 years to hear me ask.

But, always the questioner, I wondered, "Lord, what will be the evidence that you are healing me?"

"Well, hey, Bro,[7] have you been less likely to avoid confrontation lately?"

Immediately, I was able to think of several examples. Amazing how he does that. He starts to heal me so that, by the time I get around to actually praying for healing, he already has several object lessons to which he can point. His timing is exquisite!

He went on, "See, Ev, you don't need to stuff your feelings. If you act right away, you are less likely to let the anger build internally until you blow up inappropriately. You must *act*, not avoid. True, you should not act totally impulsively. Your mother was right about that. But, now that you have acknowledged your suppressed anger and I have begun to heal you, please take note in the coming days how my peace will be with you.[8] You will be emotional sometimes. Despite your mother's disdain for displays of emotion, it is better *in your case* to be yourself than to continue to pretend that you are always cool, calm and collected. I'll stay close so you won't have to worry that you will dangerously over-react."

# Healing

As I was pondering those childhood anger episodes, I thought that, perhaps, what I should have done, was take my brother to Mom and calmly explain exactly how he was provoking me. If I had, maybe she would have dealt with the boy. When I shared these thoughts with Leona, she said, "You were only a little boy. You needed adult intervention. The solution you now suggest is one we would expect of an adult, not a five-year-old."

Thus Jesus spoke truth through my wife, "It was not your fault. You needed your mother to step in and stop this cycle, but she did not." This was my *mother wound*. She failed to take effective action in this crucial area of my childhood. I was emotionally wounded as a result. For decades I have lived with the consequences. I also now live with regrets because I was often irritable with my own children, even angry, often out of proportion to what they had done. That's another story, but it is part of the accounting of my woundedness.

At one point in 2004, as I was describing the scary horse incident to Leona, I broke down and sobbed for ten minutes! She came over and sat beside me on the couch and said, "I wish I could have been there when you came in from being scared by the horse so I could have comforted you." She also pointed out that, behind the anger may have been some feelings of abandonment. I may have been somewhat generally starved for my mother's attention. My brother was born very soon after I was, Dad's health was frail and I'm sure Mother was overwhelmed.

As I relived the scary horse memory, once Jesus had dealt with my fear (Chapter 11), I then begged him to take my anger. I said, "Lord, I don't want to live with this anymore." After about ten minutes of intense prayer, Jesus gave me a mental image. He seemed to come up behind my right shoulder. Reaching down in front of me, he firmly grasped a *huge red root weed* growing out of my heart. Yielding to his steady pull, the red roots lost their grip on my heart. Jesus threw the whole weed on a huge bonfire!

# The First Test

Early the next morning, I was lying in bed having some doubts about exactly what had occurred the day before. "Lord" I prayed, "I am still afraid of my emotions. I'm still struggling with my mother's insistence that negative emotions are evil tendencies that need to be eradicated. Is there not *some* truth there? We shouldn't just go around emoting all over the place, saying everything that comes to mind, no matter how hurtful it may be to others, just for the sake of our own emotional health. After all, isn't one of the fruits of the Spirit self-control?"[9]

"True, Ev, but I am calling *you, now* to place *less* emphasis on control. In fact, as you know, *you cannot* control your real evil tendencies to be selfish and judgmental. You must turn all of these over to me. What I'm asking *you* to focus on is *fearlessly releasing* the creativity that I am pouring into your heart! I love you perfectly, Ev, my dear son, if you *believe* in my perfect love, then I will free you to be a channel for my love."

"But" I protested, "I am still tense and scared, Lord. Can you please free me of the fear of *what I might do* if I really allowed myself to feel my anger? Sometimes I scare myself!"

"Ev, I have given you a new heart. It is no longer wicked.[10] I have already removed the red root of bitterness. You need not fear your emotions. They are MINE now. Stay close to me. I will free you to be strong, wise and full of my grace.[11] As my child, you will be able to speak with authority[12] as one who is rooted in my love.[13] *I* will motivate your actions; you no longer need anger for motivation."

"Yes, Lord, I believe. Please sanctify my emotions."

## A Training Exercise

Three days later I was working out at the fitness club. At the very end, when I was most exhausted, doing my last ten of sixty calf-raises, I was rudely interrupted. I was standing on a spotter platform about one foot off the floor, heels back off the edge, both hands firmly grasping a weight bar for support. Eyes closed in concentration, dripping wet, pushing through the muscle pain, I felt a stranger tap on the left end of the bar. Impatiently, he asked if I was using the bar. What did he *think* I was doing? I was holding onto it with both hands, for crying out loud! How selfish, how thoughtless – not even willing to wait a few seconds until I had completed my set! Through the fog of my exhaustion (I couldn't even talk just then) I raised five fingers to let him know that I had only five more reps in the set. He looked puzzled and impatient, insisting that I answer him immediately, "Five what?" By then I had finished and said, "Five reps. Go ahead, I'm done." But he couldn't let it go at that. He just had to ridicule me! In a contemptuous voice he said, "I didn't know if you meant five reps, five minutes or five sets." In that split second I knew I had a simple choice. I could back down and suffer three days of self-recrimination for letting a bully best me, or I could take action. I decided to act. I interrupted his malicious mocking by looking him square in the face and in a quick, slightly-raised voice told him, "I *said* 'I am finished and you can use it now.' Did you understand *that*?" He looked somewhat taken aback and accused *me* of being a smart ass. Ignoring the obvious irony, I left the gym.

Of course, later I thought of three or four better ways I could have handled the situation. But, what happened, happened. I had what it took! I backed *him* down – without violence, *without a quavering voice.* I was not a pushover. I ACTED! As Jesus had promised, the creativity surged. Instantly, the words were there! I was no longer the four-year-old with a speech impediment. And Jesus saved me from going too far.

Jesus seemed to say, "Ev, I'm proud. You came through. You did have what it took. Don't hate yourself for reacting as you did. True, there may have been a bit more gracious way of doing it, but you did your best in a tough, fast-moving situation while you were at your most vulnerable physically. You were my MAN! I knew you could do it. Stay close and we'll work on the finesse part. No problem."

## Further Evidence

Two weeks later, in the middle of a very high-stress period at work, Jesus asked, "When was the last time you felt really angry or irritable?" I realized then that I hadn't been angry since the fitness club incident. For me to go two weeks free from what had been almost constant irritability was amazing.

Another two weeks went by and I prayed, "Lord, I was thinking this afternoon on the way home in the rush hour traffic how relaxed my chest and stomach felt. I realize now that most of my life I was carrying bitterness that caused almost constant emotional pain. About six months ago I invited you to 'help me overcome my unbelief.'[14] You must have started right away. Keep it up, Lord. I still need more work but what you have already accomplished is almost unbelievable to me. I keep thinking, 'This must be just a phase. Will the *old Everett* re-emerge shortly and I'll be right back in the *irritable dumps* once again?'"

"Hey, Bro," he seemed to reply, "I've got you covered. I AM in here working away. You'll be even more amazed when you see the results of my work in the future."

I was, and still am. I can still occasionally feel anger. But the load of rancid, caustic bitterness that I had carried for so long is gone! Hallelujah!

# 13

# Yes, I Believe, But Just Barely

## Rescue

A young man rejoiced with his bride. When their child was born, they had high hopes. At first the little fellow developed normally. But they were alarmed when they noticed that he did not startle at sharp noises. When the time came that most children begin to talk, their son only cried or made unintelligible sounds. They were just beginning to make their peace with the idea of raising a deaf child when, to their shock, the boy began to suffer spells in which his body would convulse and he would fall down, grind his teeth and foam at the mouth. As he grew, it got worse. Terrified for the boy's safety, they watched him constantly, rescuing him when his fits endangered his life. It seemed like more than epilepsy, as though some evil presence was actually trying to destroy their son! Way too often to be mere coincidence, the boy's seizures would occur at just the wrong times – near deep water or an open fire. His parents feared he would never survive childhood.

Then they heard of a man who could cast out demons. It seemed too good to be true. No doctors had been able to help. No medicine had done any good. But, the desperate father thought, *I must try, although I hold out little hope.* So he took the boy and went looking for Jesus. At first, he found Jesus' disciples. They said they had at times been able to cast out evil spirits and would be willing to try. But the demon just seemed to mock them, throwing the boy down even as they were trying to cast it out.

Finally Jesus showed up and asked what was going on. The father described the whole horrific dilemma. He came "this close" to saying, "Oh, just forget it. Everyone has his own cross to bear. Maybe this is just our thorn-in-the-flesh. Just give us the grace to face each new day, one-day-at-a-time. Who are we to expect special favors? There must be something God wants us to learn from this." But no, there was something in Jesus' eyes. *This man really cares!* the father thought. It gave him just enough faith to try one more time. *If this doesn't work,* he thought, *I'm afraid something precious and vulnerable inside me will die. But for the sake of my son, I will risk even that.*

In a trembling voice he told Jesus about his son's affliction and the disciples' failure. Jesus said, "Bring the boy to me."

Right in front of Jesus, the boy was once again thrown down. The father made his decision. "If you can do anything, take pity on us and help us," he said.

Jesus caught the "if," and confronted the father about it. He knew the father's faith was nearly non-existent. Although Jesus sometimes performed miracles for sinners who did not even know who he was,[1] in this case he chose to teach the desperate father a faith lesson. Immediately the father blurted, "I believe; help my unbelief!"[2] He must have realized that he still had reservations, and that Jesus would know.

I recognize the feeling. I find myself often praying, "Yes, Lord, I believe, but *just barely!* Please, work on my unbelief." or, "Once again, Lord, you have shown me another *knot of unbelief* in my heart. Please untie this one too!" In other words, "Lord, I desperately want to believe, but again, at this new spiritual growing edge to which you have led me, I can only believe as you grant me the grace to do so."

In the biblical story, Jesus *did* rebuke the demon. As he did, the boy let out a blood-curdling shriek. The father felt the hair on the back of his neck stand up. The boy's helpless body convulsed – then lay still and ashen. Did the father think, *Oh, well, my son is now finally 'healed,' I had hoped for healing in this life, but at least he no longer has to suffer?* We can only imagine. The Bible says almost everyone thought the boy was dead. But to the father's great relief, Jesus helped the boy stand, and he never had fits again![3] The father's weak faith had almost cost him a great blessing. Does our unbelief sometimes block blessings God wants to give us?

## Subtle Unbelief

Usually we think of unbelievers as those who willfully refuse to believe, in spite of good evidence. To most Christians, the word "unbelief" is a loaded term that we use only when referring to avowed atheists or agnostics. Instead, I want to examine subtle unbelief, into which we may have fallen unawares, even while sincerely trying to live for Christ. Such unbelief is an unintentional, often subconscious, *inability to believe*. In my experience, the spiritual maturation process involves allowing the Holy Spirit to lead us to clots of unbelief in our spiritual circulatory systems. He wants to dissolve them, so that more of his life can flow to and through us.

For example, men, do we really believe that we need intimacy with God more than we need sex? Or, those of us who love to talk, do we believe God sometimes prefers for us to be silent – to listen to his Spirit? For all of us, can we believe that God *always* has our best interests at heart, regardless of what unspeakable pain he allows to enter our lives? If we agree mentally with each premise, do we *live* that way? To the extent that we don't live it, there must still be a degree of residual, gut-level unbelief. We are not alone in this struggle to believe. Nor is it a recent development.

## Heart Disease

Our spiritual Enemy is crafty. Even in the Garden of Eden, he did not try to convince Adam and Eve that the God they communed with in the cool of the evening was merely a figment of their imaginations. No, he insinuated that this God, whom they all knew existed, was in fact holding out on them, that he really did not have their best interests at heart, and that his commandments could be ignored with impunity.[4] Then, their own fear led them to believe they could hide from God. Like children who close their *own* eyes, thinking their parents can't see them, this first couple hid. Probably without thinking it through, they were hoping for a different kind of God – a scaled-down, manageable one – a God who, if ignored just enough, would leave them alone, most of the time.

How many of us have thought, in our most honest moments, "I don't want to get too serious about getting close to and listening to God because, once I do, he will banish me to Africa for a lifetime of mission work, or he will require me to live a celibate single life" – or whatever else we most fear.

Or, how many, like me, have simply decided, "I'm tired of trying to get close to God. Trying to discover his specific will for me just seems to be a guessing game. I can't deal with the uncertainty of trying to follow Jesus step-by-step. It's not working for me. So here's what I'll do. I'll get the best job I can, make as much money as I can ethically, and try to live for the Lord in practical, everyday ways. I can't seem to think of a better approach. I'm not really cut out for this touchy-feely, twilight-zone type of spirituality anyway. I'm the practical, down-to-earth type. I need to support my family and I am doing the best I can at that, so what's the problem? I give my tithe, and then some. I always say, there are three kinds of people in this world; those who lead, those who follow and those who just want to be left alone. I am the third kind, so leave me alone, please."

## Does God Really Love Me?

Why do so many Christians believe that intimacy with God might not be safe, even if it were possible? Could it be subtle *unbelief?* Are we unable to believe that God loves us? Oh, we *say* that we do. Yet, at a deep operational level, we may be unable to believe that if we really got serious about following Jesus at every step, he would show us the *best possible* way to live! Can we believe that if he asks us to give up some of our favorite habits, he *will* replace them with something far better? *If we cannot believe God really does love us, we are in serious trouble!* Unbelief at such a basic level is devastating. Until we can get past this particular knot of unbelief, we will, at best, limp along life's journey, spiritually malnourished, even crippled. Trying to live the Christian life while not convinced that God takes personal delight in us is a monumental chore!

Why is it that even Christians who agree with sound doctrine, often struggle to believe God even *notices* them, let alone takes any particular *delight* in them? While by no means an exhaustive list, three reasons come to mind. We misinterpret biblical promises, we give up too easily, and we struggle with personal pain.

# Promises, Promises

A young woman meets a handsome guy at a church singles party. He is a Christian with a job and seems genuinely interested in her. She gives him her phone number and he promises to call. Three months go by. He never calls. She reasonably concludes that he does not care to continue the relationship.

Like the young woman, we expect that someone who cares will keep his promises. For this reason, we must interpret scriptural "promises" carefully. We must learn to read the Bible with sensitivity to its original intent, and an understanding of varying literary styles, if we hope to avoid being led by the Deceiver into a blind corner, where we begin to doubt God's love. For example, if we misinterpret a single verse in a song of praise as an ironclad, universally applicable, literal promise, we open ourselves to the suggestion that God does not keep his promises. It's hard to believe that someone who seems to break his promises truly loves us.

Let's look at one example. In Isaiah 43:2 we read, "when you walk through the fire, you will not be burned." Now let's be honest. How often in our actual experience have we touched a hot surface or strayed too close to an open flame and *not been burned?* For me the answer is *never!* And I know of only one biblical account where it happened –Shadrach, Meshach and Abednego in the fiery furnace.[5] Now compare that very rare incident to all the times Christians have been burned at the stake. According to the *Martyr's Mirror* accounts, they *were burned* and *did die* in the flames.[6] The often-used cop-out that it's always *our* fault because we have no faith, just won't do. It would be simply ridiculous to claim that all those Christian martyrs burned at the stake had no faith!

Nor can the answer be that it's not good enough to believe that God *can*, we must also believe that he *will*. In the *one case* where they *weren't* burned, the three Hebrews admitted beforehand that, although they knew God *could* save them, they did not know whether he *would!*[7]

As I struggled to understand the seemingly glaring disconnect between the "promise" and the reality, it dawned on me that many so-called promises cannot be interpreted as universal, literal guarantees of particular outcomes in this life. The "promise" of protection from being burned by fire was literally fulfilled, but only once. The context shows that Isaiah 43 is part of a hymn of praise to God's greatness.[8] The point is, we should praise God because he is *the kind of God* who can do even this physically impossible thing. We know that he already did it once, and may yet do it again, but we should not count on it in *any given case*. If we expect that each "promise" in the Bible is meant to be taken literally, to be universally applicable to all of God's people at all times, if they will only have enough faith, we will end up being disappointed with God much of the time. Or, if our theology does not allow us to express disappointment with God, we may instead agree with the Accuser that our faith is non-existent. Take your pick. Either God does not keep his promises or he withholds from us the faith we need to activate them! Neither conclusion makes it easy to believe God really loves us. Of course, since Calvary, we know God *does* love us. Therefore, as in the above example, we must learn to correctly interpret scriptural "promises."[9]

## Giving Up Too Easily

Sometimes we *expect too little* of God. Christians often emphasize that there are no easy answers or quick solutions in the matter of spiritual growth (sanctification). We are reminded that this is a life-long process. We say "experience is the best teacher" and that some folks learn best (only?) in the "school of hard knocks." But is the spiritual life *necessarily* an arduous, life-long struggle? Of course, there *are* times of testing and struggle. We can even expect those periods, well-known in Christian literature as the dark nights of the soul, when God seems to withdraw the more obvious manifestations of his presence and love.[10] But, even these times, understood correctly, are intended to *deepen* our faith through continued reliance on God's goodness and love. If instead we respond to hard times by *turning away* from God and living rebelliously according to our own agendas, and, while living this way, *use the excuse* that we should not really expect very much spiritual growth in this life, we have, in my opinion, joined the "unbelieving and perverse generation" that Jesus so emphatically denounced.[11] After all, why should we agree that experience is a better teacher than the Holy Spirit, especially if it is sinful, rebellious and prideful experience? Is it necessary that we repeat the mistakes of the stubborn mule that must be "hit up-side the head with a 2 x 4" to get his attention?[12]

What should we do if we would like to experience a life of steady, healthy, spirit-led growth in faith, hope, and love? There are practices that many Christians have found to contribute to such a life. These are the subject of the next chapter. Unfortunately, some of the traditional spiritual activities remind the average adult Christian of childhood school experiences that he may have promised himself long ago he'd never have to do again! Never mind that others have found such relatively simple daily reading, writing and praying exercises to be catalysts for remarkable spiritual growth. Apparently many just do not believe it could work for them. After all, some tell themselves, the ideal is to "pray without ceasing," so they try to be in an "attitude of prayer" throughout the day. Fine. A few spiritual giants like Brother Lawrence and Frank Laubach could undoubtedly teach us how we may eventually be able to live this lofty ideal. But, in my experience, when I was telling myself that I could be intimate with Jesus without substantial amounts of silence and solitude, it was not working. I found I had to start with very intentional, specific activities or disciplines.

Some say God calls their attention to birds, butterflies or specially shaped clouds even as they busy themselves with essential daily tasks. Great! But, if these are cited as reasons why we *never* need to slow down and pay attention to what God may want to communicate to us, are we perhaps settling for spiritual fast food when our souls crave a richer diet? Is it not true that God said "Be still and know that I am God"?[13] Didn't Jesus say "when you pray, go into your room, close the door"?[14] Jesus himself often went away to a solitary place to pray.[15]

Perhaps many have tried regular prayer and Bible study and found these activities, *as they understood and practiced them*, to be very disappointing. How many of us could say the same? But what is the proper response if this happens? Having tried and failed, should we then simply *lower our expectations?* Of course not. With faith, humility and willingness to be taught and led, ordinary Christians can grow spiritually, if we submit to God's leadership and *spend time* listening to God's inner promptings.

## Impossible? Well, Maybe.

Some who are caring for small children or invalid parents may be thinking, "Me? Spend time in solitude? What an idealistic impossibility!" In fact, it *may* be impossible for you to practice solitary, listening prayer *at all*, right now. Maybe every waking moment of your harried existence *is* totally consumed by the activities necessary to survive and to care for others. If so, I hope that God will send you great, swarming flocks of snow geese, cardinals at every turn, rainbows by day, northern lights by night – or whatever else he has been using to show you his love! However, if your busyness is an insincere excuse, if you *do* have free time that you use to watch hours of TV, surf the internet, "shop 'til you drop," or talk for hours with friends about superficial topics, then let me be so bold as to suggest that *the problem is not your schedule.*

## The Problem of *Personal* Pain

A third major reason why many folks struggle to believe that God loves *them in particular* is that he has allowed such tragic things to happen to *them*, maybe even while they were praying mightily and working-their-hearts-out serving him and others. For example, you may have been on your church's intercessory prayer team for years. You saw God do marvelous miracles in *other* people's lives. But when *you* needed his intervention for *your own* health problem, *your* struggle with unemployment or the salvation of *your* loved ones, he seemed to drop you like the proverbial hot potato. You have no problem believing God loves *other people.* He just doesn't seem to love *you!* You feel like the lost sheep Jesus did *not* come after.

Or maybe you feel spiritually numb – totally incapable of making contact with any world other than this physical one. You may look with longing at those who seem to effortlessly sense God's presence and wonder, "Why does God make it so difficult for *me* to pick up on spiritual vibes that others can so easily sense?" He seems to have singled *you* out for the silent treatment!

## What Can Be Done?

If, for these or other reasons, you simply cannot believe God loves *you*, there is really nothing *I* can say that will convince you. My only advice would be that you take your case to God in prayer. You may want to start by telling your pastor, your counselor or a trusted friend. But sooner or later, you will most likely need to "have it out" with God himself. When that time comes, find a quiet place and give yourself time. A day of silence at a retreat center may be a good way to start. Tell God exactly how disappointed you are in him. List all the reasons you can think of in your notebook or journal. Use exactly the language you must, to express your deep hurt at what appears to be his pervasive and persistent lack of concern for you as an individual. Such prayers are called laments; there are plenty of them in the Bible. Read Psalm 88 if you don't believe me. Don't worry that you will shock him. Think about it. He already knows! But he wants you to be honest with him. So go ahead, admit that you just can't believe that he loves *you!* Don't make excuses for him. Don't say, "Oh, but I'm sure you have your reasons." or "Oh, but I know you must want me to learn something from these tragic circumstances." These are just cop-outs as long as you still feel that you have been orphaned by God! *Do not lower your expectations!* Wrestle with God, like Jacob, until you *are* blessed![16]

I am not advocating a *lifestyle* of ungrateful murmuring and complaining. We know from the experiences of the Israelites in the wilderness that such attitudes and behavior can make God very angry.[17] However, Jesus knows our intentions and is very accepting of the lament of the honest seeker. If, on the other hand, your complaining is insincere and you are using it as an excuse to keep on holding God at arm's length, he will know that too! If you are not completely sure which it is for you at the beginning, just tell Jesus that, and tell him what you *want* it to be. He'll understand your limitations and give you the grace to continue the journey toward intimacy with him.

God may not improve your physical circumstances. But he does *always long* for you to know his deep love and joy.[18] Pray for a *next-step* toward that knowledge. Jesus may want you to stop some of your church activities. Are you, at least to some extent, doing them to gain his notice and approval? Until you can really believe that God loves you, your *service* may not be what he wants. After all, his *first and greatest* commandment is for you to *love* him with your whole being.[19] How can you possibly do that if you cannot believe he cares for you, personally?

## How God Did It for Me

Once I was willing to *turn toward God* and to be brutally, doggedly honest about how I felt about him, and about my total helplessness to connect with him, he began to work. He led me to exactly the right people, books, seminars and experiences that could help me begin to know and receive his love. But I had to get pretty desperate. Until then I had always told myself that there was more *I* should do to become a better Christian. I kept trying to live according to Christian principles. But the self-effort approach was just too difficult. I finally told God "I give up, it's your move." Then I prayed for months, "OK, Lord, you know where *I* am. I'm right here. If you want to have a personal relationship with me, please feel free, on *your* terms, not mine."

Over a period of several years God made it happen. He showed me his love. He communicated with me. He gave me *next-steps* personally designed for *my* growth process. I obeyed. I trusted him to get me through some pretty tough periods of "hearty renunciation" of counterfeits.[20] He showed me how to get healing and release from the mental and emotional baggage that I had carried for decades. Jesus continues to lead me. I trust my Leader and I can "hear" from him, personally! It's great to be "on-the-road" *with* him, finally.

# We Believe...But Just Barely

Lord, we do believe

Despite the seemingly overwhelming evidence

To the contrary

We do believe in your love for us

Yes, we believe, but just barely, Lord

Please batter away at our unbelief.


Improve our spiritual eyesight, Lord

Let us be still long enough

As long as it takes

To hear your still, small whisper


Reach down, Lord

And save us from sinking

We want to believe

But we can't on our own

You must form faith in us

# 14

# Spiritual Nitty Gritty

## Just Do It?

Even though loving God wholeheartedly is the *first* and *greatest* commandment, it is certainly not the *only* one. Jesus' Sermon on the Mount in Matthew 5-7 describes the attitudes and behaviors that are characteristic of a person who has grown up into Christ.[1] Jesus pointed out that, while the Old Testament law regulated external behavior, we can also sin inwardly. For example, nursing anger toward a brother is as bad in God's sight as going ahead and shooting him in the head![2] Now if I am the brother with whom you are angry, I dare say I would *prefer* that you keep your anger to yourself! But as far as *your* heart is concerned, the inner sin is equally devastating. But we often draw the wrong conclusion about how to remedy the sinful attitude. We conclude that the answer is to try even harder to *just do it*, to borrow the Nike catchphrase. Only now, in addition to the already large burden of monitoring and trying to control all of our outward actions, we must also worry about whether our inward motivations, thoughts and even emotions are pure. If this is so, it is far from good news!

# Basic Training Needed

Spiritually, the *just do it* approach does not work. Sin is a heart disease and only God can cure it. But, there is something we must do to make his work possible. We must *decide to submit* to the customized training program that God has chosen for each of us. We must be willing to engage in whatever practices and take whatever *next-steps* the Holy Spirit prescribes so that our hearts will be open to the inflow of God's grace. Only in this way can Jesus provide the power that transforms our hearts and minds. Only then will the motivations and behaviors described in the Sermon on the Mount begin to flow naturally out of our divinely transformed hearts.[3] Once we can admit to God our total inability to perform as described in Jesus' teachings, the pressure is off! We can then rest in the knowledge that the Spirit will lead us, baby-step by baby-step, until we can live authentically out of the progressively more Christlike heart that he is forming in us.

# Teaching Baby Christians

Many Christians have found certain activities helpful in opening their hearts to God's gracious transformation process. First of all, let me remind you that in Jesus' Great Commission he said we should *make disciples* **AND** *teach them to obey his commandments.* [4] In my experience, sermons on the Great Commission usually zero in on the call to evangelism, the initial making of disciples. But now let's ponder the *teaching them to obey* part. How should baby Christians be taught to obey Jesus' commandments? Certainly, the *content* of the commandments must be taught. As I was growing up, teachers, preachers and authors did an excellent job of this, except, perhaps, for an *under*-emphasis on the first and greatest commandment! However, there is more that needs to be done. The student must also be urged to actually *obey.*[5] Here again, nothing was lacking in my upbringing. The part that needed improvement was what we normally call *training.* Training is not basic education for understanding. Nor does training consist of giving pep talks or laying on guilt trips. Training is practice. It starts small – usually with demonstration of the skill by one who has already mastered it. Almost immediately, though, it gets the trainee *actively involved.* Then, step-by-step, the apprentice is led through a progressive process of growth until she has mastered the skill in question. The sports analogy is often used. A football coach who relies only on classroom lectures and half-time motivational speeches would be unlikely to produce a winning team. Physical conditioning and skills practice are also essential.

## Components of Training

The football analogy illustrates several distinct components of training. First is physical conditioning such as resistance training and running. These build muscular strength and cardio-vascular endurance. Team members are then led through drills designed to sharpen their ability to play their respective positions. Linemen practice blocking, running backs run routes and linebackers practice making good tackles. Finally, the team scrimmages. Here the offense lines up against the defense so that both can practice various plays in game-like conditions.

Core spiritual disciplines like prayer and meditation on Scripture are like the physical conditioning part of the sports training regimen. That is, spiritual exercises are those activities designed to *make possible* the growth and strengthening of the human spirit. In football, the coach can successfully train a team only if each member is alive and healthy. Proper nourishment and adequate rest are necessary starting points. It is also true in the spiritual realm. We are talking here about training baby *Christians*. These folks have had a conversion experience and are willing to regularly come to Jesus for spiritual life and nourishment. History has sadly shown that we can engage in rigorous ascetic practices without attaining transformation of our minds and spirits. For proof we need only point to the hypocritical Jewish leaders who, although they did many outward things right, failed to come to Jesus for life![6] We must think of the spiritual exercises as ways of learning to commune with God so that his grace can begin to transform us within. If instead our aim is to meet an obligation or to impress others (or God) with our dedication we are likely to miss the blessing God wants to give us.

## Fitness for Life

To complete the analogy, the football skills practice seems most like the numerous small *next-step* assignments that the Holy Spirit gives us as we walk daily with him. The Holy Spirit acts as our personal spiritual trainer or coach. The practice scrimmages correspond to trials, temptations and hardships that God allows to enter our lives as training exercises. Game day would be like the life-changing, or even life-threatening, challenges we occasionally face. For example, Queen Esther had to decide whether to risk her life to save her people.[7] But if we attempt to *just do it* in the big game without first allowing Jesus to transform our hearts and minds, we risk repeated defeat and discouragement (spiritual injury) which may, in the worst case scenario, sideline us indefinitely.

# Initial Failure

In my opinion, most Sunday morning church services address the fundamental education and motivational aspects of *teaching them to obey*, but are weak on the training part. I found this especially true with regard to training in the practices designed to facilitate the flow of divine grace. Oh, there was plenty of training going on. We learned to sit still and quiet in church, to save money, to tell the truth, to work hard and to "turn the other cheek." But we were not trained in the skills of listening and contemplative prayer or in ways to read the Bible for spiritual formation. Nor were we trained to use solitude, silence or fasting to open ourselves up to God's grace. In short, we were not given practical instruction on *how* to have a personal relationship with Jesus. Without this, I am sorry to say, the training in frugality, service and pacifism did not help me to experience God's grace. Instead, the message that came through was performance-based and legalistic. Guilt was often used as a motivator. I found this approach oppressive rather than life-giving.

Consequently, although I knew Jesus' commandments well and felt guilty when I disobeyed them, I was unable to consistently live the life, despite faithful church attendance and sincere attempts to read the Bible and pray. Why? The answer is pretty simple. I was working hard at obeying the commandments without realizing the absolute necessity of loving God wholeheartedly first. And even more basic than that, *I did not know how to live in a love relationship with Jesus.* Even Bible reading and prayer, as I was doing them, did not result in intimacy with Jesus. The lack of true, interactive communion with Jesus slowed the sanctification process to a crawl. Progress toward a Christlike heart and a transformed mind was nearly imperceptible. Therefore, my attempts to obey Jesus' commands in the Sermon on the Mount and the Great Commission were often unsuccessful.

# Frustration

How should we be teaching Christians to love and obey Jesus? For example, if I were to sit down with a new convert, what would I tell him about prayer? I know how frustrated I became as I tried to understand this most vital Christian practice. For example, the gospels frequently mention that Jesus went out to a solitary place to pray.[8] But we are not told exactly what he did out there. The only exceptions were the Transfiguration[9] and the Garden of Gethsemane.[10] In the case of the Transfiguration, what happened was so rare and otherworldly that we can hardly use it as a model for our own times of intimacy with Jesus. Similarly, the prayer in Gethsemane was on such a one-of-a-kind occasion that it seems unlikely that we were meant to emulate it on a regular basis. When the disciples asked Jesus to teach them to pray, he gave them a model prayer.[11] Although profound, it is very brief. Books have been written about this prayer.[12] Yet, Scripture does not say what Jesus did when he went out to pray all night.[13] Did he just keep repeating his own prayer? Perhaps. In Gethsemane he apparently kept repeating an even shorter prayer for over an hour.[10] I have never tried to repeat the Our Father for an hour, let alone all night. To do so would seem to be a much too literal and simplistic interpretation of Jesus' instructions on prayer.

The account of Jesus' forty days in the wilderness of temptation also lacks detail.[14] We are told that he fasted. Other than that, what did he *do* for nearly six weeks? If he took any scrolls or writing materials they are not mentioned. We can reasonably conclude by the way Jesus responded to the temptations that he had become very familiar with the Jewish Scriptures prior to the moment of temptation. He must have also learned to pray and use silence and solitude in ways that strengthened him spiritually. But, *how* he went about doing so is not revealed by the brief biblical accounts.

# I Was Puzzled

As a boy, I would sometimes hear preachers speak of having prayed for an hour or more. Judging from the brief prayers before meals and at bedtime that my parents modeled and taught, I could not imagine how anyone could possibly pray for an hour! In public prayer meetings there was singing, a devotional and sharing of requests so that the actual prayer time was about forty-five minutes. That time was filled by twelve or fifteen members praying aloud, sequentially. They usually prayed for "revival" or "the president" or for specific physical, often medical, needs that had been mentioned earlier. Although there were times, especially at meals, when we all prayed silently, there was absolutely no mention of *listening* prayer. Did Jesus practice listening prayer? We are not told. It is still a great mystery how Jesus' divinity and humanity interacted. But he was, in some way, so intimate with the Father that he knew what God was doing and how he was to join in.[15]

The only early memory I have of anyone claiming to hear directly from God was one man who seemed to have "gone off the deep end." He often appeared much too joyful for the circumstances and would occasionally claim a direct word from God during a trustee meeting where practical decisions had to be made about the maintenance of the church building. Think of the consternation this caused as others, who had *not* heard directly from God on the subject, wondered whether they dared utter an opposing opinion! Apparently it never occurred to the group to stop the meeting at that point and engage in group listening prayer, to get some sense of God's will in the matter.

# Hunger!

For years I was very suspicious of any claims that modern day Christians should expect to hear from God, other than by reading the Bible. Whenever possible, we clung tenaciously to a literal interpretation of Scripture. This was our way of avoiding being " tossed back and forth by the waves, and blown here and there by every wind of teaching."[16] As a result, I believed that a big part of being a good Christian was guarding sound doctrine. But when it became clear that such a role did not result in personal peace or holiness, I became hungry for more spiritual life and intimacy with God. I began to actively seek. I had always wondered why, in the Bible, there were many occasions when God spoke quite clearly, in contrast to the silent, distant God I had experienced. Many biblical characters argued with, wrestled, opposed or took direct orders from a very active, communicative Deity! What had changed?

# Hearing from Jesus Now?

Some teachers explained that, since we are now in the "church age," God speaks through church leadership. In our tradition, in the mid-twentieth century, this meant that whatever the Bishop Board majority voted was God's word on the issue. Or, in the case of our Catholic friends, the Pope's word was final. While I agree that some questions are best decided by the established church leadership, the practical problem with such an approach is that most of the issues of everyday life stand no chance of ever coming before the Bishop Board or the Pope. If we all tried to use this method to receive divine guidance, the church leadership would be swamped with thousands of specific questions, to which they could seldom deliver timely responses.

# Pop Quiz!

Therefore, ordinary Christians often feel confused, even lost, while doing their best to make decisions based on biblical principles, the advice of others, and feelings of peace or lack thereof. To my delight I found that we can expect much more! How about you?

1. Are you becoming increasingly convinced of God's love for you?
2. Is your love for God a genuine, palpable affection that permeates your whole being?
3. Would you say that you "know your Shepherd's voice" and are daily "following him"?[17]
4. Is your life characterized by increasing love, joy and peace?
5. Do you have increasing power to overcome sinful life patterns?
6. Do you have a strong sense of regularly being led by God to new "growing edges" of faith?

If you can answer a heart-felt "Yes!" to all of the above, you may want to skip the rest of the chapter. Otherwise I invite you to read on.

# Independent Reading

For a thorough review of the process by which a baby Christian grows up into spiritual maturity, I suggest Dallas Willard's *The Spirit of the Disciplines* [18] and *Renovation of the Heart.* [19] Also helpful are Thomas Keating's *Intimacy with God* [20] and Richard Foster's *Celebration of Discipline* [21] If you would like a resource to guide you and some fellow Christians on a journey of spiritual growth, I know of none better than the 28-week *Companions in Christ* course of private exercises and group sessions, published by Upper Room Books.[22] As you read and use these resources, you will find that each has a somewhat different list of spiritual disciplines, although some central ones like prayer are always included. You may also find that the Holy Spirit's personal training program for you will include some new ones not found on anyone else's list. I am tempted to just leave it at that and move on to the next chapter. But perhaps an overview of my own experiences with spiritual disciplines may be helpful.

# Early Attempts

My upbringing *did* emphasize Bible study and the importance of private daily devotions. Teachers at the Christian elementary school I attended sometimes asked whether we had had our personal devotions the day before! As long as I read a Bible chapter and prayed a few minutes each day I could avoid the embarrassment of having to admit that I had failed in this important *duty* of all sincere Christians. We were never asked to share what we had learned or what blessing had been given during the "quiet time." Nor were we trained in methods for finding meaning in these times of private devotion.

I suspect that many Christians wonder if it is possible to *enjoy* prayer. How can one carry on a one-sided conversation for even five minutes, let alone an hour? And then, of course, there is the startling verse that urges us to "pray without ceasing"![23] I had no idea how to pray like that, let alone how to enjoy it. My concept of prayer was much too narrow. Work and service were highly valued but sitting still to hear from God was suspect. The book of James seemed to be our "gospel." Our rallying cry was "I will shew thee my faith by my works."[24] Prayer was all about *talking to* God, not expecting him to answer, at least not personally, and in real time. We believed God spoke mainly through Bible reading.

So when I studied the Bible and ran head-on into a difficult passage, I felt betrayed. I was trying to hear from God and it was almost impossible. The King James English, the ancient setting and culture, the maddening lack of detail in many biblical narratives, my training to always strive for a literal interpretation, all worked against my sincere attempts to "hear" from the Lord. For many years I gave up, concluding that a personal relationship with the living Jesus was impossible for me. I had really tried and it had not worked. Therefore, in order to get relief from the tension caused by the huge gap between the expectation and my experience, *I lowered my expectation!* Oh, there were special times while hiking in the winter woods or listening to Beethoven's ninth symphony when I was able to connect with God for more than a few moments. But these were rare. When I was finally ready, God led me in a growth process that resulted in a precious sense of closeness with him. I now eagerly anticipate my quiet times. This chapter is not about the growth process *per se*. Rather, I simply want to describe what I have learned so far about specific activities that have made it possible for me to receive God's love and grace.

# CAUTION!

I approach this discussion with caution because I know how easy it may be to view what I'm about to write as a *formula* – or, even worse, to feel *obliged* to do the same activities in the same way. The point here is to sincerely *desire* an intimate relationship with Jesus – to *long for* it to the point that you are willing to do whatever *he leads **you** to do* so that you can learn to recognize and follow your Shepherd's voice. However, as a teacher, I do know how helpful *examples* can be. Please read the following in that light.

## What I've Learned

Let's start with private Bible reading and prayer. How can I now *enjoy* what used to be a chore? First of all, I learned that prayer is not only about *talking to* God. Yes, we are invited to present our requests to God[25] who is the giver of "every good and perfect gift,"[26] but such prayers are secondary to inviting God to bring his kingdom close.[11] Once I came to the end of my self-striving and was finally teachable, I began to learn how to recognize my Shepherd's voice. He has never yet spoken audibly to me. But I can now recognize thoughts that he places in my mind. Prayer is no longer one-sided. It has become marvelously interactive! Holy Spirit guidance and teaching have become personally meaningful. I bring real-life concerns to God in prayer and then sit expectantly, waiting for his reply. Now prayer is almost like reading an exciting mystery novel – except, in this case, it's not fiction!

## Mining Meaning from Scripture

Bible reading became much more meaningful once I learned that the Holy Spirit loves to use Scripture as a springboard for personalized teaching sessions. In other words, not only is the *writing* Holy Spirit-inspired, but so is the reading, interpretation and application to our lives.[27] Thus, if I cannot understand what I am reading, I admit that to God and take some time to "listen" to the Holy Spirit as he helps me understand. I am no longer responsible to think it through myself. I expect help and it comes to mind, regularly! I also learned a simple process for mining meaning from a passage of Scripture. It has a Latin name – Lectio Divina – meaning Sacred Reading.[28] It is easy to remember as the four "Rs": **Read, Reflect, Respond and Rest**. First, I slowly **Read** a brief biblical passage, maybe just a verse or two. There is no sense of urgency to read through the Bible in a year or even to read the traditional chapter-a-day. The idea is to slowly read for formation, not information. That is, I read until the Holy Spirit causes a word or phrase to catch my attention or perhaps I just get the sense "This verse is rich; I think I'll read it again and see what I can discover." So I read it again, slowly, and jot down any word or phrase that "jumps out at me." I record my jottings in my journal. Then I sit back and **Reflect**. That is, I take time to ponder, often writing questions or comments. I sometimes reread the passage, slowly, maybe even aloud. Then I **Respond** by writing a prayer. Often this is a request for clarification or help to make an application to my life. Sometimes the response phase develops into a multi-page "conversation" with God. For example, I may write a question that I would like God to answer. I then wait, alert for what thought comes next. Many times it is a verbal answer consistent with what I know of God's character and Word. If so, I write it down as his reply to my question. Often, though, it's a question he is asking me! In that case I also write that down and do my best to answer, also in writing. I number my journal pages and date my entries for ease of reference later. Sometimes nothing cognitive comes at all. I do not insist on any particular type of response. Some days my journal entry is just a few words. Once the two-way flow of ideas has come to an end, I enter the **Rest** phase of Sacred Reading. I actually do rest. I usually move away from the desk at which I had been doing the **Read, Reflect** and **Respond** phases and sit, or even lie down, on an upholstered chair or couch. I usually begin by thanking Jesus for his love, *inviting* him to fill me, and *consenting* to whatever work he wants to do in my heart.[20] Sometimes I repeat a focus word or phrase such as "Jesus" or "Abide in me" to help my mind settle down. At this point, thoughts about my hectic day may be ricocheting about in my head. With practice I have learned to let these thoughts flit by without paying them much attention.[29] If self-accusations or fearful "what-if scenarios" are mentally troublesome, I recognize the satanic interference and ask God to banish it. Often the Spirit suggests that I address the Evil One directly, "You must leave," I insist, "You do not belong here. This house and my mind belong to Jesus and are for his use only. I do *not* consent to your presence or interference." I don't know why I keep being amazed when it works! The Bible says, "Resist the Devil and he will flee from you."[30]

# Resting Prayer

I have learned that resting prayer can become a sweet time of intimacy with Jesus. No verbal messages are requested. None is necessarily given. After years of practice, I find that the **Rest** phase of Sacred Reading usually lasts from twenty to forty minutes. If you are just starting out, ten minutes may seem long. How do I know when to stop? It varies. Sometimes I actually doze off for some of the time. But it is not the same as just taking a nap. For me a nap can easily turn into two hours of sound sleep. This never happens to me during resting prayer. The Spirit lets me go deep for awhile and then brings me back. As I am coming out of the deep place of contemplation or "sacred sleep," Jesus often gives me a brief take-away message or maybe even a clear *next-step*. When that happens I get up and record it in my journal. Sometimes I get nothing verbal or cognitive, just a profound sense of well-being. Leona often notices that my knit brow has been replaced by an ear-to-ear grin. She might actually say, "It looks like you have been with Jesus!"

# About Time

Some may be wondering if there are any guidelines about the amount of time one should spend each day in private Bible reading and prayer. When I was starting to get serious about learning to love God with my whole being, it seemed nearly inconceivable to spend even fifteen minutes in private prayer. The goal is not to fulfill any kind of legalistic expectation. We should be willing to devote whatever time is necessary to make progress toward the intimacy with God implied by the first and greatest commandment. How often have you heard that when two human soul-mates first find one another they may talk for hours, perhaps long into the night? Or, have you ever been with a group of good friends and, even after the planned activities for the evening are completed, everyone just lingers, reluctant to allow the time of fellowship to end? We *want* to spend time with people we like. We do not think as we are approaching their house, "Oh, let me see, it is now seven o'clock. If I can just make it 'til seven fifteen I will have done my duty to this relationship and can then graciously excuse myself." The key is to take whatever time is necessary to receive a blessing from God.

# Further Examples

In addition to the above descriptions of Sacred Reading, Journaling and Resting Prayer, I will also briefly describe some other spiritual practices I have personally experienced.

## 1. A Modified Daily Examen

At the end of the day I sometimes make a list of events that happened for which I am thankful or in which I see opportunity for personal growth. On the left, I list the events. To the right of each entry I put a series of plus signs symbolizing varying degrees of gratitude for evidence of growth or, alternatively, one or more minus signs in recognition that there is still room for improvement. I may also write brief comments. This is neither bragging nor beating up on myself. It is just a tool for being honest with God and opening my heart to whatever the Holy Spirit would like to teach me about the day just past.

2. **The Jesus Prayer**

   At times when I have sinned, or if I am feeling condemned for no apparent reason, I may repeatedly pray, "Lord Jesus Christ, Son of God, have mercy on me, a sinner." The repetitive use of this prayer is common in the Eastern Orthodox Christian tradition. I have found its use calming. Praying the Jesus Prayer reminds me of my proper place before a holy God and of what Jesus has done to save me. I also find it helpful in resisting Satan's belittling accusations.

3. **Extended Periods of Silence and Solitude**

   I have participated in single- and multi-day retreats in which blocks of time were devoted to silent solitude. I usually meditate on Scripture and journal or follow the suggested worksheet, if it is a guided retreat. One time, however, I did not bring along any devotional materials. As I sat motionless for three hours in the October western Pennsylvania woods, hoping to ambush a deer, I was struck by the beauty of the yellow mountain maple leaves falling one at a time. Because I was so still, an inquisitive chipmunk felt safe enough to come within six inches of my shoulder. I saw no deer but God seemed to say, "Hey Ev, you may call this hunting, but it's really *armed solitude!*"

4. **Study**

   I often wrestle with God over the meaning of tough Bible passages and theological concepts. Chapter 3 is just one example.

5. **Laying and Praying**[31]

   This is one way to describe Sabbath-keeping.[32] Since we are currently leading spiritual formation groups on weekends (the spiritual discipline of Service, by the way), Sunday is seldom a day of rest for us. Therefore, we occasionally take part of a weekday to nap and pray. We stop all our scurrying about and lounge on sofas or comfortable recliners and intermittently doze off and pray, receptively and restfully. This is not the time for wrestling with God about tough doctrines or special needs. If the Spirit brings Monica to mind, for example, we may simply pray "Jesus – Monica," "Jesus – Monica" five or ten times slowly. This is the time for simply sitting at Jesus' feet and enjoying his cuddling love. It is wonderful!

### 6. Worship and Fellowship

In addition to glorious times of public worship every Sunday morning, I often notice God's creative masterworks. For example, Leona and I recently took a group from our neighborhood to the Middle Creek Wildlife Management Area in southeastern Pennsylvania to see the migrating Snow Geese and Tundra Swans. We also have lots of fellowship. We are participating in *six* small groups including the three *Companions in Christ* groups that we are leading.

### 7. Fasting

Like most people, I fast every day from 10 pm to 6 am! But seriously, the Lord has very recently been leading me to try an actual spiritual fast. Within the month of this writing I read *God's Chosen Fast* by Arthur Wallis[33] and the chapter on fasting in Richard Foster's *Celebration of Discipline.*[21] Three days ago at a Renovaré Conference I felt called to commit to my first ever 24-hour normal fast (water only). I picked yesterday to fast. For you champion, experienced fasters out there it must seem insignificant that I missed two whole meals, lunch and dinner. But for me it was the *next-step* to which I was called. It felt a bit like self-denial. I got a mild headache and did not sleep as soundly as usual. Leona joined me and as she said, it was kind of humbling. It felt like we were not as "in charge" as usual. Well, *good*, right? So far, the one spiritual benefit that I am aware of is something that I had never experienced before. In *God's Chosen Fast* there is a diary of a 21-day fast. This brother kept referring to having "liberty in prayer."[34] Though I am not completely sure what he meant by the phrase, during my own one-day fast I felt a new freedom to respond to the Holy Spirit in intercession for four or five specific areas of need. For two and a half hours I prayed and journaled, all of it in intercession for others. This was *new* for me! Both the length of time and the fact that it was *not at all about me* or my issues! Will I ever learn to actually *enjoy* fasting as much as I now enjoy prayer? Only time will tell.

8. **Chastity**

   I practice this spiritual discipline only in the sense that I limit the expression of my sexuality to activities I share with my wife. For me chastity includes resisting the temptation to look lustfully at other attractive women, in person or in print or electronic media.

I offer this overview only as *examples* of the means by which God's grace can break in and transform our lives. You may be much more advanced in one or more of the above. Perhaps others that I have not mentioned have been instrumental in your own spiritual journey. For example, I have not touched at all on the sacraments or the use of sacred icons. In some Christian traditions these are very highly valued means of grace.[35]

# Spiritual Rewards

In summary, spiritual disciplines are activities we *can do,* by God's grace, that make it possible for God's grace to still further invade and transform our hearts and minds. One spiritual benefit is that in times of stress the "training kicks in" and, maybe even to our own surprise, we act out of the more Christlike heart he has been forming in us. But even more basic is the benefit of intimacy with Jesus. After all, the first and greatest commandment is to be consumed with love for *him.*

# 15

# Hearty Renunciation and Spiritual Hilarity

## Payback?

Is all the nitty gritty worth it? Add up all the time spent in prayer, the scary honesty, the submission to Holy Spirit training, and the letting go of favorite coping strategies. Is there significant payback in this life? Oddly enough, renunciation of counterfeits goes hand-in-hand with living a joy-filled life. Even when we are not walking closely with God, joy sometimes surprises us – as if God wants to give us a taste, just enough to make us long for more. A moment of natural beauty takes our breath away, only to pass just as quickly. If we try later to recreate the moment, we may find the joy frustratingly elusive. At other times God asks us to make a small sacrifice, and when we do, joy floods in! Or, as if to show that the feeling itself is not the goal, the joy may be withheld for a season, even as we obey. But in general, a *lifestyle* of unbelief and disobedience eventually kills almost all the joy. Physical pleasure, sought as a counterfeit for true joy, increasingly loses its kick. If, however, we focus on learning to love and obey God, moments, even seasons of joy more and more characterize our lives.[1]

# Long Faces

Most of my life I viewed self-denial as a "necessary evil." I was convinced that Christians must be willing to give up enjoyment in *this* life for the sake of the joy that is promised in *the next*.[2] Many who take their faith seriously seem to think that the longer the face, the better the Christian. As I write, we are in a period of national mourning over the shooting deaths at Virginia Tech. The day after the atrocity I could not miss the symbolism of the Today Show anchors dressed in black. Uncharacteristically, the female co-anchor's hair was austerely tied back. Even the normally ebullient weather man was serious. Of course, it is only fitting to "mourn with those who mourn."[3] Seasons of sorrow and grief are inevitable. But, does Jesus' command to daily take up our crosses mean that we should be *chronically somber?*[4]

Any decent, empathetic human being can, over time, succumb to the notion that in a world with so much suffering, hilarity is simply unfeeling. The constant drum-beat of 24-hour media coverage of human and natural evil has led many to conclude that life is just plain awful, and that the only appropriate response is to maintain a constant attitude of "concern for those less fortunate."

# Rejoice Always!

I beg to differ. Jesus said that he came so that we could live life to the full[5] and that his joy might be in us and our joy might be complete.[6] Paul wrote that we are to "Rejoice in the Lord always."[7] But how can we live these truths in a world that is often so sad?

First of all, deep, lasting, authentic joy has only one source – Jesus. We cannot work it up. Trying to enjoy life without a vital relationship with Jesus is not just futile, but dangerous. Why do I say this? Simple. Such attempts involve counterfeits. When we don't have the real thing (and I *don't* mean Coca Cola!), we naturally crave substitutes. We may even come to believe that the substitutes are necessary – not only to enjoy life, but to survive emotionally.

# We Crave Joy

Why do we crave joy? Because God made us that way. In C. S. Lewis' *Screwtape Letters*, the elder demon, Screwtape, tells his apprentice, Wormwood, that "pleasure in its healthy and normal and satisfying form" is "His [God's] invention, not ours. He made the pleasures: all our research so far has not enabled us to produce one. All we can do is to encourage the humans to take the pleasures which our Enemy [God] has produced, at times, or in ways, or in degrees, which He has forbidden."[8] God knew that we would be unfulfilled until we found our home in him. He can use chronic lack of joy as a powerful motivator. But as long as we are using counterfeits to numb our God-given longing for joy, we are living dangerously. We leave God little choice but to allow us to suffer the consequences of our sin or to experience some life-shock, to break us loose from our benumbed bondage. This may be one reason why Jesus said that it is so hard for a rich man to enter his kingdom.[9] Anyone with plenty of money can go on for a long time, trying any number of amusements, in a vain attempt to find the joy that can come only from intimacy with God.

# Counterfeit Poisoning

Allow me an analogy from biology. We have all heard of deaths caused by carbon monoxide poisoning. Many will recall that inhaled carbon monoxide attaches itself to hemoglobin molecules on red blood cells, thus blocking some of the sites normally used to transport life-giving oxygen. As far as hemoglobin is concerned, carbon monoxide is a counterfeit. If you will pardon the anthropomorphism, hemoglobin molecules "prefer" to be bound to the carbon monoxide, which, once it has become attached, does not let go easily! Treatment for carbon monoxide poisoning is 100% oxygen. (Normal air contains only 21% oxygen.) Some studies have shown that hyperbaric oxygen, that is, pure oxygen at pressures above normal atmospheric pressure, will speed recovery.[10]

Like oxygen, joy, our source of strength,[11] can fill our lives when we are open and receptive to Jesus.[6] If, however, we choose to reject God's invitation to intimacy, we begin to suffer spiritual malnutrition. Some symptoms are: spiritual numbness, chronic discouragement and, ultimately, profound despair. This does not feel good. To alleviate the spiritual and emotional pain, we often try substitutes. Initially we do feel better, just like those hemoglobin molecules that ravenously suck up the carbon monoxide. But since the counterfeits do not nourish our spirits, the spiritual hunger soon returns. Our gracious God does not give up on us quickly. He still sends an occasional taste of joy so we won't completely forget what we are missing. Then he withdraws it again and keeps using our unsatisfied longing to draw us close.

# Treatment

Spiritually, what is the treatment for counterfeit-poisoning? Often there needs to be one or several life-shocks to awaken us to the dire condition of our souls. Once God has our attention, he may give us a *next-step*. If we obey, he may grant a taste of joy, similar to a few breaths of pure oxygen. But the treatment has only begun. There is still a lot of carbon monoxide attached to the hemoglobin. In other words, unbelief must still be uprooted, and woundedness healed. We must be transformed by the renewing of our minds.[12] If we have fallen into this spiritually anemic condition, there are two main requirements for a return to spiritual health:

1. Re-establishing the life-line to God,[13] and
2. Hearty renunciation of counterfeits.[14]

Other chapters deal with the first. Here we will explore the second.

# Hearty Renunciation

What is meant by hearty renunciation? I read the phrase first in *The Practice of the Presence of God* by Brother Lawrence. He said that "all consists in one hearty renunciation of everything which we are sensible does not lead to God; that we might accustom ourselves to a continual conversation with Him"[15] A few pages earlier he diagnosed the sad condition of many devout Christians, then and, I fear, even now. He said "many do not advance in the Christian progress because they stick in penances and particular exercises, while they neglect the love of God, which is the *end.*"[16] There you have it. Love of God is the goal. We simply must do whatever advances that quest and stop whatever hinders it! But even here we must remember that the doing is secondary to the desire.[17] God himself must give the desire. The built-in appetite for joy is one way he does so. Once we realize that counterfeits do not nourish, we are ready to pray something like this: "Yes, Lord, I want to learn to love you above all else. I have no idea *how* at this point, but I finally understand that this is the ultimate goal of my life. Now, Jesus, please show me how. What specific things must I do or stop doing to make possible growth toward the priceless treasure of intimacy with you?"

# Prerequisites

Of course, some cannot start here. Those who are severely limited mentally will certainly enjoy God's mercy. Others, suffering a severe illness, will need to be nursed back to reasonable health first. A third group, currently bound by addiction to mind-altering substances, may have to be rescued initially by special intervention techniques to give them a chance to think clearly about their choices. A fourth group has never heard about Jesus or, having heard, has never decided to follow him. These will need a deep conversion experience before this chapter can apply. The insights offered here are meant to help those who have started their walk with Jesus but now long for more intimacy.

Some committed Christians may be stymied by practical, physical issues. For example, those with a genetic predisposition to insomnia, depression or anxiety may need to seek pharmaceutical healing before significant spiritual growth is possible. Someone who is chronically sleep-deprived may be simply *unable* to focus on prayer until his biochemistry is optimized. But God knows about all these details. We can trust that he will reward all sincere seekers.[18]

# CAUTION!

Once again, as in the last chapter, I caution the reader against taking my own story as *your* word from the Lord. Consider the biblical story of the rich, young ruler. Jesus knew exactly what *he* needed to renounce.[19] For years I heard Bible teachers attempt to make Jesus' *next-step* to this young man some sort of universal requirement for all serious Christians. For some of us, material wealth may be just as dangerous a counterfeit as it was for the young ruler. But others are gifted with the ability to make money and to use it for the advancement of God's kingdom. For these, Jesus' call may be to renounce an entirely different counterfeit. Therefore, before I share my own experience, I caution you to think of it only as an *example* of how God may want to work in your life. You will be misled if you look down over my list, checking them off in your mind – "Well, I don't struggle with that one, that next one either...let's see, none of these actually give me any difficulty! I'm home free! No need for *me* to worry any more about counterfeits!" Not so fast. It may be very easy for *you* to control your sexual urges. You may actually *prefer* rabbit food! TV may bore you to tears. But you may struggle with overwork, compulsive shopping or non-stop talking. It is crucial that renunciation be directed by personal, Holy Spirit guidance. Sure, there are lists of clearly sinful activities in the Bible.[20] These are always wrong for all of us. But here we are discussing activities that are good in their rightful place but that, at any given time in a person's life, may be taking the place of intimacy with God.

# For Example

OK, now to my story. God used the deaths of my parents and my own and Leona's medical problems as life-shocks to get my attention. The September 11, 2001 attacks were also instrumental. Even though I was disappointed with what I viewed as an inadequate response by my home church, God gave me a *next-step*. In effect, he said, "Stay put, you might learn something." I obeyed and soon thereafter was invited to help teach the 28-week *Companions in Christ* (CIC) course. I agreed, mainly because I liked our co-leaders, Jim and Mary Ann Miller, and wanted to spend time with them. But, when that course was ending and the Millers asked Leona and me to teach it all over again *without them*, I didn't want to. But I gave up my personal wishes and submitted to their godly guidance. The second time through CIC was life-changing. Eight weeks in, one of the exercises was to read the story of Jacob wrestling all night with a "man" until he was blessed.[21] One of the CIC questions was, "What will you and God wrestle about?"[22] I wrote in my journal, "I want to feel close to God."

God seemed to answer, "Everett, I want that for you as well. Here is how you can have it:

1.  *Give up* recreational sex (sex as a solitary amusement)
2.  *Give up* therapeutic eating (eating to assuage emotional pain)
3.  *Give up* watching "Survivor" (the only TV program I still tried not to miss)

4. *Give up* intellectual gratification ( meaning, at that time, giving up the dream to help teach a Christian Thought course at church)"

At that point I asked, "What's next, Lord, crossword puzzles?" The thought came, "Just plain give up. Sit still and listen."

# Giving Up

As I look back now I realize that before Jesus asked me to renounce these counterfeits, he had already led me to a place of readiness to do so. The combination of my age, medication, and experiences of real, God-given joy made it possible for me to be almost relieved about items one and two. Number three was doable after several years of progressively losing interest in TV in general. In addition, I was getting tired of the backstabbing and deception that had become almost the entire focus of "Survivor." The Christian Thought course had already been postponed indefinitely. So what was I really giving up? *Reliance on counterfeits!* Jesus mentioned a few as examples, but the call was to a general giving up of anything that I had been tempted to do instead of coming to the Lord for his love. Jesus wanted me to recognize how dependent I had become on some spiritually non-nourishing physical pleasures. Once I had tasted some of the true joy only he could give, Jesus wanted me to feel some deprivation. I needed to walk more closely with him and to get healing from emotional hurts and hang-ups with which I had never come to grips. For years I had been short-circuiting the God-given early-warning system, engaging in physically pleasurable activities that, though totally legitimate in their rightful place, were keeping me from seeking the true joy I could get only from God. As my personal trainer, counselor, and Great Physician, the Holy Spirit was now prescribing, and making palatable, the very medicine I needed to get well spiritually. By the way, I am still enjoying crossword puzzles, but if I don't have time to both pray and work on a puzzle, I usually pray.

# Joy

I took God seriously. Two months went by as I renounced the "easy-outs" on which I had long relied to regulate my mood. Instead, I prayed regularly and threw myself into leading a small band of brothers and sisters who also wanted to grow closer to Jesus. Numerous moments of insight and joy began to bless my life. One in particular got my attention.

First a little background. Our church small group had given us a money gift for a tree in memory of my mother who had just died. We bought a spindly, purple-leaved redbud tree. It reminded me of some animal babies – all gangly-legged and floppy-eared. This little tree had a trunk only three quarters of an inch in diameter at the base and a mop of purple leaves each of which measured up to eight inches across! Sadly, even though we tried to protect it with several stakes and guy-wires, the gusts during one late-summer storm were just too strong. They broke the little trunk about eighteen inches from the ground. For three days it lay there, its purple-leaved top on the ground, connected to the rest of the tiny trunk by a thin strip of wood and bark. I had given up on it. I just could not bring myself to dig it out and throw it away. But Leona wouldn't have it. She had the faith I couldn't muster. She finally bought some grafting fabric and tape, straightened the tree up, bound its broken trunk together and secured it to a strong stake. Seeing that she was determined to give it another chance, I then pruned the foliage back hard, realizing that the redbud's survival depended on unburdening the infantile trunk and root system.

In the spring we waited, without much hope I'm afraid, to see if some tiny buds would amount to anything. Now it was Leona's turn to doubt. She said, "I don't think they are alive. See, when you touch them they fall off."

"Then don't touch them!" I urged. Even after all the trauma and a long, cold winter, the *bark* looked very much alive. As the weather warmed, those little buds did shoot. The tree had been saved. By mid-May it was thriving, pushing out leaf after gorgeously purple and shiny leaf. As I walked by it on one occasion, my heart overflowed with joy and hope. Jesus used that tree and Leona's faith to speak life and joy deep into my soul. I had never before felt joy that intense. I prayed, "Thank you Jesus! Thank you! Thank you! Thank you!" For the first time in my life, I wished that I had a more adequate language with which to praise the Lord Jesus. I did not laugh at this point, but the joy seemed most like uproarious hilarity! Ever since then I often find myself grinning from ear-to-ear, even in situations in which I had formerly felt tense, angry and hurt. Would I have ever experienced these spiritual highs had I not been renouncing counterfeits? I doubt it.

# Hilarity

Almost three months later, as I was working my way into the gospel of John during our summer *Companions in Christ* hiatus, I read the story of the wedding at Cana.[23] It was the occasion of Jesus' first public miracle. As we all know, he turned water into wine. How much wine did he make? The nearest I can figure, about 120 gallons! Talk about abundant provision! What a grand old time they must have had then! At first it seemed as if Jesus wanted to say "I will make no wine before my time." But instead he chose the motto, "I will make no wine unless my mother insists."

How scandalous of him! He performed his very first miracle making an alcoholic beverage for people who had been drinking for three straight days, at a rate that took their host by surprise! Jesus was not timid or inhibited. He could have made the same point by making one liter of fine wine. But NOOOOHH! He just *had* to make 120 GALLONS! Hilarious!

I prayed, "What a wild man you are, Lord!"

"Yeah, Ev, wasn't that a HOOT? You should have seen the look on the face of that banquet master when he found that not only was it excellent wine, but it had been made on the spot with no aging whatsoever, AND there were 120 gallons of it!"

"Yeah, I bet that was precious! I bet you got invited to *all* the weddings after that!"

"Well, yes, but the folks soon learned that making wine was not my life's work. One bunch of really tipsy wedding guests was enough! But it still makes me chuckle!"

# Temptation and Truth

About four months later I went to a four-day conference in Montreal. In recent years I had been taking Leona along on multi-day trips like this, but this time I was alone. I left home on a Saturday. The following Tuesday evening I read John 10:31-42. A group of people referred to simply as "the Jews" were ready to kill Jesus. Despite his many miracles, they refused to believe in his claim to oneness with God the Father. They insisted he was a "mere man." Their attitude was, "Do not confuse us with the factual evidence, our minds are made up."

As I pondered this story, a question came to mind, "Do *I* still have knots of unbelief that are just as stubborn?" Yes, I did. I realized that it was hard for me to believe that renouncing all expressions of sexuality except those I shared with Leona could really result in a better life,[5] especially when I was separated from her for days at a time. "How could having *fewer* orgasms yield a *more abundant* life?" I wondered. As travelers know, most modern hotels offer easy access to counterfeits in this area. I wished I had brought Leona along. The day before, I had fought a day-long battle over whether or not to disobey Jesus' call to renounce solitary sexual gratification. Even though I had already experienced numerous examples of true spiritual exhilaration that I knew were made possible, in part at least, by my willingness to obey this divine directive, I had been tormented all day by a *compulsive urge* to fall back into old patterns. I craved the control and predictability of the self-induced, counterfeit joy. As it turned out, I fought off the temptation by working out at the hotel gym immediately after the last afternoon conference session and then going to dinner. By the time I returned to my room the urge had passed and I was able to sleep peacefully.

Nevertheless, having to battle all day was evidence that I did not yet have complete peace and calm in that area of life. It was not even what Ed Smith calls "tolerable recovery."[25] It was more like intolerable *full-fledged spiritual warfare!* It felt like I was still believing some sort of lie. In fact, it almost seemed as if the Holy Spirit had set me up for a training session. First came the call to renunciation, then the time away from Leona, then he allowed the strong temptation. Actually, I could almost say that "Everett was led by the Spirit into Montreal to be tempted by the Devil!"[26]

The following evening I felt a call to pray for insight and healing. "Dear Lord, what is wrong with me? I do not have a strong *physical* urge right now but the mental battle can still be intense and persistent when I am separated from Leona. I know from experience that were she here, I would not give the in-room movies a second thought. I do not think the difference is merely that my physical needs would have been met by marital intimacy. No, it seems like a *switch in my mind is activated* by the mere fact of the separation. Am I onto something here, Lord?"

I went into resting prayer at this point. After a time I began to write. "I was raised by parents who seemed to believe that sexuality was shameful and should not only be kept secret, but avoided altogether as much as possible. As I was growing up I couldn't help but notice that they slept in different rooms, or at least different beds, most of their married life. This pattern started soon after all three children were born."

"However," I went on, "*I* am *very* sexual. I was early in life and have been ever since. I must still believe, though, that sex is shameful because it is very hard for me to talk about sex, even with Leona. Even to write this down in my journal is a struggle. I mean, what if someone found this thing? Suppose our children, while going through my things after my death, should read that Dad struggled with these 'shameful' urges, what would they think?"

That's all it took. I wrote, "What a crock of [scatological reference deleted]!"

Immediately Jesus said, "Amen, brother, who do you think *made* you a sexy man in the first place?"

"You, of course, Lord. How *dare* I call your very own hilarious, joyful invention shameful?!"

I had to stop writing because, at this point, I broke out into spontaneous, belly-shaking, falling-down, rolling-in-the-aisles, side-splitting, helpless, raucous laughter! It's a wonder the guys in the adjoining rooms didn't call the fellows in the white coats! Once I was able to calm down to just intermittent fits of giggles, I went back to writing. Addressing our Enemy I said, "Why you silly [expletive deleted], you!"

Just think of it! All those years he had me believing that the sexual Everett was shameful and had to be *kept separate* from the "pure, non-sexual" Everett. What a stupid fantasy that second Everett was! Ha! Of *course*, I'm sexy. Of *course* my procreative instincts are designed so that my race will "be fruitful and increase in number; fill the earth and subdue it."[27] I love being a normal man in this way. But I also know that if I indiscriminately indulge these very natural, God-given urges, my spirit will die."[28] Later I prayed more about that dilemma but, at that point, there was real healing. It seemed that once I realized the two-Everett lie (one sexual and one "pure"), I could almost hear two parts of my mind come together with a smooth, solid *Ker-Chunk!* The truth is, the real Everett is sexual. God made me that way and he is totally able to see to it that my sexuality will enrich rather than destroy my life.

# Real Healing?

I tell this story here to make the point that, had I not been obeying Jesus' call to renunciation, I would most likely have missed taking a major step forward in the transformation of my mind and emotional make-up. How do I know the healing was for real? Here's how.

Although I still like sex, the compulsion is gone. When marital intimacy is not practical for a little while, I can think of times of involuntary arousal as mildly pleasurable, a sign that I am not dead yet, unlike in the past when the same sensation triggered a mild panic, "Oh, no! Here comes that bad Everett, rising up again!" Also, since I have given God first place, he has freed me from the old desperation – as if I am missing out on something of *supreme importance* – whenever sexual expression is delayed a bit.

# Freedom Demonstration

How much freedom did I get? A recent business trip to Las Vegas was telling. First, let me explain briefly about my medication status at the time. Antidepressants can reduce libido. However, for the six months just prior to this trip, I had taken no antidepressants. I had decided to try doing without them over the spring and summer months. Therefore, what I am about to describe cannot be attributed merely to a medication side-effect.

I went to Vegas on a Wednesday to staff a trade-show booth. The first evening I went to dinner with colleagues but Thursday and Friday evenings I was alone. Normally, I would have expected a major battle with temptation in such surroundings. But this trip followed considerable emotional healing and lots of experience with hearty renunciation. I felt no desire to go out on the town and see the sights. True joy triumphed right there amid the glitz of sin, the pretend joy, and all the trappings of a counterfeit paradise. I understood that the physical beauty on parade, the promise of instant wealth, the good food on an expense account were invitations to settle for less than the best. I felt no anxiety, no need for physical gratification, just a restful gratitude that I was loved extravagantly and steadily.

Thursday afternoon, when I was alone at the booth, I heard a woman's voice giving some sort of joy holler. I couldn't help but be curious. I soon spotted a showgirl wearing what appeared to be a pheasant-feather headdress, and not a whole lot more, going around the huge exhibit hall having her picture taken with various show attendees. For about forty minutes she took up a position just to the right of my booth. As I sat on the booth stool I could not see her. I could have easily stood up, taken two steps forward and feasted my eyes. I had already seen her walk by the booth and knew that she was quite attractive, but I chose to remain seated. Although this was definitely an example of hearty renunciation of lustful looking, I was amazed to find that I felt peaceful rather than deprived.

## Joyful Self-denial?

So how do Holy Spirit-directed self-denial and God-given joy correlate? It partly depends on how we define joy. If we mean by it a sense of intense spiritual exhilaration, I would have to say that as long as I was trying to *avoid* renunciation, joy was practically non-existent. Once I was able to begin practicing renunciation, spiritual highs that felt a lot like hilarity, and sometimes even resulted in hearty laughter, became more common. Of course, we could not survive constant exhilaration. But if we are supremely happy only once a decade, something probably needs fixed (as they say in Pittsburgh).

If, however, we define joy as a general lightness of spirit and freedom from gloom, self-condemnation and pessimism, then I would say that, for me, when I don't have joy in this sense, I take it as a signal that I need to spend more time in close communion with Jesus and/or I need to ask him if there is anything blocking the joy. If it is something I am doing instead of walking closely with Jesus, I have found that stopping that activity, as directed and enabled by the Holy Spirit, often results in a return of joy.

Can joy actually be experienced during demanding, stressful, and perhaps even painful life circumstances? I leave this question for the next chapter.

# 16

# Joy and Suffering

## Where is the Joy?

A man of God once asked, "Would you say your life is joyful?" The twenty or so men gathered that Sunday afternoon looked stumped. We could not honestly answer yes. After some thought, I realized that until then my life had been characterized by mild to moderate depression, punctuated by rare moments of joy. Around that same time I saw several young Jesuits being interviewed on TV. Their faces absolutely beamed! When asked about their joy, they described a life that most of us would find boring, even tedious – prayer, meditation on Scripture, fasting, celibacy, manual labor – the typical monastic routine. In contrast, I had a well-paid career, a beautiful and loving wife, a great home in an upscale neighborhood, and fantastic children and friends. But joy seldom shone from my face. I wanted the joy Jesus promised.[1]

## Spirit Fruit

What *is* joy? It seems not to fit with the rest of the fruit of the Spirit.[2] We can *work at* being loving, gentle peacemakers. But how can we make ourselves more joyful? All the rest seem to be virtues of Christian character, things we can practice, but how does one practice joy? If joy is a fruit of the Spirit, when is it in season? What Christian would say it is

OK to show love or self-control only a few times a year? Yet we seem willing to go for long periods without joy. The Bible says we should rejoice with those who rejoice, but mourn with those who mourn.[3] Where is the verse that says, "Relax with those that are at peace, be tense with those in a tizzy"?

People often distrust someone who smiles a lot. They assume that no one can be *that* happy. The smiles are often taken as evidence of insincerity or a hidden agenda. Although God *can* give us joy in the midst of trying circumstances, acting joyful when we are really crying inside is hardly a fruit of the Spirit. Jesus wept over Jerusalem,[4] agonized in Gethsemane,[5] and cried out on the cross "My God, my God, why have you forsaken me?"[6] The prophet Isaiah described the Messiah as a "man of sorrows and familiar with suffering."[7] And yet, the Bible admonishes us to "Rejoice in the Lord always"[8] and to "Be joyful always."[9] But then, as mentioned above, we are urged to "mourn with those who mourn." Unless we can figure out how to mourn joyfully, it seems we are at an impasse. Let's see what Jesus had to say on the subject.

# Jesus' Joy

In John 15:11 we read, "I have told you this so that my joy may be in you and that your joy may be complete." The Greek verb for "be complete" means to "fulfill, make full, to be filled, full, complete" and is often used with reference to the fulfillment of Old Testament scriptures.[10] It does not necessarily mean continuous, intense or exhilarating. Could it mean "as much joy as we can contain"? Perhaps God knows just how much joy is possible for each of us and, to the extent that we follow closely, listen carefully, and obey consistently, we experience the *full measure* of the joy God knows we can contain.

# Always?

Must we adopt a literal, legalistic interpretation of Scriptures that seem to *command* that Christians be "always" joyful?[8, 9] Could it be that such verses are simply good, practical advice rather than laws to be obeyed legalistically? In other words, was this just Paul's way of saying, "Don't always be 'bringing people down' with your constant griping and complaining"? Might he have continued, "Lighten up, look at life with Jesus as an exciting opportunity, look for evidence of his blessing and point it out to others. Be grateful. Do not be faithless, but believe that he really does have your best interests at heart"?

# Christian Joy

## The emotion:

What then is the nature of Christian joy? The plain meaning of the Greek word "chara" is "joy, rejoicing, happiness or gladness."[11] This is not complicated. On the surface, joy is clearly an emotion and as such is not completely under rational control. We cannot typically *decide* to feel joyful. Joy comes and goes, varies in intensity and is to some degree dependent on external circumstances. It is just as pathological to pretend that we always feel joyful as it is to deny and suppress all feelings of anger. However, if joyful feelings are very rare, we should probably ask Jesus why.

## The attitude:

At a somewhat deeper level, Christian joy is a mental attitude of childlike playfulness, maybe even a somewhat bemused life-outlook. We enjoy spending time with people whose eyes sparkle mischievously and who seem ready to break into a little dance at the slightest provocation. Unlike the surface feeling of gladness, joy in this sense is more affected by the condition of the inner spirit and is less a product of circumstances. Not so much an emotion, this joy is a predisposition to see the good in others and in our environment. Biological factors at least partially explain such a cheerful attitude. The correct neurochemical balance is a wonderful thing. But it is also true that one's personal belief system can have a strong effect on joy. Someone who is carrying a load of unresolved bitterness, fear and guilt is unlikely to be predominately cheerful.

## The Spirit-fruit:

Still deeper is joy as Spirit-fruit. This one is hardest of all to put into words. I believe it is a deep, abiding *sense of well-being* grounded in the conviction that God is good. Once we are given the grace to begin to fathom God's love,[12] we can start to relax into a deep soul rest. Yes, we can still feel pain, but our profound trust in God's good intentions toward us maximizes our ability to find enjoyment in life.

All three aspects of joy are present, with a lot of overlap, in the life of the mature Christian. If the *emotion* is present only rarely, and the *playful attitude* and *sense of well-being* are almost completely absent for months at a time, we should make it a serious prayer concern. Habitual somberness (lack of joy) is no more commendable than lack of patience. It is *not* OK for joy to be the one Spirit-fruit that seldom shows on the outside. But, is joy *always* possible, even in suffering?

# Joy in Suffering?

Some defend the concept of joy-in-suffering by explaining that, as we endure unavoidable hardship, we can be at least partially consoled by hope of a better future. But this is not the same as actually enjoying the hardship. Likewise, trusting that in all things God is working for our good[13] is not quite the same as enjoying the process. Another idea that is sometimes called joy-in-suffering is merely learning to find joy in life circumstances that had formerly caused only suffering. But again, this is not actually enjoying suffering. Instead, it is an example of our hearts being transformed so that we can now see the good in situations that previously seemed only painful. When this happens it is marvelous. But can there ever be joy *during* suffering?

In order to answer this question we need to think clearly about what we mean by "suffering." Much of what we call suffering falls into a category we commonly call inconvenience or annoyance. This includes everyday, petty setbacks, interruptions or unkind words or deeds we may endure as part of life in a sinful world. We may also include here instances of hearty renunciation to which God may call us, or even cases where God is asking us to delay or forego personal wishes or preferences in order to love someone else. Physically, a bad paper cut, an infected in-grown toenail or a speck of dirt in the eye could represent this level of suffering. Let's call this **Type 1** suffering.

**Type 2** suffering would then be bearable but potentially joy-killing maladies such as sharp, shooting pains or a constant, throbbing ache. Emotionally, **Type 2** suffering is characterized by an ongoing sense of loss or deep heartache such as can linger for months or even years after the death of a loved one. Alternatively, it could be a persistent sense of being misunderstood, unappreciated or simply ignored. Such emotional suffering can be caused by unresolved emotional woundedness from traumatic childhood events. I would also put in this category the feelings of loss associated with severe permanent disability, even if the victim has no physical pain.

Finally, **Type 3** suffering is like sustained, severe pain such as can be experienced by persons in the final stages of certain cancers. Emotionally, it could be represented by the crushing grief and regret felt by someone who had caused the death of a child by his own carelessness, or simply by a series of preventable, tragic events.

Fortunately, most suffering is of the first type. All three types of joy outlined earlier (the emotion, the attitude and the Spirit-fruit) are possible, with God's help, during **Type 1** suffering. During **Type 2** suffering, only joy as Spirit-fruit, a deep sense of well-being, can be reliably present. God may grant moments of exhilaration but don't be surprised if they are rare. Joy as a playful attitude may be possible with much practice and while communing closely with Jesus. Causes of **Type 2** suffering, especially those related to unresolved emotional woundedness, should be faced and brought to Jesus for healing.

Is any type of joy possible during **Type 3** suffering? It is very hard to find actual examples. Jesus certainly did not seem to enjoy his evening in Gethsemane.[5] C. S. Lewis suffered great emotional distress after his wife's death. *A Grief Observed* makes clear he did not enjoy *that* experience.[14]

It is probably true that we often suffer more than necessary because we give in to fear, anger and a rebellious attitude, rather than relaxing as much as possible in God's tender care. To the extent that we focus on the storm and fail to look to Jesus,[15] we miss out on some of the comfort, perhaps even moments of joy, that Jesus wants to give us, even as we live through severe hardship. But the pain itself is not enjoyable, especially severe physical pain. God can and sometimes does miraculously remove pain, but failing that, it should be viewed as a medical emergency and treated accordingly. After all, pain is there for a reason, to let us know we are not healthy and to motivate us to take effective action.

# Why Suffer?

Given the state of modern medical science, no one should have to endure severe physical pain over an extended period. The Agency for Health Care Policy and Research states that "The ethical obligation to manage pain and relieve the patient's suffering is at the core of a health care professional's commitment."[16] The patient may choose, as Jesus did on the cross,[17] to refuse relief for a higher purpose. For example, she may want to be mentally alert for a period of time to complete a symphony, painting, or book. However, if she becomes so pain-wracked that all she can think about is the pain, why not seek the *joy of relief?* God sometimes grants pain-relief through medication. Crushing grief and other severe forms of *emotional* pain may be more amenable to spiritual and emotional cures. Usually though, a period of time must pass before anything resembling joy can return.

## The Paradox of Suffering, Love and Joy

Nevertheless, it is also true that trying to avoid *all* suffering is a hallmark of a selfish lifestyle. A completely self-absorbed person, like the priest and the Levite in the story of the Good Samaritan, makes it a priority to avoid not only his own pain, but also any involvement with the pain of others.[18] The paradox is that seeking happiness selfishly yields diminishing returns. Alienation from others results when they realize that the selfish person does not really care about *them.* Conversely, by being willing to be inconvenienced, even marginalized, in order to show love to others, we often receive, as an unintentional by-product, more joy and love than we had ever thought possible. Most people like receiving loving attention from someone who has no selfish, hidden agenda. They naturally want to befriend and repay such a person. Genuinely unselfish behavior seems so rare that most people instinctively try to encourage it. Though receiving love in return should not be our *motive* in loving others, it is an almost inescapable *result.* It's just one of the ways life works.[19] But how can we become unselfish? God must give us love on the inside. We become unselfish by getting a new heart, one that is willing to be inconvenienced because of the strength of the compassion that God has poured into it. If this transformation is what some mean by joy-in-suffering, I am all for it!

Although clearly still in basic training on this Spirit-fruit, I have had just enough first-hand experience to know that love of God and others leads to joy, and that joy, in turn, is a source of great spiritual strength.[20]

# 17

# Playing Joyfully Outside

## Playing in God's Neighborhood

Iremember how delightful it was to have a friend show up at the door and ask my mother, "Can Everett come out and play?" Similarly, God wants each of us to come out and play in his neighborhood.[1] Do we sometimes decline the invitation out of fear? Are we busy with what may amount to a virtual-reality religious video game? In any case, if we could trust God enough to step over the threshold, perhaps we would find that not only can he keep us safe; it may even be more fun out there!

## Released

Jesus said that he came to "proclaim freedom for the prisoners"[2] I can't remember any cases where he literally bailed anyone out of jail. But he did free many from sin, disease, disability and evil spirits. Is Jesus still in the freedom business? Absolutely. In earlier chapters we have seen examples of how Jesus can free us from unbelief, fear, bitterness, compulsive behaviors and chronic lack of joy. This chapter is about being released for ministry. In other words, how does Jesus free us to serve in his kingdom – either at a secular job or in some other setting? He often starts by freeing us inwardly – then the freedom begins to show on the outside.

For example, let me tell you a story about one of my first grade teachers. Let's just call her Mrs. Gurrness. Although she caused me a lot of emotional trauma, God did use these painful memories to teach me a valuable life-lesson. Here is how it happened.

A few years ago, after I had received considerable healing and given up a number of counterfeits, I still had to admit that I could not always obey Jesus' second most important commandment – to love my neighbor as myself. There were a few "neighbors" (not those who lived next-door, as it happened) that I could not love. Honestly, the thought of befriending certain folks depressed me. I *hate* feeling depressed. But, even worse, I feared that if I shared these thoughts I risked being scolded for being unloving. I *hate* having strong feelings that I cannot express. I also hate being scolded! So I asked God (I can't remember the last time *he* scolded me!) what he wanted me to do about my predicament. After about ten minutes he seemed to say, "Go tell Leona how you feel." Leona offered to lead me in a Theophostic Prayer Ministry (TPM) session. Here is how it went.

**Presenting Emotions**: I felt stuck, conflicted, drawn to the possibility of helping others through TPM, but when I thought of ministering to a really needy person, I got depressed. I feared that even if I was doing my best to help others I would be misunderstood. They might be so insecure that they would always find a way to twist my well-intentioned efforts into something bad. I was afraid I would fail. It seemed hopeless.

**Memory Picture**: As I allowed Jesus to lead me back in time I arrived at a memory in first grade. After three months at one school, our family moved and I had to start over. To make matters worse, my new teacher, Mrs. Gurrness, seemed to instantly dislike me. Things did not go well at all. On one occasion the boy who sat behind me was doing something to aggravate me. I must have reacted overtly. The teacher noticed and banished us both to an empty classroom next-door with strict orders not to talk. As I recall it, the other guy started talking loudly. I could not believe he had the nerve to be so disobedient. I had just begun to tell him to stop it when, wouldn't you know it, Mrs. Gurrness appeared in the doorway, saw *me* talking, jumped to the conclusion that *I* was the one who had been doing all the loud talking, and called me a liar when I tried to explain what had actually been going on! At that point she allowed my tormentor to return to the classroom and made me stand out in the hallway. I felt a tremendous sense of injustice. I felt hopelessly misunderstood. After what seemed to be about two hours (probably only 30 or 40 minutes), I convinced myself that she must have forgotten I was still out there or that, if I just had one more chance, I could better explain what had happened and thus remove the stain from my six-year-old reputation. So I knocked on the door. Well, of course, this just enraged her even more. She again accused me of being a liar and a generally bad kid and made me stay out in the hall for another long time.

**Lies I Believed:** Others will always believe me to be bad no matter how hard I try to be good. It will never get better – the situation is hopeless. Since I had let the other kid so easily get me into trouble and since I naively believed I could reason with Mrs. Gurrness, I must be stupid as well.

**Truth Received:** Jesus seemed to say, "If you had to go through life with a name like Gurrness, you might be grouchy too!" I laughed out loud! This was one of the first times I realized that Jesus could be funny.

Then Jesus gave me a mental picture. I was sitting dejectedly on the floor in the hallway after the final banishment. My head hung down hopelessly. Then to my left I "saw" Jesus bustling down the hall towards me. He stopped, stretched out his hand and said, "Let's go for a walk! Let Mrs. Gurrness worry about it. Why do you want to go back into that room anyway?" We left the building, sprinted across the street to the park and started playing on the merry-go-round. I hung on with my legs and let my arms fly out while Jesus pushed. He ran at top speed around the dusty circle. His long hair flew. His beard parted at the chin and blew back on either side of his face. His robes flapped. His sandals flop-flop-flopped as he kicked up a big cloud of dust! *I was in heaven!* What a *joy* to be *outdoors* on a school day playing, expressing all my pent-up, fierce physical energy, *with Jesus!*

I kept thinking, "Any time now Mrs. Gurrness will come out looking for me." But she never did. And, best of all, I realized that the other boy was still cooped up in the classroom *with Mrs. Gurrness!* He still had to sit still and be quiet. I had actually gotten the better deal. And Jesus kept glancing over at me with the most mischievous, infectious grin that I had ever seen.

I shouted to him, "Hey, Jesus, you wild man, we're going to have to get you a pair of Nikes if you keep this up!" We both laughed heartily.

# Jesus is Fun!

Suddenly I realized that I no longer cared what Mrs. Gurrness thought of me. Jesus loved and enjoyed my fierce energy. I was not really in trouble. And, even if I had been too naively trusting, it did not matter because Jesus *liked* that about me. He saw it as my capacity to meet life with an open, trusting, and joyful outlook. Mrs. Gurrness had tried to shut me out – to make me feel odd, hurt, and misunderstood, but that was OK, because Jesus was out in the hallway with me all along. He wanted to take me even *further outside!*

This Theophostic parable not only healed deep woundedness, it also impressed on me how much fun Jesus could be! This was not the only time Jesus showed up playfully in memories Leona and I worked through over that time. In fact, it became a kind of *theme* during four or five different TPM sessions. In addition, it got me thinking. Could this newfound inner freedom have a practical application? What might it mean to be invited even further outside with Jesus?

# Orders from Headquarters

At that time I was trying to decide how much longer I should work at a career in which I felt both dead-ended and burnt-out. About two years before, I had turned down a chance at an early-retirement buy-out because I felt I would simply have been motivated by a desire to escape, with no real sense of purpose or calling to do something else with my life. Two years later, however, I was starting to get a sense of call to spend significant amounts of time leading small groups, practicing contemplative prayer, studying and writing. I prayed, "Lord, you know how much time I have left. How do YOU want me to spend it?"

Very clearly, two words came to mind, "Play joyfully!" It was almost like he was quoting from *Bill and Ted's Excellent Adventure*, "Party on, Dude!"

"Whaaa...?" I was speechless.

Jesus clarified slightly, "Throw yourself unreservedly into the *Game of Life!*"

# Outside

At about the same time, the Holy Spirit gave me an insight that conceptually connected two of my most traumatic childhood memories. In both the "scary horse" (Chapter 11) and the "Mrs. Gurrness" memories, I was *shut out* and wanted desperately to get back in. But what Jesus showed me in both instances was, "Ev, you were *made* for the outside, it is more *fun* outside, and I can keep you *safe* outside. In other words, I made you to pioneer, to think outside the box, the warehouse, sometimes even the whole industrial park! Let me use your gifts to break through to some of my loved ones who also need to be freed to come out and play."

Of course I replied, "Yes, Lord, please do." But then I added, "But, Lord Jesus, what does 'outside' mean right now – outside the security of my job?"

"Well, Ev, my man," he seemed to say, "when it gets to the point that you are so 'pregnant' with a calling to something else that you feel you can no longer afford to spend time working here, I will make a way for you to leave." And that was all he would say at that time. So for months my journal entries were full of accounts of my trying to understand if "outside" meant at my job in the business world, or at another place altogether. In a sense it was both, sequentially. First, for about a year, I benefited from various Holy Spirit training sessions during which he taught me how to find joy amid some massively stressful workplace challenges. One major life-lesson was how essential it is to surrender my plans for the day into his hands and to be accepting and compassionate while being interrupted and having to work with people quite different from me. As long as I kept trying to hold onto control of my daily agenda, I felt aggravation instead of joy. As long as I kept complaining about how hard it was to work with people whose thought processes were very different from mine, I had very little joy. But once I turned over control to Jesus, he started to show me how to enjoy working with some of the very folks that I had found most irritating before! I hope some of them noticed that I had become a bit easier to work with as well.

# Making Tents

About six months before I knew that retirement was imminent, I was reading in Acts 11:19-30 about numerous early Christians who were serving the Lord with great effectiveness. They taught large numbers of people, saw many repent at their preaching, and made predictions that came true. After prayerfully pondering this passage, I was struck by the comparative ordinariness of most modern Christian's lives. So I asked Jesus, "Lord, what about those of us who spend our days writing Material Safety Data Sheets, watching toddlers, driving forklifts, lifting pitch forks, listening to pitches from tuning forks, pitching fork balls or pitching crab pot buoys off pitching trawler decks? What about us, Lord, are we all just chopped liver here?"

The thought soon came, "No, Kiddo, of course not. I love you all. Even Paul himself was a tent maker.[3] But how often need that be said? It would have made no sense for Luke (the writer of the Book of Acts) to repeatedly mention Paul's daily routine. Imagine how ludicrous it would have been had he written, "Paul got up out of bed and made more tents." And again in the next chapter, "Paul made three tents last week and is just now starting another one." And two chapters later, "You should *see* the tent Paul has just finished! By the way, is anyone on the market for a new tent?"

I agreed, "I suppose you're right, Lord. That would have been just silly. But the fact remains, Paul did get up, many days, sat down and made tents. Did he advertise, I wonder? Did he perhaps hang out a sign, "Apostolic Tents"? Did he buy a small ad in the "Corinthian Chronicle" urging "Trying to make your own tents may make you too tense. Relax, let the tent making to Paul!" Despite his "thorn in the flesh,"[4] was Paul able to make tents joyfully? How many hours a day did it take for him to earn his living making tents? Did he make tents in prison? How did he have enough time to do all the traveling, preaching, teaching, letter writing and church planting if he was constantly cutting and sewing tent fabric?"

Jesus seemed to answer, "You're a hoot, my man! I enjoy your slightly irreverent questions. You're living this very mystery right now yourself, aren't you?" (Notice, he didn't bother to answer any of my questions. Instead he cut right through to the motivation behind them.)

"You bet, Lord" I replied, "and it's frustrating. I want to study, pray and write full-time, but my job is getting in the way. What do you want me to do about it, Lord?"

"Well, Ev, relax. That's *my responsibility* and I'm working on it. Just stay close, be patient, do what you can in your spare time and let me work out the details of this particular life-puzzle, OK?"

"Fine with me, my King. Lead on."

# Joyful Work

A few months later Jesus made it clear that, for me, at that time, "outside" did mean study, prayer and writing instead of continuing to work at my job. But many others are still working full-time at boring and stressful jobs that take time from what they'd rather be doing. I am talking about other types of productive work or ministry, not just their favorite recreational activities. I can only say that, based on my experience, if God has actually called you to a particular work for a time, and if you stay close to him, you may be surprised at how much joy he can bring, even in situations that, naturally speaking, are less than ideal. But it may also be that, after you have walked closely with Jesus for a while, he will make it clear that he is calling you further outside. If he means by that a major change in how you spend your time, he can also make it feasible and fun.[5]

# 18

# The Creator's Delight

## You Expect Me to Believe That?

How can God possibly be delighted with us? Over and over the Bible speaks of God's wrath at our sinfulness.[1] Yet, personally, I have found Jesus to be as tender as a doting grandmother. Think of all the grief God has suffered because he made us. The theologians say God doesn't need us. If he had been somehow incomplete all those eons before he created us, he would not be God, they say. God "has life in himself."[2] God is self-sufficient. If so, why does he get so upset when we act up?[3] Why does he grieve when we ignore him?[4]

There is a sense in which it is not about us; it's all about God.[5] But then, why did he bother to create us at all? Our purpose is to glorify God.[6] OK. But why? Wasn't he already perfectly glorious and didn't he already know it? How can anything we sing, write or do possibly add to his glory? God is done, stick a fork in him, some theologians seem to imply. Any change would only detract from God's perfection. But, I ask, how can any mere creature, expert or not, presume to define perfection where God is concerned? Could it be that, in God's case, perfection means continuing to become more glorious, infinitely? In other words, is

God's "completeness" continually expanding? Is it part of his glory that he can keep *redefining* perfection? If so, maybe God created us partly because he wanted to see what *we* would come up with. Could God be so great that he is able to make creatures who can dream up something even God had not yet thought of? Can our creativity *enrich* God in some mysterious manner? Can our voluntary love make him even more glorious? I have no idea. I'm just asking. But, if I were an expert theologian, I would ponder carefully before deciding what is *impossible* for God! Yes, I know the Bible verses that say God doesn't change.[7] But what exactly do they mean? Certainly not that he is totally aloof and emotionless.[3, 4] One possible meaning is that he is not fickle or capricious; we can rely on him. Certainly God's moral standards do not fluctuate based on what is socially acceptable in any given culture. Yet he interacts personally with his creatures.[8] It seems to me that a totally self-sufficient and unchanging God would not.

For those who believe that God could never grow or change in any way, I have a question. What was the nature of Jesus' resurrection body? Did he always live in such a body, or was it something new? If he always *did* have that body, were the nail and spear wounds always evident?[9] Even now, at the right hand of the Father,[10] is Jesus a disembodied spirit, or does he still live in his resurrection body? If he is a spirit, what happened to his resurrection body? Just something to think about – for those who believe they have God figured out.

# Are We Special?

Why are we worth even a second of God's "time"? One possible answer is that, since the fall, we deserve *no attention* from him at all. The apostle Paul implies in the early chapters of his letter to the Romans that, without God, human beings are rotten to the core.[11] In chapter one he lumps all humans into the same category as the worst among us. In the second chapter he states that anyone who passes judgment on someone else is (secretly?) doing all the same bad stuff as the openly wicked.[12] Paul does not say whether this is also true of those who do *not* judge others, or if there even *is* such a group. Does this mean God loves us because of who *he* is, not because of any value he sees in us? Perhaps. Yet God seems smitten with love for us.[13] He pays attention to what happens to every sparrow.[14] But he did not die for the sparrows. If we do not praise him, the very rocks would cry out.[15] But Jesus did not die for the rocks. He called the rest of his creation "good," but it was only after he had created humans that he pronounced it all "very good."[16] He said that we were to "rule over...all the earth,"[17] that we are "a little lower than the angels,"[18] and that we will some day be co-rulers with him.[19] He said nothing of the sort about dolphins. He put himself out big-time to come and save us. If we are such worthless creatures, why would he not just start over, or forget the whole idea and just go back to the perfection and completeness he always had before *we* messed everything up?

# Why *Did* God Create Humanity?

Perhaps it would be useful to list some possible theories and briefly evaluate each in light of biblical and experiential evidence.

1.  **God has a cosmic case of Attention Deficit Hyperactivity Disorder.** He made humans on a whim but has since lost interest. Present at the beginning, he now prefers to remain distant. He wound up the universe and is now letting it run down on its own. **Response**: Every time God seems to ignore one of our fervent petitions we can be tempted to view him in this way. It may well be true that God does not micro-manage every detail of his creation. For example, God may usually allow natural forces to control the weather. But to generalize from these experiences, concluding that God takes no interest in *any* of the specifics of our lives, does not square with the biblical description of a God who remembers every sparrow and who keeps a running tally of the number of hairs on each of our heads.[14]

2.  **God has a sick sense of humor.** He made us for the amusement potential. To such a god, watching a bunch of bumbling bumpkins try to make sense of what happens to them could sometimes be laughable. One might imagine that a cruel god would say to an angel, "Watch this, let's see what they do when we make Mount St. Helens blow up – *sideways!* I *know* they're not expecting that!" **Response**: This one just seems like malicious slander – a devilish lie. Although, from an earth-bound perspective,[20] it could at times be tempting to believe this about God.

3.      **God is the ultimate "500 pound gorilla."** He made us just because he wanted to. **Response**: While this certainly is true (well, not the gorilla part), it does not answer the question, "Why did he *want* to?"

4.      **God is vain and self-absorbed.** He made us so there would be a race of creatures that could write books, sing, and preach about how "it is all about him." **Response**: Oh, please!

5.      **God is lazy and dictatorial.** He created humans to *serve* him. By this view, we should search the Scriptures for things God wants us to *do,* and then we should *get busy* because God, the ultimate task-master, is watching, ever poised to punish the slacker. **Response**: As repulsive as this sounds when put into writing, I suspect quite a few raised under the Protestant Work Ethic still feel in their gut that there may be some truth in this one. However, if this *were* the main reason God created us, why isn't the first and greatest commandment "Run errands for God with all your heart, soul, mind and strength"?

6.      **God was lonely.** He made us to keep him company in this vast, empty universe. **Response**: It is much more likely that he has always had perfect unity and communion within the Trinity. (See Chapter 21)

7.      **God is creative.** He enjoys dreaming up and making new stuff. He likes a challenge and is always up to something. Even after the initial creation, he continues to work.[21] **Response**: Now we seem to be getting somewhere. A possible corollary here is that *God has big plans.* Therefore, life here on earth is a *test* to see how we will fit into his plans for the afterlife.[22] But, why wouldn't an all-knowing God already know that? (See number 8.)

8.      **God is curious, even playful.** He wanted to see what we would come up with. **Response**: This pre-supposes a self-limiting omniscience. But how could God decide what *not* to know without first knowing it all? Can we imagine that God could choose to be temporarily unaware of at least some of our choices? At first it feels like a monumental conceptual stretch but, when we think about it, *this is the God who became a*

*man!* For a time Jesus chose to subject himself to at least some of the limitations of his assumed humanity. As a two-day-old baby, was Jesus divine? Most conservative Christians would say yes. Did Jesus know everything at that point? Probably not. In Luke 2:52 we read that "Jesus *grew in wisdom* and stature, and in favor with God and men." (emphasis mine) Therefore, God demonstrated an ability and willingness to, at least temporarily, remain unaware of some knowledge.[23]

Some theologians think God chose to give us real freedom of choice. Consequently, some future details are undetermined. By this view, God's foreknowledge is of two types. His *definite* foreknowledge consists of those events that God has decided to bring about on his own. His *indefinite* foreknowledge, on the other hand, encompasses a range of possible outcomes depending on the choices humans make. In the latter case, God has chosen to allow us areas of true choice *within* his comprehensive plan. In these areas of human choice, God still knows all he *can* know. But, given that he has decided ahead of time to let us participate in the decision-making process, he cannot know that part of the future because it does not yet exist.[24] Without some such arrangement, it seems to me that what we think of as freedom-of-choice is an illusion, simply an artifact of God's having withheld from us the knowledge of our own future choices, while he, all the while, knows *exactly* how we will choose, or by a strict predestination view, has actually *predetermined* what we will decide.

Of course, this whole discussion hinges on how we think about time. Most Christians believe that God is not limited by time. He is living in the "eternal now." However, he has obviously chosen to place humans in a time-bound world. Without past, present and future, without sequential events, how can there be an interactive love relationship? For that matter, how can there be story, journey or growth? I do not know. But for now God has chosen to interact with me as if we *both* have a past, present and future. Given that, I believe he can respond to my thoughts and prayers, just as if he were walking with me through this temporal life. As he does, can he take delight in or enjoy what I come up with? All I know is that Jesus seems to get a charge out of me! God seems to often chuckle, even laugh heartily, when we spend time together. Would he do that if he already foreknew every word I would ever say?

9.   **God is love.** God loves to love and wanted to expand the ultimate communion of the Trinity to many more sentient, creative and free creatures. This reason explains why it was not enough for God to have created just rocks, sparrows and dolphins. God wanted to dote on creatures who could be aware he was doing so and who could love him in return. **Response**: Of this whole list, this one seems to ring most true and to fit best with what I know of the God of the Bible and my personal experience.

# Divine Delight

So the creative, loving God made us. How can we be sure he takes pleasure in us? Well, we know God made us in his image.[25] *He put value into us!* He also gave us the ability to make choices. We made some really bad ones. In so doing, humans became unfathomably sinful compared to God's holy perfection.[26] But we also know that he loves us to a degree we cannot begin to imagine.[27] The Bible also says that God's wrath comes on all of us because of our sinfulness.[11] Given how often we mess up, how is it possible that God can delight in any one of us?

How do I *know* that he is pleased with *me?* Here is how. In all of my personal experience with Jesus, he has never scolded me. Wrath and condemnation just have not entered the picture.[28] Unlike the rebellious religious leaders who felt the sting of Jesus' displeasure,[29] I have sensed only his compassion, encouragement and good humor. Scripture reveals that God is clearly *capable* of denouncing and punishing open rebellion and stubborn, ungrateful griping.[30] But, he can also be amazingly gentle with those who have screwed up their lives but are now seeking him.[31] God responds to human attitudes and actions in reasonable ways. In my case, since I was already his and was finally earnestly seeking him, I was pleasing to him, in spite of my sin and brokenness. He ran to meet me while I was still a long way off.[32] And, just as he did at Jesus' baptism, my Daddy God said, "Ev is my beloved son, in whom I am well pleased."[33] Why was that possible? Jesus' blood had already washed my soul clean.[28] Now my mind needed to be transformed and my lie-based emotional woundedness had to be healed. Jesus was delighted because he knew that I was about to *let him do* what he does best, set captives free![34]

I understood a little better once I had grandsons. It really *is* possible to be delighted with someone who is far from perfect. Sure, open rebellion hurts, and, it's even worse if one of them walks off and ignores me when I am offering a hug. But they still make me smile with delight, almost all the time. Why? I understand that it is hard being small and that in time they will learn to love better. And they're just so unbelievably cute!

## Oh, So *That's* What You Intended, Lord?

Not only does God put value into human beings in general, he also builds *specific giftedness into each of us.* The Holy Spirit wants to guide us into truth about how God views each of us. Let me illustrate once again with a personal experience.

At the end of the Mrs. Gurrness Theophostic Prayer Ministry (TPM) session, (Chapter 17), Leona asked me if I still felt tense when I thought about befriending certain individuals. I admitted that I still had some feelings of inadequacy. This time the Holy Spirit led me to memories, many of them, in which I seemed to be impulsive. Usually I was not intentionally being naughty, but my natural curiosity and tendency to experiment often got me into trouble. Here is just one example. When I was about seven we lived in a second story apartment with an outdoor staircase. For some strange reason I wondered what would happen if I held a black crayon against the white cement-block wall as I walked up the stairs. So I tried it. Well, you can guess the rest. My parents did not care for the somewhat jagged, black step-pattern on the white wall and made me clean it off. Thus ended my budding career as a graffiti artist.

I was *always* doing stuff like that! I remember thinking over and over, "Well, it will take some time to live that one down." A month or two later I'd be slowly rebuilding my reputation as a "nice boy" and I'd again do something unconventional, maybe even embarrassing. I'd have to start counting days of "nice-boyness" all over again. It reminds me of a friend from a rural part of West Virginia who moved to the Pittsburgh area to work. One day he told me that he seldom drove in downtown Pittsburgh because, as he put it, "Every time I drive in Pittsburgh, I have to start my Christian life all over again!"

At any rate, the lies that took root from all these childhood experiences were:

1. There is something wrong with the way I am "wired."
2. My natural curiosity and action-oriented nature are bad.
3. I will always embarrass myself and be considered naughty or weird.

The truth that came was in the form of a mental picture. Jesus was working on an intricate machine, with infinite care and great precision. As I "watched," I discovered that he was not repairing it, he was *inventing* it. In fact, *I* was the machine. He was building me from scratch, exactly the way he had designed me long ages before. He was making me to be "at home" in new, wild places. He intended for me to crave adventure and to think creatively and unconventionally. Consequently, I should not be too surprised or embarrassed when others are not quite sure how to take me. Jesus knows how that feels. He was always shocking people and getting into trouble.[35] It can be great fun. But it can also make it difficult to be "best friends" with some folks. However, Jesus showed me that I don't necessarily have to be "best friends" with people in order to help them. For example, people I never met, even some who have already died, have helped me immensely through their writings. I seem to be called to pray, think, write and set an example. Sometimes Jesus wants me to say a few words, or just to be a good listener.

# God Delights in Each of Us

I hope that by sharing these thoughts and experiences I may have inspired you to seek *your own vision* of how much God personally values *you*. It is one of Satan's goals to have us disrespect God's handiwork. We should not agree with the Accuser when he belittles us. Jesus said "love your neighbor as yourself."[36] If we habitually devalue ourselves, we won't love others very well either. Yes, our sin needed to be dealt with, but it had to be done *once* and Jesus himself said "It is finished."[37]

God is not angry with me. My heart is no longer desperately wicked.[38] My Creator takes delight in me. I am his precious child. If you have given your life to him, you can say the same. Humility and self-respect are not mutually exclusive. Seek God earnestly. Resist the Devil and all his picky put-downs. It is no longer true that there are no righteous human beings. In fact, technically, it was not true even as Paul was writing Romans 3:11. Paul, and well over three thousand souls, had already been washed clean by then.[39] True, none of us is morally perfect apart from God, but, as believers, we are righteous in God's eyes.[28] If you are still straining, trying hard to measure up, please relax. Be assured that we become less sinful by marinating in God's love, spending time with him, letting his favor saturate our souls. (Chapter 14) God created us because he wants to dote on us. We should let him.

# 19

# Of Course You Realize, This Means War

## What War?

Iremember the little flutter of delight I felt whenever my favorite cartoon rabbit crossed his "arms," tapped his big furry foot and said, "Of course you realize, this means war!" I knew exactly what that meant. Justice was about to be done. Evil would get its comeuppance. Joy and good humor would win out over whatever dastardly villain had been running amok. And the whole story would come to a satisfying, even amusing, conclusion in a few glorious moments.

Ah.... if only it could be so uncomplicated in real life. Most adults think of war, at its best, as a necessary evil, certainly never amusing. But I'm not talking about physical war. To borrow the *Star Wars* terminology, I am referring to the struggle against "the dark side."[1] Is this just the stuff of fantasy? Are villains simply created to make a good story, to generate suspense so that movie goers and novel readers won't lose interest? Or, do story tellers include them, at least partly, because they resonate with our intuitive sense about how the universe operates?

# Evil, What's That?

In today's polite society, we almost never talk about evil. Instead we speak of inappropriate behavior, bad choices, personality disorders, and acts of Mother Nature. On a societal level, the most reprehensible trait seems to be intolerance. We desperately want to believe that the vast majority of humans mean well but, because of childhood trauma and/or adult life stresses, are driven to occasionally misbehave. Leona is a psychiatric nurse. She never sees evil mentioned in the diagnoses or treatment plans she and the psychiatrists develop for their patients. I worked for years in corporate middle management. Our training emphasized the need to address behavior, never motivation or attitude. The theory worked pretty well on a day-to-day level. If the employees understood what performance was expected and met that standard, we could avoid the hurt feelings and time-consuming debates that tend to accompany accusations about unobservable attitudes and feelings. As managers, we were not expected to play psychologist. The "why" questions of human behavior were left to professionals, trained to delve into the inner workings of the human psyche. Even when we would hear a news report of one of the very rare occasions when unaddressed inner turmoil erupted into workplace violence, we would be very reluctant to blame it on evil. The perpetrator was thought of as a "very sick puppy." We all wracked our brains about how future incidents could be avoided by better awareness of early warning signs. In the much less drastic but far more common cases in which, for example, an employee was cruel to subordinates or made inappropriate sexual advances, he was often sent to sensitivity training or sexual harassment awareness classes – as if the problem was merely a lack of knowledge.

Likewise, many of us these days simply do not want to talk about war. We are anti-war. We want peace. It is popular to believe that everybody just wants to live in a stable society and enjoy family life. We yearn for "a small world after all" in which we "join hands across America." "Can't we all just get along?" some plead.

# Reality Check

Well, no, I'm sorry to say, we can't. Haven't you heard? Some people are using butcher knives to hack off the heads of helpless victims. Others are sending their children out to blow themselves up in crowded market places. Fathers are abandoning their wives and children for a second chance at personal happiness. Mothers are "choosing" to terminate the development of their inconvenient, unborn children. Twenty-four hour "news" channels repeatedly broadcast the most lurid crimes. The media networks know that people are morbidly fascinated with stories about bizarre, violent behavior, especially if it involves sexually titillating details. Such stories are used over and over to keep people watching, in the hope that they will see the commercials, buy the products and keep the networks in business. This seems like ghoulish greed to me. It must gratify Satan to get so much free publicity.

## Progress?

Yet, we prefer to deny that evil exists. Our current, secular worldview is that, with hard work and good education, we will slowly but surely continue to make *progress* toward a world in which more and more of us will be able to "just get along." Intolerance is public enemy number one. Ignorance and violence vie for second place.

Some believe that enlightened government is the answer to our woes. According to them, if we could just convince enough people to vote for bright, well-educated, well-intentioned public servants, they could take over the reigns of political power and bring about a near-paradise on earth by a combination of the force of law and the persuasive power of the "bully pulpits" of public office. With the unquestioning assistance of a co-operative media and entertainment industry, such an approach wields considerable power for change. But, as Stalin's subjects found out the hard way, this approach can all too easily result in the violent deaths of millions. So far, in the USA, there is a system of government that helps to ensure that no one political group can fully implement a utopian, secular-humanistic dream for societal self-improvement. In my opinion, this is a good thing. Why? Because I think the basic premises of this worldview are faulty. Although education and tolerance are important, neither gets to the basic cause of our problems.

## Basic Evil

According to my understanding of divine truth as revealed in the Bible, neither intolerance nor ignorance, nor even violence, are the basic evils at work in the universe. Instead, there are two types of evil, personal and impersonal. I define *personal evil* as the bad choices of sentient, free, created beings, whether angelic, human or others we don't know about yet. *Impersonal evil* has natural causes that do not directly depend on specific bad human choices. Yet, even though we can't point to a personal decision that caused the natural catastrophe, most would agree it is not a good thing when one's house is buried under scalding volcanic ash, especially if one is in it at the time. I'll discuss impersonal evil a bit more later.

I believe that the Bible teaches that the most basic bad choice is to fail to love God with all of one's being. (Chapter 7) Usually this takes the form of simply saying no to God. Instead of accepting our place as beings created to enjoy, love and obey our Creator and King, we believe we can do better by striking out on our own. This is true idolatry. We will live life our way, thank you very much! The sobering thing about such basic evil is that it does not require that we stand up and shake our fists at the sky and scream our blasphemies for all to hear. It can be as simple as a quiet inner decision to be in charge of one's own life. We like our independence. We think freedom means *we* get to decide how we spend our time, money and talent. Oh, we can be completely tolerant of how other people live *their* lives, but they had better not tell *us* what to do! Do we include God when we say "Back off, guys, I don't need you to tell me how to run my life"? While sometimes appropriate when addressing meddling humans, this boundary-setting sentence should never be used in prayer.

# Origin of Evil

Why do I say that usurping God's place in one's own life is a more fundamental evil than intolerance and violence? Well, let's think it through a bit. Although intolerance and violence *can* be the horrendous out-workings of idolatry, they can also be good in some settings. Intolerance of anarchy or child abuse, for example, would be considered good by most. Likewise, use of force (controlled violence) to restrain a gun-wielding madman intent on shooting dozens of people at the local mall, would be a good thing. Just ask those in the field of fire!

According to the Bible, the first evil was introduced into God's good creation when Lucifer, the most glorious and powerful of all created beings, decided to rebel. The few details given in Scripture about Satan's beginning indicate that his sin was his decision to "make [himself] like the Most High."[2] God *did not tolerate* Lucifer's impudence and *violently* threw him and his rebellious followers out of heaven.[3] Clearly, the evil here was not God's intolerance and violence, but Lucifer's (now Satan's) rebellion. The sin in the Garden of Eden was totally *non-violent*.[4] Adam and Eve's rebellion and disobedience, however, were judged to be so evil that they were barred from paradise and cursed.[5] Therefore, we see that whether intolerance and violence are considered evil depends on the setting in which they operate. Idolatry, on the other hand, is always bad. The Old Testament is full of accounts of how the children of Israel repeatedly broke God's heart by paying homage to false gods. Judas, Ananias and Sapphira,[6] Herod[7] and many of the Jewish religious leaders are examples of New Testament characters that also rebelled against God.

# Alternative Views

## Atheistic evolution

There are, of course, alternative worldviews that reject divine revelation. One that is popular among secular thinkers is atheistic evolution. By this theory, impersonal mechanisms such as spontaneous mutation and natural selection (survival of the fittest) have, over time, resulted in the steady improvement and progress of the human species. Such a worldview should logically define evil as any action that would threaten the long-term viability of humanity. For example, basic evil should be any action that would protect weak, diseased or dysfunctional individuals. If such should not be killed outright, they should at least be sterilized. Powerful tyrants should be praised and supported since they have proven themselves most fit to survive. In fact, the ideal social unit should be the group in which all males remain celibate except the alpha male. He alone would impregnate all the strong, intelligent females, as often as possible, thus passing along only the best genetic material.

I reject this worldview for a number of reasons. First, it does not answer the question of origins. Where did matter and energy come from? Why are so many natural characteristics so perfectly fined-tuned so that life could develop and thrive?[8] Secondly, I question the premise that the ultimate good is the long-term *physical* survival of the species. I believe it is more likely that this physical world is only a small part of reality. Jesus taught that in the kingdom of God, physical survival takes a distant second place to spiritual salvation, growth and preparation for an eternal afterlife.[9] Third, the cold-blooded brutality of the "might makes right" ethic that grows naturally from this worldview goes against not only biblical moral teachings, but also the evidence of the human conscience.[10] Lastly, when we think of the social experiments that were based on such principles, the track record is abysmal. Names like Adolf Hitler and Josef Stalin come quickly to mind.

## Secular humanism

I will deal with only one more alternative view. Secular humanism objects to any appeal to the supernatural as a standard for what is good. Proponents believe that we, as intelligent and well-intentioned humans, are perfectly capable of figuring out the principles of ethical conduct. By diligent study of what has worked well or gone wrong in the past, we can continually improve our ability to structure society in such a way that we can make steady progress toward near-paradise on earth. This philosophy has appeal since it does not require convincing anyone of the truth of invisible, otherworldly sources of good or evil. Likewise, by this view, no all-powerful being or creator need be taken into account or obeyed. Thus, this is the ideal ideology for idolaters.

But, again, I reject this for a number of reasons. First, like atheistic evolution, this one does not answer the origin questions. Secondly, since there is no ultimate source of moral law, the question becomes, "Who gets to decide what is 'good'?" The answer, unfortunately, is "Whoever is in power at the time." So, once again, we are right back to the "might makes right" position that has caused so much trouble in the past. Thirdly, since morality is based on societal norms, it is relative to a given place and time. How do we deal with the inevitable disagreements as we move about doing business in different parts of the globe, or as we move through time? Lastly, peoples raised in vastly different cultures will forever frustrate optimistic attempts to arrive at moral certainty by human discussion alone. Think about something as simple as laws against price-fixing. The same actions that threaten business leaders with large fines and possible imprisonment in the United States, are considered perfectly legitimate when taken by OPEC.

If evil is relative from place to place, no wonder the concept has become so bankrupt that it is seldom used anymore in everyday speech. Once again, idolaters love this philosophy. It puts us in charge, we think. If the Bible is right, however, this worldview puts us right back to the original sin, eating from the tree of the knowledge of good and evil, telling God to go pound sand.

# Why Does God Put Up with Evil?

There is one question, though, about the Christian view of good and evil, that has long badgered thoughtful seekers. How can an all-powerful, all-loving God countenance a universe in which there is so much evil? Some have argued that it is none of our business to try to explain or justify what God predetermines or allows. Perhaps not, ultimately, but since I am on this quest to learn to love God more completely, I need to be sure that I am not harboring any unnecessarily harsh views of how God interacts with his creatures.

First of all, the Bible teaches that an eternal, all-good God created initially innocent angels and humans, giving both the freedom to choose good or evil. At some point, Lucifer and some other angels chose to rebel, thus introducing evil into God's creation for the first time. Adam and Eve also disobeyed God. For some reason, Lucifer's rebellion did not corrupt all the angels, although Adam and Eve's fall did mess up all subsequent humanity as well as the physical creation.[4, 11] Why the difference? The Bible does not say and I have no further insights at this point.

In any case, since Lucifer's fall, God threw him and his followers (fallen angels/demons) out of heaven, but did not destroy them.[3] Since then, God has allowed Satan to mess with humans.[4, 12] Thus, Christians see our current situation as a modified dualism in which the more powerful eternal source of good (God) temporarily is tolerating, and perhaps even at times using, the weaker source of evil (Satan). There are some hints in Scripture as to why God is allowing Satan to continue his nefarious activities but, in specific cases, it is often hard to know what God is up to. We don't know the future and cannot see into human hearts. Nor can we grasp how completely and gloriously God will "restore...the years that the locust hath eaten"[13] The apostle Paul points out that God will abundantly make it up to any who suffer for his sake.[14]

The biblical evidence is that God chose to create angels and humans with the freedom to choose good or evil. Why would he do that when he must have known how much suffering would result? The only answer that makes sense is that God decided that the *good of freedom* outweighed the evil that would result. Only God could make such a judgment. He has, and here we are. However, I cannot accept that God would actually plan and author specific evil actions.[15] For example, I cannot believe that God would predestine a man to rape a woman. I can, just barely, accept that he would stand by and let it happen, knowing that he will be able to bring good from it. But, to imagine that he planned for it and personally caused it to happen just seems out of character. If God's ways are *that* different from my own moral sense, which the Bible says came from God in the first place,[10] how would it ever be possible for the two of us to have any sort of relationship, let alone one characterized by an all-consuming love? Therefore, since the first and greatest commandment is to love God whole-heartedly, I am compelled to adopt a free-will, modified dualism interpretation of Scripture to answer the question as to why God allows evil.

## Bad Weather

As mentioned earlier, it is difficult to see how the above approach explains what I have called *impersonal evil*. Tornados, tidal waves, volcanic eruptions and earthquakes, to name just a few, cannot easily be blamed on human choice. There are biblical accounts that ascribe to Satan the ability, when permitted by God, to cause tornados, lightning, floods and disease.[16] In addition, natural catastrophes may also be indirectly attributable to the fact that original sin caused nature itself to be "subjected to frustration."[11] While I suspect that specific natural disasters are rarely caused by direct satanic action, the biblical evidence does not allow us to rule it out. Practically, it would almost always be unknowable and, even if we knew it, what difference would it make? We can always pray for supernatural intervention, but statistically, it is unlikely in any given instance. As Jesus suggests in the parable of the two builders, it is better to build your house on solid, high ground, than to build it on the beach in the hope that God will always steer the hurricanes around it.[17]

## Spiritual Warfare?

With this background, let us consider spiritual warfare. Unlike Elmer Fudd, Satan is not always easily routed. The last thing he wants is for Jesus to receive the glory that results when his children voluntarily love and obey him. So, expect Satan to put up a good fight. If he can make us believe he doesn't exist, he can operate as an under-cover agent, making his suggestions seem like reasonable thoughts of our own. Failing that, once he knows we are "on to him," he has numerous tactics he can use. As I have already hinted, I believe that Satan is glad to use 24-hour "news" coverage to dishearten many. What better way is there for the

Devil to convince millions that *evil is winning* than to constantly broadcast all the worst crimes and natural disasters. Movies and TV shows run a close second. And don't forget easy access to pornography, alcohol, drugs and even good food. For many Christians, busyness, yes, even over-commitment to "church work," to the exclusion of time spent developing intimacy with Jesus, can be a devilish trick. Yes, this means war. Even the most gentle and non-violent among us must face the fact that evil humans and fallen angels do not wish us well. The Bible urges us to "resist the Devil"[18] and to "put on the full armor of God."[19] God himself is a warrior.[20] The war between good and evil is a constant theme in Scripture as well as in almost all stories told in secular plays, novels and movies.[21] Yet, we often resist the notion as we go about our daily routines. "Who me? A warrior? What over-dramatic claptrap! Why, I just do my job, collect my paycheck, mow the lawn, and try my best to live a respectable life."

I empathize. Even now I feel a little silly holding forth about warfare as I sit here in my suburban home, typing. But then again, if the pen is mightier than the sword, perhaps, at times, the word processor can be more effective than the M-16. Although a guy with an M-16 could make *me* stop typing, God could raise up someone else to do the writing, maybe much more effectively.

# See No Evil?

The trouble with the head-in-the-sand approach about evil is that, every so often, an atrocity occurs that reminds us that all is not well with the world. Suddenly, we are yanked out of our musings about exactly how many days the hotel heiress must spend in jail and are slapped in the face with the fact that a nine-year-old girl was snatched screaming from her front lawn, and dragged away to be tortured and killed. "What is going on?" we ask. "What ever happened to the 'progress' we thought we were making?"

I know, some will argue that, as a whole, life is far less "brutish and short" than it was in the past. We are just much more aware of each incident because of modern broadcasting technology. Most of these over-publicized "news" events are given so much attention exactly because they are so rare. On the other hand, millions can die by out-of-control genocide in Africa with hardly a mention on American TV. Whatever we conclude on the subject of "progress," we certainly must admit that all is not sweetness and light. Sometimes I think, "How can

God stand it? Isn't it about time for some fire and brimstone? Or even better, a few well-aimed cases of antibiotic-resistant, flesh-eating infection, like the one that felled Herod?"[22] Who knows, maybe such judgment happens more often than we are aware. In any case, there are laws and police forces and, according to Romans 13, societies do have responsibilities to control evildoers. This chapter is about *spiritual* warfare. What is it and what is our role?

# Back Story

As I read Scripture, we are living in the period after which Jesus' death and resurrection have disarmed Satan.[23] However, he has not yet been bound or destroyed. He is therefore free to move about and to do his worst to deceive humans.[24] He can still take advantage of harbored resentment and bitterness[25] but he is not the only source of evil. We can be tempted by our own evil desires, without Satan's personal involvement.[26] He acts like a fierce, man-eating lion[27] but apparently it's a bluff, because, if we resist, he runs away![18] Since he is not allowed to force the will of a child of God,[28] he must work primarily by deception or through humans who *have* been deceived or who are *knowingly* serving him. He is not omni-present,[18, 27] but he and/or his demons can at times influence our thoughts.[29]

# Public Evidence

The book of Acts gives many examples of how adamantly the enemies of Christ opposed the growth of the early church. The apostles fought many a spiritual battle against Satan and his servants, human and spiritual. Almost all of the early church leaders died untimely and violent deaths at the hands of humans in Satan's service. The battle continues today. In many parts of the globe, Christians are still tortured and killed for their faith. In the USA right now physical persecution is practically non-existent. But spiritually, politically, and socially we are still under attack. For example, consider the persistent campaign to banish anything Christian from all aspects of community life except churches and private homes. Artists often enjoy shocking people by showing blatant disrespect for Christian symbols. Only Christians can be consistently mocked without creating a public uproar from the guardians of political correctness.

# Inner Battles

Personally, I find that the internal battle takes place almost daily. At this point, Satan usually cannot make much headway in the areas of lust or anger that he had used on me so successfully in the past. Now he tempts me more often to be proud, judgmental or self-absorbed. Failing that, he or his evil spirit servants use a grumpy, petty drumbeat of belittlement. I am getting better at recognizing these assaults on my heart, and often tell him to get lost, but, if I'm tired and a bit under-the-weather emotionally, he can still give me a pretty nasty fight in this area.

I'll give just one example. Recently our pastor preached a sermon about loving others. One of the points was that we should be careful what we say, because our words can really discourage others. Well, that kind of shook me. I felt like the disciples must have at the Last Supper when they asked, "Lord, is it I?"[30] During the next several days, accusatory thoughts kept ricocheting in my head. One recent event, where I had blurted out some thoughts, not realizing how hurtful they could have been for one person in the group, kept coming to mind. I allowed the Evil One to harass me for almost three days until I finally brought it to Jesus in prayer. He reminded me that the very night I had said those things, before I had even left the building, I had apologized for how critical it had sounded and was assured that there were no hard feelings. I finally realized that I had suffered several days of discouragement about something that was not even about me! I am just starting to learn that when that sort of condemnation thinking begins, I need to say to Satan, in the name of Jesus, "If you have something to say to me, out with it! I will no longer accept these vague insinuations. I do not agree to wrack my brains, trying to think of what I may have done to deserve such condemnation. It's not always my fault." Instead, I need to ask the Holy Spirit to give me the true picture, to convict me of any specific sin, and to let me know if there is anything I should do to make things right. If no such guidance comes, I need to forget it and go *love someone else* – show interest in *them*. It's amazing how well that works to get me out of one of those self-belittling, self-absorbed downward spirals.

# Our Mission

As Christians then, our mission is to choose to love and obey God and to resist the opposition. Those who play down the warfare model have a point. The first and greatest commandment is to love God, not to hate the Devil. Yet, there is ample biblical evidence that good people have repeatedly been required to stand up to, and yes, even battle evil. God and his angels have fought major battles against opposing evil forces.[31] It stands to reason that twenty-first century Christians would become involved in the struggle as well.

# Rules of Engagement

I still wonder about some details though. What are the rules of engagement where Satan and his demonic servants are concerned? We are told to resist and Satan will flee. But how far does he go and how long is it until he returns? Does he send a lesser demon while he is away? Why aren't they required to wear bells so that we can be alerted as soon as they come back? How can we co-operate with the Holy Spirit to limit the frequency and duration of their visits? The Bible says that sometimes God gives specific permission for Satan to harass a particular person.[32] There are also times that God's Spirit actually uses Satan to test, or even help with the training of, some of God's own.[33] At other times, our own rebellion, such as harbored anger or refusal to forgive, creates an opportunity for Satan to mess with our minds.[25] It may even be that refusal (or inability) to deal with our inner woundedness sometimes opens us to continued deception, and negates or diminishes our ability to experience spiritual power, love, joy and peace.[34]

# Is Satan Always Involved?

One question that Christians have debated is "How much do we *invite* open spiritual warfare by giving Satan too much 'credit' for what may be at times simply our own fallen nature?"[26] It is often hard to tell, but here are a few thoughts. If, for example, in a quiet moment, maybe even when I am practicing contemplative prayer, my mind begins to imagine a lustful or violent scenario, what should I conclude? In the past I sometimes thought, "Oh, that is just my desperately wicked heart expressing itself again!" Now I realize my heart is no longer desperately wicked.[35] So, if I have not been indulging in lustful looking, I can be pretty sure that the lustful thoughts came from outside my own heart, namely, from Satan or an underling. On the other hand, if I had been recently harboring resentment toward a particular person and entertaining thoughts of how I might retaliate, Satan doesn't have to do much. He may choose to suggest some ideas as to *how* I might carry out my own evil desire. However, if I am not currently harboring a vengeful attitude, any thoughts of scary scenarios are probably being placed in my mind by a fallen angel.

# Battle Plans

It may not always be crucial to determine the *source* of such thoughts in order to get freedom from them. However, sound thinking about such questions can be helpful, just like good intelligence makes physical warfare easier. For example, if I am entertaining lust I need to confess it, get forgiveness and stop it. If I find that I *cannot stop it*, I need to seek help to get emotional and spiritual healing so that I am once again free to decide not to lust. If, however, I have not been encouraging lust in any way, but I still find that lustful thoughts have entered my mind, I need to resist the Devil. That is, I need to stand in the authority Christ won for me on Good Friday and Easter and tell Satan, "You are not welcome in my mind. It belongs to Jesus. Just leave. I do not agree with those thoughts." Then I must turn to Jesus and pray, "Lord, I acknowledge your presence and invite you to fill me with your life and godliness." This simple act of the will can work wonders because *God takes action* once we say no to Satan and yes to him.

A second question comes to mind, "Do we sometimes encourage overt manifestations of demonic presence and influence by letting the evil spirits know that we *expect* a big ruckus?" Yes, I believe this can happen. I especially like Dr. Ed Smith's advice to deal with demons by calmly standing in one's authority as Christ's servant and telling them that you will not allow them to act up.[36] At this point, though, I must admit that I have absolutely no experience dealing with any physical manifestations of demonic activity. I find that the mental battle is quite enough. I need no further convincing.

# Let's Go on the Offensive!

Remembering once again the delight I felt when I first heard those words as a child, "Of course you realize, this means war!" I ponder the difference. Why was that a delight when, in most cases, thoughts of spiritual warfare now seem scary? Yes, I know, it was just a cartoon. There wasn't much at stake. But I think there is something else. The Bible says that "the fear of the *Lord* is the beginning of wisdom,"[37] *not* the fear of the Devil. When Bugs Bunny declared war we knew that the good guys were about to make life miserable for the bad guys, not vice versa! Jesus demonstrated how that is supposed to work spiritually. He said that he saw Satan fall from heaven when he sent the disciples out to minister.[38] And that was even before the resurrection and Pentecost. It seems to me that we need more Christians who can recognize Satan's attacks, disagree with his suggestions, stand against his condemnation and move with Holy Spirit power into what Satan had always thought was *his* territory.

# 20

# A Sweet, Smooth Roar

## Power

Do you have the power? In his last words on earth Jesus said to his disciples "you will receive power when the Holy Spirit comes on you."[1] Shortly before that he told them "Do not leave Jerusalem, but wait for the gift my Father promised ... in a few days you will be baptized with the Holy Spirit."[2] They waited. There was the sound like a jet engine, flames of fire settled on each head and they were given the ability to miraculously speak foreign languages.[3] Did God ever repeat this exact manifestation of his power? If so, there is no record of it. Speaking in tongues is mentioned on numerous other occasions but not the loud roar or the flames. To my knowledge, no modern-day Christian has ever gone to Jerusalem to wait for the power. Yet many would say that they *are* receiving Holy Spirit power.

I'm sure I have power that had been missing for decades. I can now successfully resist temptation. I can love those with whom I thoroughly disagree politically. My waistline is four inches less ample with almost no effort on my part. For the first time in my life I am not worried about money. I can actually *enjoy* prayer for over an hour a day! I can sense God's love for me and "hear" from him regularly. To me, these are signs of miraculous spiritual power. While not as outwardly spectacular as tornado sounds, flames on heads, healing of quadriplegics or resurrections of buried corpses, my own experiences of God's power are just as real, to me, and to those who know me well.

# Miraculous Healing

As I began to write this chapter, it seemed I could not escape the issue of miraculous physical healing. For no obvious reason, people kept bringing me books on the topic. So I read them. My best friend kept mentioning his struggle with the issue. I listened, I hope sympathetically, but had no good answer to the dilemma of pleas for divine physical healing that were clearly answered in the negative. Can some people be used by God today to miraculously heal others? It certainly seems so. Some "healers" may be faking it. But I personally know and trust some individuals who tell of personal healings that were instantaneous, and confirmed by the most up-to-date medical imaging techniques. Yet, at least one such walking miracle has now aged and is having heart and lung problems; so far these have *not* been miraculously healed. Another friend has seen miraculous healings as a result of his ministry. Yet his wife, a woman of great faith, has suffered multiple painful illnesses for years.

Cessationists believe and teach that all miraculous signs and wonders, including supernatural healing, ceased with the death of the last of the apostles, defined as those who actually saw Jesus in the flesh. I cannot agree. There are just too many credible supernatural healings. Yet, how can we explain their relative rarity today compared to Jesus' earthly ministry? Some claim that God wants to heal everyone but cannot because of our doubt.[4] This cannot be the whole answer. The idea that God wants us all forever physically healthy inevitably runs aground on the shoal of human mortality. It stretches credulity beyond the breaking point to imagine that all believing Christians are meant to live completely healthy lives and then, like Enoch, to be simply transported to heaven without a moment's illness.[5] If this were God's intention, why did he create viruses? Why wasn't a spiritual giant like Joni Eareckson Tada healed years ago? Why would God have allowed Satan to give Job a painful skin disease?[6] Why would he have refused three times to take away Paul's "thorn in the flesh"?[7] Was Paul's faith defective or missing? No, in fact, it was not a matter of faith at all. The condition was given to keep Paul humble. In Ms. Tada's case, in her own words, her tragic injury was "God's plan for Joni and Friends to reach disabled people around the world with His gospel."[8]

I am driven to the conclusion that neither the cessationist nor the charismatic faith healer has the whole truth. A third possible answer comes to mind. Perhaps, at this time, God has chosen to manifest his power primarily by freeing us from spiritual and emotional bondage.[9] Let me illustrate.

# Object Lesson

Even as I write, Jesus is giving me an object lesson. I have a fever, sinus congestion, a headache and a bad cough. I have prayed earnestly for physical healing. It has not happened. However, just two evenings ago, as Leona and I were sharing, she mentioned her strong feelings about not being considered pretty in elementary school. I have told her many times how attractive I find her. But this head knowledge had not reached the root of the issue. So, after a brief discussion, as physically weak and sick as I was, I obeyed the Spirit's gentle nudge and offered her a Theophostic Prayer Ministry session. Leona agreed and after some work she was willing to give to Jesus the bitterness that she had been carrying for fifty years. It was basically, "It is not fair, God, that you made other girls pretty so that they had boyfriends while you made me unattractive." She was not sure at first that she was willing to give up the resentment. She thought she might feel defenseless without the coping mechanism on which she had long relied. I told her it was her choice but I kept asking, "Do you really want to keep carrying this for the rest of your life?" As soon as she decided to give the anger to Jesus, she noticed the feeling of abandonment that had been hiding behind the anger all those years. I asked her what she believed was true. She said, "I was all alone." I asked Jesus if he would come and bring her truth. I just waited. After about a minute of silence, she smiled and said, "He is showing me that he was right there, hurting right along with me. And, now I feel a strong sense of his presence and love!"

Two days later, she now tells me with a big smile, "I have gone back to those memories a number of times since the TPM session the other evening, and I can no longer feel any strong emotion at all. I have the same memories, but the emotional baggage is gone. It is like a large room that had been full of junk has now been swept clean!"

# Possible Answers

So I ask, "Why would Jesus so adamantly refuse to take away my flu symptoms, but so readily show up to heal Leona emotionally and spiritually? And not only that, why did he use the physically sick person to help the emotionally hurting one?"

A possible answer to the first question is that Jesus knows we have limited time and resources. He wants us to focus right now on inner healing, so he reinforces the behavior he wants to encourage. Emotional healing and mind transformation[10] affect parts of us that will live forever, while our bodies are perishable and will have to be replaced anyway.[11] As to the second question, "Why did he use the physically sick guy?" – perhaps it was another example of the "My grace is sufficient" principle.[12] Or maybe it was just God's sense of humor. The point seems to be, God performs miracles of healing – emotional, physical or spiritual – whenever *he* decides to do so. Sometimes he responds to prayers of faith,[13] sometimes he heals those who don't even know him[14] and sometimes he says "No, my grace is sufficient."[12]

# Greater Things

When we think of divine power, we tend to think first of visible signs and wonders that have no apparent natural explanation. But God looks on the heart.[15] Many who emphasize faith healing of bodily illness use John 14:12 where Jesus says, "I tell you the truth, anyone who has faith in me will do what I have been doing. He will do even greater things than these because I am going to the Father." It seems not to compute. If anything, it seems like what we do is far less than what Jesus did. I recently received an insight about the possible meaning of this verse as I was praying through the story of the raising of Lazarus. As I pored over the details, I was struck by how much Jesus knew. He knew *that* Lazarus would die,[16] *when* he would die[17] and *that he would be able to raise* Lazarus.[18] In comparison, I seem to stumble through life nearly blind.

I prayed, "Lord Jesus, your spiritual vision seems so impossibly superior to anything I have experienced. I am strongly tempted, therefore, to disbelieve that we mere humans could ever 'do even greater things.' I am very close to explaining your signs and wonders by appealing to the Jesus-was-God-and-I'm-not argument. Dear, Lord, can I dare hope that John 14:12 means us in the 21ˢᵗ century? If it is true, why aren't resurrections commonplace?"

During Jesus' ministry they were rare. In addition to Lazarus, only two others are recorded, Jarius' daughter,[19] and the widow's son.[20] Two additional raisings are recorded in Acts – Dorcas[21] and Eutychus.[22] I have never heard of mass resurrections. If we are to do greater things, why can't we go to a cemetery and go down the row bringing the folks back? I asked Jesus what John 14:12 means.

"Lord Jesus," I prayed, "from *your* perspective, what 'greater things' were done by your disciples?"

The thought came almost right away, "Well, now, my son, as you know, I value *spiritual life* even more than physical life.[15] Therefore, I was really whooping and shouting, laughing for joy and high-fiving every angel in sight when those *three thousand souls were saved* after Peter's sermon on that first Christian Pentecost![23] To me, that was most definitely a 'greater thing' than a few people being brought back to life physically!"

## Tentative Conclusions about Power

So what can we conclude about God-given power in the life of the believer? Here is my list, for now:

1.  God has power and is the Source of all we have.[24]
2.  God is sovereign, mysterious and infinitely creative.[25] We should not feel bad if we cannot always predict what he will do.
3.  It may be that each of us has as much miracle-working power as God can trust us with at the moment.[26]
4.  Our first priority is to love God and others, not to perform miracles. (Chapter 7)
5.  God uses his power to promote voluntary, loving relationships.[27] Therefore, I believe he may at times arrange events to *thwart* our attempts to go it alone.[28] For example, he may heal when a cessationist thought he would not, and refuse to heal when a charismatic was sure that he would. If he always followed the same formula in such matters, many of us would be tempted to think we did not need to abide intimately in him.
6.  At certain periods in history, or places on the globe, God chooses to step in and do more frequent visible signs and

wonders when, in his judgment, it is necessary to call attention to a new work he is doing.[29]

7. Our job is not to predict what God will do in any given circumstance. Rather, we should seek such intimacy with him that we will more often be able to sense *how he wants us to join him in what he is already up to!* Hint: be on the lookout for opportunities to help others experience spiritual and psychological healing.[30]

8. Our personal power can be choked off by sin or by simple neglect of the practices to which the Holy Spirit has called us – practices designed to keep the life-line to God clean and open. (Chapter 14)

9. If we love the power Source more than the manifestations, our lives will increasingly be characterized by the sweet, smooth roar of uninterrupted power. Not in the sense that there will be no surprises. He will not always do what we had hoped. But as we seek earnestly to love God and others, we will become more-and-more aware of his power.[31]

Of course, this chapter is a snap-shot in time, heavily influenced by what I have experienced, read and heard of God's power *so far.* Does he have much more to show me? I am certain of it.[32] I can hardly wait!

## Bonus (with Warning)!

I include the following for those who enjoy the challenge of a mechanical repair job. If you have no idea what a gasket is, or if the phrase "fuel pump" makes you slightly queasy, perhaps you should just skip to the next chapter.

## A Sweet, Smooth Roar

Useless

Completely worthless

Couldn't even give it away

Too heavy to even load and haul.

New battery worked fine.

Starter motor turned engine over

And over…and over

The 18 horse Briggs and Stratton Twin fired

Ran unevenly, for 10 seconds

Then just died

As though strangled

Again battery and starter worked

Unsuccessfully

Didn't even try

Flooded?

Tried again an hour later

Ran haltingly, missing badly

Died again

Abruptly

Numerous attempts over next 2 days

Nothing

Wife said

"You're still a man."

I replied,

"Yes, I'm a man,

But that's not a mower!"


Amateur diagnosis

Not getting fuel

Tractor sat too long, unused

Gas went bad

Mechanic could have overhauled it

Looked around

No mechanics in sight!

Tried disassembly

Dropped tiny fuel pump spring

Never saw it again
Ordered new carburetor
Complete with fuel pump!

Removed old carburetor
Very carefully
Made written notes
What attached where
Measured exact point to clamp choke cable
Careful of the gaskets
Bolted on new carburetor
Drained old gas
Installed new fuel filter
Reattached air cleaner
With new air filter
Added fresh gas
Set throttle to "Run"
(Picture of rabbit)
Pulled choke
Turned key to "Start"
Fuel flowing
Engine turning
At first nothing
Then it caught
AAAAH!
The sweet, smooth roar of uninterrupted power!
No longer useless
A mower once again!

Like my heart, Lord

Its connection to you fouled by disuse and neglect
Misfiring often
Sometimes altogether passive
Sometimes angrily protesting your coyness

Touched by the Master
No amateur this time
Scary surgeries
Parental funerals
Given the gift of longing
Taught by the Spirit
A vision of what might be
Grace to admit need
Weekend retreat
Lectio divina
Good books
Medical help
Spiritual friends
*Companions in Christ*
Twenty-eight weeks, twice!
Giving up counterfeits
Time
Pastor's advice, "Learn to pray."
Writing

The Lord
Spiritual mechanic
At my invitation
Working on my unbelief
Healing heart brokenness

Tuning and repairing
Parts I can't even see
And finally
The sweet, smooth roar of uninterrupted power!

Power to be his son
To act in spite of fear
To love
To confront evil
To create
Power to see tiny hints of his beauty
As much as I can stand

Oh, to be used daily
In tune with the Designer's purpose
To hear in my heart always
The sweet, smooth roar of his uninterrupted power!

# 21

# Trinity, Unity and Us

## What Jesus Wants for Us

In John 17:20-23 Jesus says "I pray...for those who will believe in me... that all of them...may be *one*, Father, just as you are *in me* and I am *in you*. May they also be *in us* so that the world may believe that you have sent me. I have given them the glory that you gave me, that they may be *one as we are one: I in them and you in me.*" (emphasis mine)

In addition to the obvious sermon on Christian unity so often found in this passage, did you see what I saw? Did someone very important just invite us *into the Trinity*? Although this passage mentions only the Father and the Son, a similar one in John 14:15-20 includes the promise of the "Spirit of truth" who will live with us and in us. In what sense have we humans been invited into the Trinity? Clearly, we do not become divine. But Jesus seems to reassure, "You're right, of course, the invitation is not to assume divinity, but, don't worry, there is plenty of room for growth in intimacy without fear of overstepping any divine/human boundaries. Resisting unity with God is a far greater human problem than getting too close will ever be!"

# God Present

Some time ago, I came to my prayer time and admitted feeling lonely. I asked, "Lord, what do you want me to know about my tendency to feel abandoned?" These thoughts came:

"First of all Ev, you are not alone. I AM here with you! I love you more than you love life itself and I will never leave you nor forsake you.[1] You should get to know me. I AM God the Holy Spirit."

I answered, "I would love that, Mr. Holy Spirit? I mean no disrespect, but it is hard to feel intimate with a person whose name starts with 'the.' It's like trying to develop a friendship with 'the teacher' or 'the boss.' Is your name Immanuel, Lord? As I understand Scripture, you are most definitely 'God with us' now that Jesus has ascended. But Immanuel was the name given to the virgin's son.[2] Then why did everyone call him Jesus? Help, Lord!"

He seemed to reply, "Well, Ev, my boy, as you know, I AM one God. I have chosen at this time not to be present in human form on the earth. However, you and I can be close. When you open yourself to me, I can communicate with you, mind-to-mind. I am very pleased with your passion to learn to recognize my voice as distinct from your own thoughts or the suggestions of the Enemy. It is not so important exactly which names we use. I am your God and you are my precious child. *Let's just enjoy being together.* Let's revel in closeness. Can you simply *rest* in the intimacy that is my gift to all who put me first? In other words, don't worry so much about *understanding* our oneness, *just live it, enjoy it!* If I had wanted you to understand the Trinity, I would have given you more intelligence. For now just think of 'us' (the Trinity)[3] as a mystery that symbolizes the ultimate oneness of holy intimacy, into which you have been invited!"

# Trinity

One God

The great I AM

The Father, Son and Holy Spirit

Picture of ultimate oneness

Gift of matchless unity

Offered to me

Certified loner no longer

Now included in the only in-group that counts!

Where lack of "cool" matters not a whit.

That, Lord, is indeed cool!


What can it possibly mean to be invited into such an in-group? Jesus said at one point that the only way to enter the kingdom of God is to "receive [it] like a little child."[4] People were bringing children to Jesus for his touch. The disciples objected but Jesus said "Let the little children come to me, and do not hinder them, for the kingdom of God belongs to such as these."[5] In my mind's eye I can see him now, down on his haunches, with a twinkle in his eye, motioning for them to come. I see big grins on their faces as they totter, plod and scamper over to him. He embraces them into the warm, secure folds of his tunic. The big sleeves hanging from his arms wrap soothingly around them as they giggle and squeal with delight!

I have found that in order to receive his invitation to intimacy, I need to be willing to admit my need, and, as children do so instinctively, to beg him to bless me, just like Jacob. He wrestled with God all night, refusing to let go until he was blessed.[6] On one such occasion, while grieving my parents' deaths, I sat in my prayer chair and prayed repeatedly, "I am desperate for you, Lord Jesus" and "Hug me, Daddy God" and "I love you Holy Spirit of God." After about ten minutes a mental image came. Three robed figures stood with arms on each other's shoulders, enjoying a group hug. I saw myself as a thigh-high toddler and begged "Let me in, let me in, let me in!"

They broke the circle and with out-stretched arms looked at me and said "Welcome home, Evy!" I began to join the hug, holding onto their knees, but I became aware of other children looking on longingly. I said, "Can the rest come too?" They answered with hearty good humor, "Of course, the more the merrier!" My heart almost bursts with gratitude even now as I remember!

Not only do children readily admit their need, they also are naturally open to this great new adventure called life. They are filled with awe at the wonders revealed or hinted at each day. Recently I was playing "tractors" with my two-and-a-half-year-old grandson when he informed me that his tractor had stopped working. I pretended to examine the tiny Farmall engine. After a moment, I announced that the fan belt had torn. His eyes grew wide with wonder and delight. I am certain he had no idea what a fan belt was, let alone how it helps to cool a tractor engine. But his lack of understanding of the details didn't get in the way of his sense of awe. He seemed to be thinking, "DadDad knows about tractors! It's going to be great fun playing 'tractors' with DadDad!"

Like children, we must recognize and accept out need. We must expectantly beg him to let us in. We must believe he can fill our overworked, cynical adult minds and hearts with a fresh sense of wonder and joy. For me, it took some time. Years of left-brain tyranny had taken their toll. But it was not hopeless, and the resulting intimacy and joy were well worth the effort.

## What about Us Introverts?

Can this sense of acceptance by God make social situations more comfortable, even for shy people? Remarkably, yes. Let me illustrate. After considerable awakening to the joy of hearing from God through others, and even after much inner healing, I am still an introvert. So when Leona and I were invited to a church-sponsored square dance, I was leery. Let's face it, I am rhythmically-challenged. My attempts at dancing have been clumsy at best. Square I may be, but I had never square-danced. But I agreed to go anyway. My "dancing" amused some folks, but I was amazed to discover that I actually enjoyed it! What a delight to find that Jesus can take a shy, uncool introvert, give him love and healing, and change him into a person who can actually enjoy meeting strangers at a square dance! Though still not gregarious, I no longer dread parties. Jesus' John 17 prayer for oneness is being answered for me even in this ordinary sense.

## Can Community Happen at the Detroit Airport?

Over a twenty-eight year career I spent way too much time at the Metro airport in Detroit, Michigan. But one such occasion was memorable. As I sat waiting for my flight, I was opening myself to the Holy Spirit by musing on this prayer that he had given me earlier that day:

## Invitation

Lord, you are invited

Come to dinner at our house

Walk on our pond

Climb into our boat

Drive your breakfast wagon onto our worksite

Show us as much of your beauty as we can stand

Heal our hearts, Lord

Batter away at our unbelief.


Charm your children, Lord

Let us laugh loudly

And live lovingly

As your kingdom comes!

Amen


A most amazing thing started to happen. I became aware of a group of young men jokingly ribbing one another behind me. Ten feet off to my front right was a group of three men and a woman similarly enjoying each other's company. One young lady sat on the floor to my front left, her back resting against a big, round concrete pillar, contentedly typing on her laptop. Three seats to my right was an absolutely gorgeous young woman. She wore very little make-up and was dressed modestly, but she was clearly fit and had the face of an angel! Suddenly it seemed like Jesus was showing me how he saw all of these dear folks – with heart-felt delight in them, his very own precious children. It was as though his presence packed that grungy, old, rancid-smelling gate area with warm good humor and beauty. I have no idea whether my prayer in any way contributed to that scene, or whether it simply made me aware of God's love and presence. Either way, I boarded the plane that day with a new appreciation of God's love for *all* his human children. It seemed like he had given me just a hint of what he had intended when he created us.

Frank Laubach tells of experiences where he had prayed for people in public places and noticed a remarkable improvement in their mood immediately afterward.[7] In this case I was inviting God to "charm his children" in a general sense, not aware of these particular folks initially. But God seemed to want me to know that he agreed with my wishes, or better, that I was in-tune with his, right there in that unlikely place. Was the young woman to my right *really* an angel? I don't know. Maybe I'll ask Jesus sometime.

## A Wideness in the Oneness

Reared a Mennonite, I heard a lot about our denomination's distinctive beliefs. I believe many Christian groups place too much emphasis on the boundaries – on who's in and who's out of their particular variety of the Christian faith. If, instead of focusing on the fringes, we would all look to Christ, I believe he would see to it that we were brought closer together, progressively nearer to the oneness with him and each other that is his will. While studying the book of Acts several years ago I was intrigued by the story of Cornelius in the tenth chapter. Here is the account in the New Alliterative Paraphrase version:[8]

# Cornelius

Cornelius the Caesarean centurion

Vividly viewed a vision

Scared, he stared at the seraphim

In severe fear he queried

"What is it, Lord?"


"Your alms and psalms were seen," he said,

"So send men to Simon at Simon's domicile by the sea."

When the speaking seraphim had split
He sent several servants and a swordsman
To the seaside Samaritan city of Joppa.

When Pete[9] reached the roof he was ready to eat
He fell into a spell and saw a big sheet
Full of four-footed furry fellows as well as
Snakes, snipes, whip-poor-wills and spoonbills.

"Slaughter, sauté and swallow."
Was God's command. But follow?
Not Simon. Said he sincerely
"Only approved appetizers need apply!"

Three times God tried
Then the meat sheet rose to the sky
And the Spirit said to Simon,
"Go down and see several servants and a swordsman
From Cornelius the Caesarean centurion
A devout donor to the destitute
A sheep of another fold
Whose heart is pure gold."

So Simon said, "OK"
And asked them in to stay
As guests that very day.

People are different, God made them that way
What fun it can be as we work day-by-day
As a tightly-knit team of toilers who take time

To talk and walk together and, Hey!
What a hoot to have a whole host of
Heaven-dreamed helpers!

I hope we all have the same home.

# 22

# There's Got to Be a Sequel

## Good Riddance

Keys are important; we need them constantly. Losing them can cause near panic. Metaphorically, we like understanding a key concept, playing a key role or occupying a key position. Yet, when we stop to think about it, why are keys necessary? That's right, because we have to lock things. Will we need keys in heaven? I can't imagine why. There will be no thieves. No one will be rude enough to barge unannounced through a closed but unlocked door. I know I won't miss carrying my bulky key ring or looking for lost keys, worrying who found them and may be planning to invade my home.

What else won't bug us in heaven? Wouldn't it be great if we never again needed insect repellent, pesticides or weed killers? How nice to have no more budgets, mortgages, car payments or taxes? Oh, and just think, no deadlines, monthly reports, staff meetings or performance reviews. Some people will be out of work: dentists, insurance salesmen, funeral directors, police officers, cancer researchers, pharmacists, game wardens, even evangelists.

In such a world there would be invention without necessity, warmth without sweat, light without glare and roses without Japanese beetles. There will be no waiting in line, traffic jams, flies on our food or oil drips on the garage floor. We'll no longer need to put up with incompetence, rudeness, or green lights that turn yellow at just the wrong instant. We won't have to fear what unkind words the rest of the group may say about us after we leave. No one will assign selfish motives to actions we meant only for good. Pastors will no longer struggle to unite congregational factions who disagree about how to arrange the seating.

Wouldn't it be nice to stop worrying about global warming, carbon footprints, sustainable development and genetic engineering? Oh, and how about no more senior moments, Freudian slips or typos? We could forget about things that go bump in the night, ghosts, and alien abductions. And, oh yeah, no more pompous snobs, entitled freeloaders or folks who are too easily offended.

What if the spirit world was no longer such a mystery and we could know God's will as clearly as the date and time? We could happily do without paradoxes, moral dilemmas and trade-offs. Imagine the relief if we no longer had to battle temptation or watch a loved one die.

I realize, of course, that some items on this "good riddance" list would seem trivial to those who face rape, torture, imprisonment and death because of religious, ethnic or tribal conflicts. How can we keep hope alive in a world with so much misery? Well, at least part of the answer is that there is more to reality than what we see on CNN or read in Newsweek.[1] While it is certainly true that decent people and governments should do everything possible to minimize human cruelty,[2] there really *is* "pie-in-the-sky-by-and-by." And, guess what, it's cherry pie with a big scoop of Häagen-Dazs, and much, much more! In previous chapters we have examined practical issues of *this* life. There is certainly hope each day as God works to bring good out of every situation.[3] God's kingdom is already here, including some spiritual pie a-la-mode right here on earth.[4] But, compared to what is in store, we "ain't seen nothin' yet!"[5]

## Biblical Hints about Heaven

But what *will* we do in heaven? Most are familiar with the biblical passages that rule out lying, impurity, idolatry, pain, crying and death.[6] There are also texts that foretell singing,[7] worship,[8] public speaking,[9] eating and drinking,[10] seeing and knowing God intimately,[11] ruling,[12] serving,[13] incense burning,[14] and trumpet playing.[15] Some passages suggest heavenly contemplation (at least there will be silence for half an hour),[16] writing,[17] exotic zoology (observing talking eagles and other strange beasts),[18] surveying,[19] and construction.[20] Jesus has promised that we can spend time with him in heaven.[21] Those of us with a philosophical bent will enjoy a new way of knowing.[22] Those who like to observe human behavior will no doubt join the "great cloud of witnesses" cheering on those who are still running the race.[23]

How much of this should be taken literally is open for debate. For example, I have often wondered about the Scriptures that speak of being co-rulers with Christ.[12] Who or what will we rule? Will some who have become spiritual giants be given the privilege of helping others, who still may have a long way to grow? Will we perhaps rule over animals and plants like Adam and Eve before the fall?[24] Will we rule over other races of God's creation? Will we help govern brand new universes? In what sense may the parable of the talents apply to heaven?[25] If the kingdom of God is like a boss who gives more responsibility to those employees who make the best use of what they had already been given, what is the nature of the expanded sphere of influence? We are not told. But it is intriguing to imagine.

Judging from the nature of Jesus' resurrection body, it makes sense that we would be able to eat,[26] even though we will probably not need to.[27] Therefore, perhaps those who enjoy gourmet cooking or baking "heavenly" desserts may find that they can continue their hobbies in heaven, although I'd be surprised if they had to wash dishes. (Might there even be weed-free farming, with no worries about fuel or fertilizer costs and no concern over less than ideal weather, or fluctuations in the price of beef?) Like Jesus after his resurrection, we will probably be able to touch one another[28] and inanimate objects.[29] Yet our new bodies will allow us to move unhindered through "solid" objects if we choose to do so.[30] How can this be? From chemistry we learn that only a tiny fraction of the space taken up by an atom is occupied by the nucleus and the electrons orbiting it. For example, a hydrogen atom's diameter is 100,000 times greater than that of either its proton or electron. In other words, if the proton were the size of a ping pong ball, the single electron orbiting it would be comparable in size but would be buzzing around at a distance of at least a half mile from the proton.[31] Think of all the "empty space!" If we were somehow able to synchronize the movements of all the affected electrons, there would be *plenty of room* for objects to move through one another. Apparently the risen Jesus knew how! (Yes, I know about wave-particle duality. Certainly, it would be just as easy for the Creator to manipulate waves in energy fields as to negotiate between speeding particles.)

# Baffling Questions

**1. Strange images:** Of all the topics I've tackled in this book, this one seems most intractable. The Scriptures that talk of the afterlife, if taken literally, reveal a strange mixture of bliss, horror and what, at first glance, seems to be downright silliness. The book of Revelation speaks of a lot of shouting, singing and chanting, in the company of the scariest menagerie of hybrid monsters ever described. It seems at times like a huge, over-crowded church service. Then the next thing you know there are horrific judgments, tormented sinners and a great, cosmic war. Jesus' own teachings point to judgment,[32] construction of mansions or rooms,[20] and sitting on Abraham's lap while carrying on a conversation with a sinner in hell![33] How big is Abraham's lap, anyway? Do we all get a turn? And what kind of heaven would allow for conversation with a tormented hell-dweller? Yes, I know it was a parable, not actual historic narrative. But still, Jesus named a well-known historic figure, the Father-of-the-Faithful, no less. It seems unlikely that Jesus would try to make a serious spiritual point using an illustration that had no basis in fact. That would be like a person trying to explain cold weather to a visitor from the tropics by likening it to sitting on Santa Claus's lap at the North Pole.

So what could Jesus have possibly meant by "Abraham's lap"? Is it metaphorical language for the place "the faithful" go after death? Perhaps. But then what is this about seeing another guy in torment and conversing with him across an unbridgeable canyon? Is this referring to a time *before* God wipes away all tears and banishes all pain?[34] It seems to me that anyone who had even *begun* to love his neighbors and enemies would certainly be pained by even the thought, let alone an actual conversation, with a fellow human in torment. How could that be heaven? (Chapter 3) Perhaps the story is just an allegory, as if Jesus were saying, "Imagine what these two guys might say if they *could* converse."

**2. Time:** But, for me, the most unimaginable aspect of heaven is what it will be like to live in eternity. Whenever I think of this topic the first two lines of James Milton Black's "When the Roll Is Called up Yonder" play over in my mind:

"When the trumpet of the Lord shall sound, and time shall be no more,

and the morning breaks, eternal, bright and fair..."

I had always assumed that the part about time being no more had an ironclad scriptural basis. The verse Mr. Black probably was thinking about is Revelation 10:6 where, in the King James Version, an angel declares that "there should be time no longer." I remember numerous sermons using this text to support a concept of heaven in which time does not exist. Somehow, we will live in an "eternal now," whatever that means. But then I happened to reread this verse recently in the NIV and was amazed to see it rendered "There will be no more delay!" The Greek word is "chronos." It means "time," not "delay."[35] But still, in the context, it's possible that it was being used in the sense that a harried tour director might urge, "Hurry back to the cruise ship, folks, there is no more time!" As Randy Alcorn puts it, Revelation 10:6 does not mean "that time itself will cease, but that there is no time left before God's judgment is executed."[36]

Psychologists sometimes counsel clients to "just live in the present." After all, they reason, the past is gone and the future is not yet here. We can do nothing to change either. But, have you ever tried to follow such advice? What *is* the present? In clock time, it is an infinitesimally small point. No sooner have you identified it than it becomes the past! Without memory of the past or imagination of the future, we have no more awareness than an amoeba. Therefore, trying to imagine heaven as a timeless "eternal now" is unhelpful.

Let's try another approach. We have already seen how Jesus' resurrection body could touch "solid" objects if he so chose, or alternatively, at will, he could walk right through them. Similarly, it may be that in heaven we will be able to experience time without being *stuck* in it. For example, when we need time for relational purposes, so that we can experience a progression of events and personal interactions, it will be available to us. If we want time to slow down or even stop for a while so that we can savor a particularly "good time" we are enjoying, time will do our bidding. In a world that would give a brand new meaning to the phrase "flex time," we may be able to move backwards to reconnect with a particularly meaningful experience. Could it be that we may even be able to look or even move forward in "time"? In other words, will we be able to push the "play," "rewind," "pause," and "fast forward" buttons in real life, not just when viewing a videotape? How such a system could work without utter chaos I cannot imagine. In our present world, with so many independent, selfish wills operating all at once, giving each the ability to manipulate time would be catastrophic. But in heaven, where unselfish love reigns, it just might work.

For those who wish to tackle a more rigorous treatment of this topic, I recommend Peter Kreeft's fascinating book, *Everything You Ever Wanted to Know about Heaven...But Never Dreamed of Asking.*[37] He says that what we usually think of as clock time is the fourth dimension (length, width and thickness being the first three). He then introduces the fifth dimension as "human time." This is what we refer to when we say things like "We had a wonderful time on vacation." It is clock time that has been filled with meaningful content by human activity. This is also the time that the psychologist is thinking of when she advises her client to live in the present. The present, in human time, is the activity that we are enjoying presently. For example, I am writing this paragraph on Labor Day afternoon, 2007. For me, this period of several hours of clock time is my "present" right now. In a "human time" (fifth dimension) sense, I am fully engaged, having a "great time." So far, I can follow Professor Kreeft's reasoning. But then he defines the *sixth* dimension as "eternity." It's here that he loses me. I won't even try to summarize his description. Read it for yourself. He may be exactly correct; I just don't seem to have the intellectual equipment to grasp his argument. All I end up with, having read Kreeft repeatedly, is a mental picture of eternity as the point at the center of a sphere. To me, this image of eternity seems just as limiting as thinking of it as a point on a line. As Kreeft himself says, heaven cannot possibly be less than what we experience in this life.[38] At least Kreeft and I do seem to concur that, from the perspective of eternity, time becomes "malleable."[39]

Biblically, there is some evidence that heaven is not completely timeless. In fact, according to the Revelator, there was "silence in heaven for about half an hour."[16] In addition, "seals" were opened, trumpets sounded and "bowls" poured out sequentially, over a period of time.[40] I must admit, though, that for me, this topic is one of those cases where God's knowledge is "unsearchable" and "beyond tracing out."[41]

**3. Free will:** Another such mystery is how to think about freedom in heaven. Since I believe, as Alcorn does,[42] that "the capacity to choose is part of what makes us human," I wonder if we will still be capable of sin in heaven. Alcorn says no. As he points out, the Bible promises no more death[43] and since sin results in death,[44] there can be no more sin in heaven. Furthermore, since we will be raised incorruptible,[45] "our risen bodies...will be immune to corruption."[46] Alcorn goes on:

> "The inability to sin doesn't inherently violate free will. My inability to be God, an angel, a rabbit, or a flower is not a violation of my free will. It's the simple reality of my nature. The new nature that'll be ours in Heaven – the righteousness of Christ – is a nature that cannot sin, anymore than a diamond can be soft or blue can be red."[42]

Although I find this comforting, and I believe biblical, I am still left with the question, "What *does* freedom of choice mean in heaven?" If it no longer means freedom to make a basic moral choice between good and evil, between love and rebellion, exactly what are we free to choose? If we will be merely able to choose among an array of similarly good options, won't our ability to be free moral agents be reduced to that extent? If so, is this the one exception to the principle that heaven cannot be less real than what we experience in this life? Alas, yet another "unsearchable" mystery![41]

# The Essence of Heaven

Personally, my heart does not warm to some of the traditional descriptions of heaven. The idea of heaven as a humongous cube[47] with streets of gold and pearly gates,[48] no night,[49] and huge, noisy crowds[50] does not exactly appeal to this wilderness-loving contemplative who revels in the stillness of a deserted winter woods, or the coziness of a dark evening before a crackling fire. The biblical descriptions may charm those who would love to travel to New York City to join thousands of fellow-citizens in the Times Square New Year's Eve celebration. But the rest of us may well wonder, if heaven is such a wonderful experience, why is it so difficult to imagine as a favorite destination?

One reason may be the lack of emphasis on heaven in many seminaries and churches.[51] Sermons about the afterlife seem to be rare these days. It would do most of us good to think about heaven more often. Paul advised the Philippians to think on whatever is true, noble, right, pure, lovely, admirable, excellent and praiseworthy.[52] Heaven qualifies. We do well to remind ourselves and others of the "lively hope" that we have in Christ Jesus because of his resurrection from the dead.[53]

However, some may believe that it is presumptuous to try to imagine heaven. After all, Paul says in 1 Corinthians 2:9, "No eye has seen, no ear has heard, no mind has conceived what God has prepared for those who love him." At first, this seems to explain why we have trouble imagining heaven; we were not *meant* to understand it. But wait, in the very next verse, Paul says, "But *God has revealed it to us by his Spirit.*" (emphasis mine) Really? How could I have missed that? So I read on. Paul says that the Spirit "expresses spiritual truths in spiritual words" and "the spiritual man makes judgments about all things,"[54] and that "we have the mind of Christ."[55] So we see with delight that this passage, sometimes wrongly used to warn *against* trying to imagine heaven, actually supports opening our hearts and minds to the Spirit's teaching on the subject! The challenge seems to be, how can we, as spiritual persons, make judgments about heaven, in a way that maximizes heaven's appeal without degenerating into mere foolish speculation? Very prayerfully, that's how. We should pray that God would both empower us to understand as much as possible, and forgive where we may misread his guidance.

Let's go back to the question, why don't the biblical descriptions of heaven sound appealing to some of us? It could be because we try to interpret the passages too literally. If, way back in Paul's time, *God had already revealed what he had prepared for those that love him,*[56] why is it still such a mystery 2000 years later? Probably because we have not thought clearly enough about exactly what it is that God has already revealed. What God has made possible in Christ is a *heavenly quality of life* characterized by an intimate, loving relationship with God and others. Once we begin to experience this *kingdom life* here and now, we can begin to grasp the *essence of heaven*. The questions about how our heavenly bodies will interact with space, time and matter are fascinating to consider, but the really *important* questions about heaven have to do with how we will relate to God and our fellow heavenly citizens.

## Heavenly Relationships

So what can be said about the nature of divine and human relationships in the kingdom of heaven, now, as well as in the afterlife? One reason it may be difficult to imagine heaven is that awe and godly fear are inspired in us as we contemplate meeting God face-to-face. A few lines from W. Chalmers Smith's majestic hymn come to mind:

Immortal, invisible, God only wise

In light inaccessible hid from our eyes,...

Great Father of glory, pure Father of light,

Thine angels adore thee, all veiling their sight;

All laud we would render: O help us to see

'Tis only the splendour of light hideth thee.[57]


Is it possible that many of us will not be ready for the full splendor of God's presence when we first enter heaven? Peter Kreeft believes in three types of heavenly experience. In the first, we will do the work necessary for self-understanding, inner healing and spiritual formation (sanctification) that many of us neglect in this life.[58] Secondly, and overlapping with the first stage, we open ourselves to one another. The vulnerability, and loving listening, of this stage further deepens our own self-understanding and prepares and strengthens our spirits for the ultimate stage, face-to-face intimacy with God

This description rings true for me. The themes and activities of the three stages fit with experiences that I have already tasted, as a fledging citizen of the kingdom of God. Of course, there is a sense in which we have already "seen the Father" as shown to us in Christ's incarnation.[59] However, God's transcendent power and dangerously brilliant beauty (glory), fully revealed, would certainly do us in.[60] Paul wrote that God's ways are far above ours.[41] Isaiah was "undone" by his vision of God.[61] God put Moses in a cleft in the rock and covered him with his hand as he passed by, removing the protecting hand only after he had passed, so that Moses saw only God's back.[62] As God said, "you cannot see my face, for no one may see me and live."[63]

The Person whose power spoke the universe into existence may need to *always* protect us from a major portion of his energy. We cannot even look directly at just one of the trillions of stars God created without risking permanent eye damage – and that is from a distance of 93 million miles! Think what incredible radiation God himself would emit if he ever fully revealed himself! But we need not fear. He knows our weakness and is fully capable of optimizing intimacy without incinerating us. He became a man and walked among us, after all. But there seems to be good evidence that, as our spirits become more robust through more time spent close to God's heart, we progressively become able to safely experience more of God, and thus more bliss.[64] We become-and-more like the "solid people" of C. S. Lewis' *The Great Divorce*

–increasingly able to inhabit the bright and substantial reality of our ultimate home.[65]

As we do, I suspect that we will care less-and-less whether we live in a room prepared for us in a cubic, golden city, *or* in a rustic log mansion, built on a 10,000 acre tract of pristine wilderness. It will not matter whether we serve God day and night in his temple, or fly our heavenly star cruiser to the far reaches of a brand new universe, that we are helping God govern. It will be the love that matters.[66]

# A Hope-filled Head-Start

During all this searching about the nature of heaven, I am learning once again about *hope* right here on earth. Leona and I are currently working through a modern adaptation of the *Book of Exercises* originally written by Ignatius of Loyola.[67] We are being led by the Holy Spirit and by a great spiritual director. Just a few days ago the Scripture was from Isaiah. "Woe to him who quarrels with his Maker, to him who is but a potsherd among the potsherds on the ground."[68] Since there have been times when I have quarreled with my Maker, I found this verse troubling. A potsherd is a broken piece of already fired clay pottery. Unlike fresh, un-fired clay, a potsherd cannot be reshaped. This picture became a symbol for me of parts of my relationship with Leona. At that time Leona and I had just had a recurrence of our most common conflict. Even though I have gained much freedom in the area of my food choices (Chapter 9), it is still a sensitive topic for me.

While we were enjoying one of our local bountiful buffets, Leona asked whether I had eaten any salad. I said it was none of her business. Neither of us could enjoy the rest of *that* silent meal! This recurring rough spot in our relationship made me think of a useless piece of broken pottery on the floor.

Why do we keep irritating each other like this? We're not sure, but we believe God will do the impossible. He will turn this potsherd into fresh, workable clay. In my mind's eye, it's as though a dried, surface scale is cracking and falling away, revealing a healthy, pink glow.

Jesus seems to say, "This is a picture of what I will do for you and Leona. I will breathe newness and life into this part of your relationship. I will free you from this brokenness."

And I reply hopefully, "Yes, Lord, I believe. Please have your way with this piece of clay."

And I'm sure that he will, both in this life and the next. Each day, moment-by-moment, the sequels keep coming!

# EPILOGUE
## Does God Like Pizza?

At first, I was going to make this question the title of the book. But then I thought, *How are people going to find it when they do an online book search?* Those doing a search on "pizza" will most likely be looking for cookbooks. But I still like the question. It seems to capture the divine-human mystery, in much the same way as when Jesus used everyday objects to illustrate great truths. Would the stupendous, unimaginable Creator ever choose to chat with me over a pizza supper? How well do I know him if I can't ask him a simple question like, "Do you like pizza?"

Recently, as part of the Ignatian Exercises, I was pondering Jesus' resurrection. My spiritual director had said to expect the risen Lord to make an "appearance" in a way that would be unmistakable, though not necessarily dramatic. For me, this seemed just a bit contrived. I was accustomed to conversing with Jesus whenever I felt like it. Now I was supposed to think of him as dead, in the tomb, the Saturday before Easter. It was hard for me to imagine.

After several days, I finally prayed, "OK, Lord, what am I to do about this?"

The thought came, "Read your Bible."

"Yes, Lord, what should I read?"

"Read about eating fish."

"OK, which occasion?"

"Behind locked doors, after I arose."

"Alrighty then," I agreed, and read from Luke 24:41-42 where Jesus, knowing some of them still did not believe it was him, asked, "Do you have anything here to eat?" They gave him a piece of broiled fish, and he took it and ate it in their presence.

Then I said to Jesus, "So, Lord?"

"Don't you see?" he asked. "If it had been 2008, you would have probably given me pizza!"

"So, what of it, Lord?"

"Dead men don't eat fish *or* pizza, my son!"

"Very true," I acknowledged, but aching for still more closeness, I pressed on, "But Lord, *I* have never seen your hands, feet *or* side. Nor have I *seen* you eat fish, pizza, scalloped potatoes or hot dogs – not even in my 'mind's eye'!"

Now it was his turn to ask, "So?"

"Well," I replied, "I've been told to expect you to 'show up' in some unmistakable way."

"Really? Who said?"

Somewhat exasperated with his feigned ignorance, I exclaimed, "My spiritual director, that's who!"

"Oh, yeah. You know, Ev, I really *like* her! Let's see, now. What are we going to do about this dilemma? Hmmmm. I wonder what would be acceptable."

"Lord, this conversation is starting to sound ridiculous!"

Jesus just said, "Hey, hand me a little more of that pizza, while I give this some thought. Do you have any ideas, Ev? I'm drawing a blank, here."

"Oh, Jesus! You're getting sillier by the second!"

Jesus sat there, calmly chewing the last bit of deep-dish, meat-lovers pizza. "By the way, Ev," he finally said, "this is really good pizza. You have any more?"

"No, I'm afraid that's it, Bro."

"Do you think Domino's would deliver – in thirty minutes?"

"You tell me, Lord. I am totally stupefied."

With a twinkle in his eye he glanced over at me and said "But you *do* have a smile on your face, my son!"

"That I do, Lord, that I do!"

# NOTES

## Preface

1. John 5:39-40

## Chapter 1: Chatting With an Invisible Friend

1. John 10:10
2. 1 Kings 19:12
3. Romans 8:16; 1 Corinthians 12:8
4. Acts 4:15-17
5. John 10:11
6. John 10:4
7. John 10:16
8. John 10:27
9. John 16:12-13
10. Genesis 1:26
11. Galations 1:9; Revelation 22:18-19;
12. James 1:14
13. 1 Thessalonians 3:5
14. Acts 17:11
15. What happens when Jesus "loves on me"? As I sit quietly in my "prayer chair," my spirit calms and slowly a sense of peace, belonging, and well-being settles over me. Perhaps I am experiencing what the apostle Paul wrote of in Romans 8:16. "The Spirit himself testifies with our spirit that we are God's children."
16. Romans 5:8
17. Matthew 22:37-38; John 15:4
18. Numbers 22:21-35
19. Dallas Willard, *Hearing God* (Downers Grove, Ill.: InterVarsity Press, 1984)
20. Thomas à Kempis, *The Imitation of Christ* (Peabody, Mass.: Hendrickson Publishers, 2004)
21. Robert Don Hughes, *Questioning God* (Grand Rapids, Mich.: BakerBooks, 2005), p.143.

# Chapter 2: Awesome Mystery

1.  Matthew 7:7
2.  Romans 11:33-34
3.  Colossians 1:17; Hebrews 1:3
4.  Luke 12:7
5.  John 11:48
6.  Romans 5:12; 8:20
7.  John 11:6
8.  John 11:17
9.  1 Corinthians 13:12
10. John Eldredge, *Epic*, (Nashville, Tenn., Thomas Nelson, 2004)

# Chapter 3: Who Are You, Lord?

1.  Acts 9:5
2.  Matthew 22:37
3.  1 Samuel 2:2; 1 John 4:8
4.  Isaiah 54:8
5.  Matthew 7:13-14
6.  Matthew 25:46
7.  Edwards, Jonathan. "Sinners in the Hands of an Angry God." Preached July 8, 1741. *Christian Classics Ethereal Library*. *www.ccel.org*. (Accessed October 16, 2007)
8.  Randolph J. Klassen, *What Does the Bible Really Say About Hell?: Wrestling With the Traditional View*, (Telford, PA: Pandora Press, 2001), pp. 31-36
9.  Luke 15:1-7, 11-32
10. Matthew 18:22 KJV
11. Mark 3:5
12. Luke 16:19-31
13. Romans 11:33-34
14. C. S. Lewis, *The Great Divorce*, (New York: Macmillan, 1946)
15. Ibid., p. 8
16. Hebrews 10:26-31
17. Genesis 3:22
18. Matthew 25:46
19. John Stott in *Evangelical Essentials: A Liberal-Evangelical Dialogue*, (Downers Grove, Ill., InterVarsity, 1988), pp. 319-320
20. Edward W. Fudge, *The Fire That Consumes: A Biblical and Historical Study of the Doctrine of Final Punishment*, (Lincoln, NE: iUniverse.com, 2001)

21. Ephesians 1:10
22. John 12:32
23. Philippians 2:10-11
24. James 2:19
25. Mark 10:27
26. Randolph J. Klassen, *What Does the Bible Really Say About Hell?: Wrestling With the Traditional View*, (Telford, PA: Pandora Press, 2001)
27. Acts 10:2
28. Acts 10:34-35
29. Acts 10:44
30. John 3:16
31. Luke 12:47-48
32. Romans 1:20; 2:13-16
33. John 5:27
34. John 5:30
35. Mark 3:1-5

## Chapter 4: The Divine-Human Dance

1. Revelation 3:20
2. 2 Corinthians 5:17
3. Revelation 3:19
4. Act 3:17
5. Luke 3:7
6. Matthew 23:27
7. Revelation 3:16
8. John 14:23
9. Revelation 3:21
10. Exodus 32:32
11. Genesis 1:26
12. James 1:17
13. Matthew 16:23
14. Matthew 26:42
15. Isaiah 55:8-9; Romans 11:33-34
16. Dallas Willard, *Renovation of the Heart*, (Colorado Springs, NavPress, 2002)
17. Thomas Keating, *Intimacy with God*, (New York, The Crossroad Publishing Co., 1994), p. 143

18. Adele V. Gonzalez, "Prayer and the Character of God", *Companions in Christ: Participant's Book*, (Nashville, Tenn., Upper Room Books, 2001), p. 113

19. Thomas `a Kempis, *The Imitation of Christ*, (Peabody, Mass., Hendrikson Publishers, 2004), p. 42

20. John 16:12-13

## Chapter 5: No Longer Willing to Miss Out

1. Philip Yancey, *Reaching for the Invisible God*, (Grand Rapids, Mich., Zondervan, 2000), p. 15

2. Gerrit Dawson, et. al., *Companions in Christ: A Small-Group Experience in Spiritual Formation*, (Nashville, Tenn., Upper Room Books, 2001)

3. Psalm 139:13

4. Dallas Willard, *Renovation of the Heart*, (Colorado Springs, Col., NavPress, 2002), pp. 144-157

5. John Eldredge, *The Journey of Desire*, (Nashville, Tenn., Thomas Nelson, 2000)

6. 1 Corinthians 15:52-54

7. Numbers 22:28-30

8. Acts 9:3-6

9. Jonah 1:17 and 2:10

10. 1 Kings 19:12

11. Acts 8:26-40

12. Genesis 32:26

13. Genesis 32:29

14. Genesis 32:25

15. Acts 13:49-52

16. John Eldredge, *The Journey of Desire*, (Nashville, Tenn., Thomas Nelson, 2000), p. 182

17. Genesis 3:8

18. Luke 2:22-38

## Chapter 6: Imagination and Faith

1. Exodus 3:1

2. Richard Baxter quoted by E. Glenn Hinson, "Directing Imagination," *Companions in Christ: Participant's Book*, (Nashville, Tenn., Upper Room Books, 2001), p. 96

3. Luke 24:30-31

4. Acts 9:1-19

5. 2 Kings 5:1-14
6. Exodus 4:10
7. Judges 6:12
8. Judges 6:36-40
9. Hebrews 11:1
10. 2 Corinthians 5:7
11. Mark 5:34; Luke 8:48
12. Acts 6:7
13. 1 Corinthians 13:12
14. Matthew 22:37
15. Thomas Keating, *Intimacy with God*, (New York, Crossroad Publishing, 1994), p. 123

## Chapter 7: The Two Most Important Things

1. Luke 10:25-28
2. Matthew 22:34-40
3. Deuteronomy 6:5; Leviticus 19:18
4. 1 John 4:19
5. Luke 14:26-33
6. Matthew 5:22
7. Matthew 13:46
8. Matthew 7:12
9. John 15:11
10. John 5:40
11. Luke 3:23
12. Luke 2:41-49
13. Luke 4:1-13
14. Luke 6:12
15. John 4:34; 5:36
16. Mark 6:31-32
17. Mark 6:46
18. Mark 6:34
19. Acts 9:17-18
20. Galatians 1:11-18
21. Luke 14:26
22. John 14:15
23. John 21:15-17
24. Matthew 28:19
25. Philippians 2:13

# Chapter 8: Can We Talk?

1. Ephesians 6:4
2. James 2:18
3. 1 Corinthians 11:5-6
4. 1 Thessalonians 5:17
5. 1 Corinthians 11:7
6. 1 Peter 3:3-4
7. Proverbs 16:18
8. Revelation 21:8
9. James 1:27
10. John 3:3
11. Psalm 119:11
12. Matthew 5:44
13. Philippians 3:4-8
14. Romans 8:32
15. John Eldredge, *Waking the Dead*, (Nashville, Tenn., Thomas Nelson, 2003), p. 132
16. Ibid., p. 134
17. Romans 7:14-19
18. 1 Corinthians 11:1
19. 2 Timothy 4:7
20. Edward M. Smith, *Theophostic Prayer Ministry: Basic Seminar Manual*, (Campbellsville, Kentucky, New Creation, 2005), p. 21-22
21. Edward M. Smith, *Healing Life's Deepest Hurts*, (Ventura, California, Regal, 2002), p. 106
22. Ibid., p. 180
23. Ibid., p. 181
24. Romans 8:37
25. Jeremiah 18:1-6
26. Romans 7:10-11
27. Isaiah 64:6
28. 2 Corinthians 5:17
29. 1 Corinthians 15:19

# Chapter 9: Heart Healing

1. John Eldredge, *Wild at Heart*, (Nashville, Tenn., Thomas Nelson, 2001), p. 69
2. Dallas Willard, *The Great Omission*, (San Francisco, Harper, 2006), p. 94

3. Hebrews 11:37
4. Hebrews 11:33
5. Luke 12:24
6. Luke 12:33
7. Luke 12:30
8. 2 Thessalonians 3:10
9. Stephen D. Bryant, et.al., *Companions in Christ: Leader's Guide*, (Nashville, Tenn., Upper Room Books, 2001), p. 107
10. Gerrit Scott Dawson, et.al., *Companions in Christ: Participant's Book*, (Nashville, Tenn., Upper Room Books, 2001)
11. Ibid., p. 81
12. Romans 7:14-25
13. Gerrit Scott Dawson, et.al., *Companions in Christ: Participant's Book*, (Nashville, Tenn., Upper Room Books, 2001), p. 197
14. Ibid., p. 34
15. Ephesians 6:11
16. Luke 13:10-17
17. Luke 9:42
18. Edward M. Smith, *Healing Life's Deepest Hurts*, (Ventura, CA, Regal Books, 2002)
19. Mark 10:46-52
20. Edward M. Smith, *Healing Life's Deepest Hurts*, (Ventura, CA, Regal Books, 2002), p.12
21. Edward M. Smith, *Theophostic Prayer Ministry: Basic Seminar Manual*, (Campbellsville, KY, New Creation Publishing, 2005), p. 33
22. Edward M. Smith, *Healing Life's Deepest Hurts*, (Ventura, CA, Regal Books, 2002), p.19
23. Jeremiah 29:11
24. 75 milligrams Bupropion per day
25. John 5:6-9
26. John 5:13
27. John 5:14
28. Jerome P. Wagner, *Wagner Enneagram Personality Style Scales*, (Los Angeles, CA, Western Psychological Services, 1999)

## Chapter 10: Lies That Bind

1. John 8:31-32
2. Edward M. Smith, *Healing Life's Deepest Hurts*, (Ventura, Cal., Regal Books, 2002), p. 51ff
3. Philippians 4:7

4. Romans 12:2
5. Edward M. Smith, *Theophostic Prayer Ministry: Basic Seminar Manual*, (Campbellsville, KY, New Creation, 2005), pp. 104-106
6. Psalm 139:15
7. Edward M. Smith, *Theophostic Prayer Ministry: Basic Seminar Manual*, (Campbellsville, KY, New Creation, 2005), pp 312-313
8. Romans 8:33-34
9. Romans 8:1
10. Genesis 3:5
11. James 1:5
12. Ephesians 4:15
13. Thomas Keating, *Intimacy with God*, (New York, Crossroad, 1994)
14. Tony Jones, *Soul Shaper*, (El Cajon, Cal., Youth Specialties, 2003), p. 98

## Chapter 11: Enjoying Life in a Scary World

1. 1 John 4:16
2. Psalm 111:10
3. "What does the Bible say about fear?", *Got Questions?org*, www.gotquestions.org (December 20, 2006), p. 1
4. James Strong, et. al., *The Strongest Strong's Exhaustive Concordance of the Bible*, (Grand Rapids, Zondervan, 2001), pp. 387 and 1652
5. Ibid., pp. 387 and 1600
6. 2 Timothy 1:7
7. Psalm 27:4-5
8. 1 Samuel 18:7
9. Romans 13:4
10. Matthew 5:44
11. "Arminianism", *Wikipedia, the free encyclopedia, en.wikipedia.org* (December 21, 2006), p. 1 ; Hebrews 10:26; 2 Peter 2:20-22
12. Philippians 1:6 and Jude 1:24

## Chapter 12: The Red Root of Bitterness

1. Genesis 3:18
2. Ephesians 4:26; Psalm 37:8
3. John Eldredge, *Wild at Heart Field Manual*, (Nashville, Nelson Books, 2002), p. 79
4. Ibid., p. 96
5. John 2:15
6. Matthew 23:27

7. Romans 8:29
8. John 14:27
9. Galatians 5:22-23
10. Ezekiel 36:26
11. Luke 2:40
12. Luke 10:19
13. Ephesians 3:17
14. Mark 9:24

## Chapter 13: Yes, I Believe, But Just Barely

1. John 5:1-14
2. Mark 9:24 (Revised Standard Version)
3. Mark 9:14-27
4. Genesis 3:4-5
5. Daniel 3:27
6. Thieleman J. van Braught, *The Bloody Theater or Martyrs Mirror of the Defenseless Christians Who Baptized Only Upon Confession of Faith, and Who Suffered and Died for the Testimony of Jesus, Their Savior, From the Time of Christ to the Year A. D. 1660*, (Scottdale, Penn., Herald Press, 1987)
7. Daniel 3:18
8. Isaiah 42:10
9. 2 Timothy 2:15
10. Thomas Keating, *Intimacy With God*, (New York, Crossroad, 1994), pp. 97, 98 and 162
11. Matthew 17:17
12. Dad, unpublished aphorism!
13. Psalm 46:10
14. Matthew 6:6
15. Mark 1:35
16. Genesis 32:29
17. Numbers 11
18. John 15:9-11
19. Mark 12:29-30
20. Brother Lawrence, *The Practice of the Presence of God*, (Peabody, Mass, Hendrickson, 2004), p. 17

## Chapter 14: Spiritual Nitty Gritty

1. Ephesians 4:15
2. Matthew 5:21-22

3. Ezekiel 36:26; Matthew 12:35
4. Matthew 28:18-20
5. James 1:22
6. John 5:40
7. Esther 4:14
8. Mark 1:35
9. Mark 9:2-9
10. Matthew 26:36-44
11. Luke 11:1-4
12. Max Lucado, *The Great House of God*, (Nashville, Tenn., W Publishing, 1997)
13. Luke 6:2
14. Matthew 4:1-11
15. John 5:19-23
16. Ephesians 4:14
17. John 10:2-4
18. Dallas Willard, *The Spirit of the Disciplines*, (San Francisco, Harper, 1988)
19. Dallas Willard, *Renovation of the Heart*, (Colorado Springs, NavPress, 2002)
20. Thomas Keating, *Intimacy with God*, (New York, Crossroad, 1994)
21. Richard J. Foster, *Celebration of Discipline*, (San Francisco, Harper, 1978)
22. Gerrit Scott Dawson, et. al., *Companions in Christ: A Small-Group Experience in Spiritual Formation*, (Nashville, Tenn., Upper Room Books, 2001)
23. 1 Thessalonians 5:17 (KJV)
24. James 2:18 (KJV)
25. Philippians 4:6
26. James 1:17
27. Stephen D. Bryant, et. al., *Companions in Christ: A Small-Group Experience in Spiritual Formation, Leader's Guide*, (Nashville, Tenn., Upper Room Books, 2001), p. 58
28. Gerrit Scott Dawson, et. al., *Companions in Christ: A Small-Group Experience in Spiritual Formation, Participant's Book*, (Nashville, Tenn., Upper Room Books, 2001), pp. 91-93
29. Thomas Keating, *Intimacy with God*, (New York, Crossroad, 1994), pp. 123-124
30. James 4:7

31. "Laying and Praying" is not original with me. I would love to give credit if I could think where I read it! (Yes, I know it is grammatically incorrect, but I don't care!)

32. Eugene H. Peterson, *Christ Plays in Ten Thousand Places*, (Grand Rapids, Mich., Eerdmans, 2005), pp. 109-110

33. Arthur Wallis, *God's Chosen Fast*, (Fort Washington, Penn., Christian Literature Crusade, 1968)

34. Ibid., p. 123

35. Tony Jones, *Soul Shaper*, (El Cajon, Calif., Youth Specialties Books, 2003)

## Chapter 15: Hearty Renunciation and Spiritual Hilarity

1. Matthew 16:25
2. Isaiah 53:3; Hebrews 12:2; Romans 8:18
3. Romans 12:15
4. Luke 9:23
5. John 10:10
6. John 15:11
7. Philippians 4:4
8. C. S. Lewis, *The Screwtape Letters*, (New York, Macmillan, 1959), p. 49
9. Mark 10:25
10. "Carbon monoxide poisoning", *Wikipedia, the free encyclopedia*, en.wikipedia.org/wiki/Carbon_monoxide_poisoning (April 18, 2007), p.7
11. Nehemiah 8:10
12. Romans 12:2
13. John 15:4 and 5
14. Luke 9:23; 1 Corinthians 9:27
15. Brother Lawrence, *The Practice of the Presence of God*, (Peabody, Mass., Hendrickson, 2004), p.17
16. Ibid., p.15
17. John 6:44 and John 12:32
18. Hebrews 11:6
19. Mark 10:21
20. Exodus 20:1-17; Romans 1:22-32; Colossians 3:5-9; Revelation 21:8
21. Genesis 32:22-32

22. Gerrit Scott Dawson, et. al., *Companions in Christ: A Small-Group Experience in Spiritual Formation, Participant's Book,* (Nashville, Tenn., Upper Room Books, 2001), p.81
23. John 2:1-11
24. Gerrit Scott Dawson, et. al., *Companions in Christ: A Small-Group Experience in Spiritual Formation, Participant's Book,* (Nashville, Tenn., Upper Room Books, 2001), p.198
25. Edward M. Smith, *Healing Life's Deepest Hurts,* (Ventura, Cal., Regal, 2002) pp. 37-38
26. Matthew 4:1
27. Genesis 1:28
28. Galatians 6:8

# Chapter 16: Joy and Suffering

1. John 15:11
2. Galatians 5:22
3. Romans 12:15
4. Luke 19:41
5. Luke 22:44
6. Mark 15:34
7. Isaiah 53:3
8. Philippians 4:4
9. 1 Thessalonians 5:16
10. James Strong, et. al., *The Strongest Strong's Exhaustive Concordance of the Bible,* (Grand Rapids, Zondervan, 2001), pp. 424 and 1637
11. Ibid., pp. 627 and 1653
12. Ephesians 3:18
13. Romans 8:28
14. C. S. Lewis, *A Grief Observed,* (San Francisco, Harper, 1961)
15. Matthew 14:30
16. Sandra H. Johnson, "Disciplinary Actions and Pain Relief: Analysis of the Pain Relief Act," *Journal of Law, Medicine and Ethics, 24,* no. 4 (1996): 319-327
17. Matthew 27:34
18. Luke 10:31-32
19. Luke 17:33
20. Nehemiah 8:10

## Chapter 17: Playing Joyfully Outside

1. Eugene H. Peterson, *Christ Plays in Ten Thousand Places*, (Grand Rapids, Mich., Eerdmans, 2005)
2. Luke 4:18
3. Acts 18:3; 1 Corinthians 4:12
4. 2 Corinthians 12:7
5. Matthew 11:29-30

## Chapter 18: The Creator's Delight

1. Romans 1:18-20 and 2:5
2. John 5:26
3. Romans 1:18; John 2:13-17
4. Matthew 23:37
5. 2 Corinthians 4:5-11
6. Romans 15:5-9
7. Malachi 3:6; James 1:17
8. The Bible (start with the gospels)
9. John 20:27
10. Mark 16:19
11. Romans 1:28-32; Romans 2:1; Romans 3:9-18
12. Romans 2:1
13. John 3:16; Romans 5:8
14. Luke 12:6-7
15. Luke 19:40
16. Genesis 1:4, 10, 12, 18, 21, 25, 31
17. Genesis 1:26
18. Hebrews 2:7
19. Revelation 3:21
20. Ecclesiastes 1:13-14
21. John 5:17
22. Rick Warren, *The Purpose Driven Life*, (Grand Rapids, Mich., Zondervan, 2002), pp. 42-44
23. Some may object that, although Jesus was not omniscient as an infant, God the Father nevertheless was, at that same time. They may be right. However, Jesus himself said, "Anyone who has seen me has seen the Father." (John 14:9) If we cannot learn about God's nature by careful study of the biblical record of Jesus' life, what hope is there of understanding God at all?

24. Christopher A. Hall and John Sanders, "Does God Know Your Next Move?", *Christianity Today 45*:7, May 21, 2001, p. 38
25. Genesis 1:26
26. Isaiah 6:1-7; Luke 5:8; Romans 1-3
27. Ephesians 3:17-19
28. Romans 8:1
29. Matthew 23:27
30. Numbers 14: 26-35
31. Luke 7:37-50
32. Luke 15:20
33. Matthew 3:17
34. Luke 4:18-21
35. Matthew 10:34-39
36. Matthew 19:19
37. John 19:30
38. Ezekiel 36:26
39. Acts 2:41

## Chapter 19: Of Course You Realize, This Means War

1.  Strictly speaking, I do not subscribe to the "Star Wars" worldview. By this philosophy, called *monism*, there is one "force" with two sides. We can choose to operate on either side. If we choose the "dark side," we become "evil." Evil, by this view, always was and always will be inseparable from good. But, what *is* the force? Where did it come from? I find the prospect of connecting with a half-good, half-evil fuzzy something-or-other simply uninteresting. I just can't convince myself that it would be a good thing if the ultimate source of all that I see around me were inextricably contaminated with evil. However, I cannot buy a strictly dualistic view either. Dualists hold that there are two co-eternal, equally powerful, opposing beings or forces. Thus the struggle between good and evil represents an ontological dichotomy that can never be resolved. Christians who over-emphasize Satan's power and importance can unwittingly adopt such a misconception. Instead, I believe the Bible reveals a modified dualistic interpretation of reality. I describe it briefly, later in this chapter.
2.  Isaiah 14:14; Ezekiel 28:12-19
3.  Revelation 12:1-9
4.  Genesis 3:1-6
5.  Genesis 3:16-19 and 23

6. Acts 5:1-11
7. Acts 12:23
8. Hugh Ross, et. al., *Lights in the Sky and Little Green Men*, (Colorado Springs, Colo., NavPress, 2002), pp. 171-192
9. Matthew 10:28
10. Romans 2:14-15
11. Romans 8:19-22
12. Job 1:6-19 and 2:7; Matthew 4:1-11, 9:32-33, 15:22, 16:23; Mark 4:15, 5:3-4, 7 and 13; Luke 4:34-35, 9:39 and 42, 13:10 and 16; John 13:2 and 27; 1 Chronicles 21:1; Revelation 12:9-17
13. Joel 2:25 (KJV)
14. Romans 8:18
15. William Hasker, "A Philosophical Perspective" in Pinnock's *The Openness of God*, (Downers Grove, Ill., InterVarsity Press, 1994), p. 152
16. Job 1:16, 19 and 2:7; Luke 9: 39 and 42, 13:10 and 16; Revelation 12:15
17. Matthew 7:24-27
18. James 4:7
19. Ephesians 6:11
20. Exodus 15:3
21. John Eldredge, *Epic*, (Nashville, Tenn., Nelson, 2004), pp. 28 ff
22. Acts 12:23
23. Colossians 2:15
24. 2 Corinthians 11:14; 2 Thessalonians 2:9; 2 Timothy 2:25-26
25. Ephesians 4:26-27
26. James 1:14
27. 1 Peter 5:8
28. 1 John 5:18
29. Acts 5:3, 19:15-16
30. Matthew 26:22 (KJV)
31. Daniel 10:13; Revelation 12:7
32. Job 1:12
33. Matthew 4:1; My temptation in Montreal (Chapter 15)
34. Edward M. Smith, *Theophostic Prayer Ministry: Basic Seminar Manual*, (Campbellsville, Ky., New Creation, 2005), p. 226
35. Ezekiel 36:26
36. Edward M. Smith, *Theophostic Prayer Ministry: Basic Seminar Manual*, (Campbellsville, Ky., New Creation, 2005), p. 230
37. Psalm 111:10
38. Luke 10:18

## Chapter 20: A Sweet, Smooth Roar

1. Acts 1:8
2. Acts 1:4-5
3. Acts 2:1-4
4. Reginald Cherry, *Healing Prayer*, (Nashville, Tenn., Thomas Nelson, 1999), pp.102-103
5. Genesis 5:24
6. Job 2:6-8
7. 2 Corinthians 12:7-8
8. Joni Eareckson Tada, *Welcome to Joni and Friends International Disability Center*, http://www.joniandfriends.org (August 11, 2007), Home page
9. Luke 4:18-19
10. Romans 12:2
11. 1 Corinthians 15
12. 2 Corinthians 12:9
13. Matthew 9:2, 22 and 29; 15:28
14. John 5:11-15
15. 1 Samuel 16:7
16. John 11:13
17. John 11:11
18. John 11:4 and 11
19. Matthew 9:8 and 26
20. Luke 7:11-15
21. Acts 9:40
22. Acts 20:9-10
23. Acts 2:41; Luke 15:10
24. 2 Peter 1:3; 2 Timothy 1:7
25. Romans 11:33-34
26. Peter Kreeft, *Everything You Ever Wanted to Know about Heaven...But Never Dreamed of Asking*, (San Francisco, Ignatius, 1990), p. 112
27. Ephesians 3:14-19
28. John Eldredge, *The Journey of Desire*, (Nashville, Tenn., Nelson, 2000), pp. 89-105
29. David L. Edwards and John Stott, *Evangelical Essentials: A Liberal-Evangelical Dialogue*, (Downer's Grove, Ill., InterVarsity, 1988), pp. 217-219
30. Francis MacNutt, *The Healing Reawakening: Reclaiming our Lost Inheritance*, (Grand Rapids, Mich., 2005), p. 226
31. Matthew 5:8
32. John 16:12-13

# Chapter 21: Trinity, Unity and Us

1. Deuteronomy 31:6, Hebrews 13:5
2. Isaiah 7:14, Matthew 1:23
3. Genesis 1:26
4. Luke 18:17
5. Luke 18:15-16
6. Genesis 32:24-26
7. Frank C. Laubach, *Prayer: The Mightiest Force in the World* (Old Tappan, New Jersey, Revell, 1946), p. 74
8. Don't waste *too* much time looking for the NAP! So far, only Acts 10:1-35 has been rendered in this version.
9. Since it is OK to call Almighty God "Daddy" (Romans 8:15), it should be no problem calling Peter "Pete".

# Chapter 22: There's Got to Be a Sequel

1. Romans 8:18
2. Romans 13:4
3. Romans 8:28
4. Matthew 10:7
5. Revelation 21:1-7
6. Revelation 21:4, 27; 22:15
7. Revelation 5:9-13
8. Revelation 4:8-11; 19:1-8
9. Revelation 5:2; 12:10-12
10. Matthew 22:1-14; Revelation 19:9; 21:6; 22:17
11. 1 Corinthians 13:11-12; Revelation 22:3-5
12. Daniel 7:18-28
13. Revelation 7:15
14. Revelation 8:3-4
15. Revelation 8:7,8,10,12; 9:1,13
16. Revelation 8:1
17. Revelation 5:1; 14:13
18. Revelation 4:6-8; 8:13; 13:1-2
19. Revelation 21:15-17
20. John 14:2
21. John 14:3
22. 1 Corinthians 13:12
23. Hebrews 12:1
24. Genesis 1:26; 2:19-20

25. Matthew 25:14-23
26. Luke 24:42
27. Peter Kreeft, *Everything You Ever Wanted to Know about Heaven...But Never Dreamed of Asking*, (San Francisco, Ignatius, 1990), p. 95
28. John 20:24-28
29. Luke 24:30
30. John 20:19
31. Robert C. Smoot and Jack Price, *Chemistry: A Modern Course*, (Columbus, Ohio, Merrill, 1975), p. 122
32. Matthew 25:31-46
33. Luke 16:22
34. Revelation 21:4
35. James Strong, et. al., *The Strongest Strong's Exhaustive Concordance of the Bible*, (Grand Rapids, Zondervan, 2001), pp. 1214 and 1654
36. Randy Alcorn, *Heaven*, (Wheaton, Ill., Tyndale, 2004), p. 258
37. Peter Kreeft, *Everything You Ever Wanted to Know about Heaven...But Never Dreamed of Asking*, (San Francisco, Ignatius, 1990), pp. 151-171
38. Ibid., pp. 153-154
39. Ibid., p. 171
40. Revelation 6-16
41. Romans 11:33-34
42. Randy Alcorn, *Heaven*, (Wheaton, Ill., Tyndale, 2004), p. 301
43. Revelation 21:4
44. Romans 6:23
45. 1 Corinthians 15:52
46. Randy Alcorn, *Heaven*, (Wheaton, Ill., Tyndale, 2004), p. 300
47. Revelation 21:16
48. Revelation 21:21
49. Revelation 21:25
50. Revelation 7:9-10
51. Randy Alcorn, *Heaven*, (Wheaton, Ill., Tyndale, 2004), pp. 8-10
52. Philippians 4:8
53. 1 Peter 1:3
54. 1 Corinthians 2:13-15
55. 1 Corinthians 2:16
56. 1 Corinthians 2:9-10
57. 1 Timothy 6:16
58. Peter Kreeft, *Everything You Ever Wanted to Know about Heaven...But Never Dreamed of Asking*, (San Francisco, Ignatius, 1990), p. 62
59. John 14:9

60. Revelation 1:16-17
61. Isaiah 6:5 KJV
62. Exodus 33:22-33
63. Exodus 33:20
64. 1 Corinthians 3:10-15
65. C. S. Lewis, *The Great Divorce*, (New York, Macmillan, 1946), pp. 26-31
66. 1 Corinthians 13:13
67. Tony Jones, *Soul Shaper*, (El Cajon, Calif., Youth Specialties Books, 2003), pp. 98 ff
68. Isaiah 45:9

# About the Author

Trained in the biological sciences, **Everett Myer** earned his DDHS* in the School of Hard Knocks. The stresses of decades as a corporate middle manager drove him to seek intimacy with Jesus. He was a missionary teacher in Somalia, has served as an ordained pastoral elder, and leads spiritual formation groups. Everett and his wife Leona enjoy crossword puzzles, spending time with their five grandchildren, and "playing house" together in Manheim, Pennsylvania.

*Daily Disciple of the Holy Spirit

www.ingramcontent.com/pod-product-compliance
Lightning Source LLC
Chambersburg PA
CBHW022122080426
42734CB00006B/221